PIOTR OLENDER

RUSSO-JAPANESE NAVAL WAR 1904-1905

VOL. 2 BATTLE OF TSUSHIMA

STRATUS

Romanization used in the book.

BGN/PCGN romanization system for Russian is a method for romanization of Cyrillic Russian texts, that is, their transliteration into the Latin alphabet as used in the English language. It is used by the Oxford University Press. Romanization of the Russian ships' names were published in vol. I.

Russian names used in the book.

Е.И. Алексеев	E.I. Alekseev	Н.Г. Лишин	N.G. Lishin
А.П. Андреев	A.P. Andreev	А.А. Ливен	A.A. Liven
Г.П. Беляев	G.P. Belyaev	М.Ф. Лощинский	M.F. Loshchinskiy
В.И. Бэр	V.I. Ber	С.О. Макаров	S.O. Makarov
А.М. Безобразов	A.M. Bezobrazov	Н.А. Матусевич	N.A. Matusevich
П.А. Безобразов	P.A. Bezobrazov	В.Н. Миклухо-Маклай	V.N. Miklukho-Maklay
А.А. Бильдерлинг	A.A. Bil'derling	М.П. Молас	M.P Molas
Ф.Э. Боссе	F.E. Bosse	Н.И. Небогатов	N.I. Nebogatov
В.А. Бойсман	V.A. Boysman	М.В. Озеров	M.V Ozerov
Н.М. Бухвостов	N.M Bukhvostov	В.А. Попов	V.A. Popov
И.И. Чагин	I.I. Chagin	Ф.В. Раден	F.V. Raden
Н.К. Чернышев	N.K. Chernyshev	О.Л. Радлов	O.L. Radlov
Н.Д. Дабич	N.D. Dabich	Н.К. Рейценштейн	N.K. Reytsenshteyn
Л.Ф. Добротворский	L.F Dobrotvorskiy	А.А. Родионов	A.A Rodionov
Е.Р. Егорьев	E.R. Egor'ev	З. П. Рожественски	Z.P. Rozhestvenski
О.А. Энквист	O.A Enkvist	В.Ф. Руднев	V.F. Rudnev
Н.О. Эссен	N.O. Essen	В.Ф. Сарычев	V.F. Sarychev
Д.Г. Фелькерзам	D.G Fel'kerzam	П.И. Серебренников	P.I. Serebrennikov
В.Н. Ферзен	V.N. Ferzen	Э.Н. Щенснович	E.N. Shchensnovich
Б.А. Фитингоф	B.A Fitingof	С.П. Шеин	S.P. Shein
А.В. Фок	A.V Fok	Г.К. Штакельберг	G.K. Shtakel'berg
А.А. Гинтер	A.A. Ginter	М.Ф. Шульц	M.F. Shul'ts
К.А. Грамматчиков	K.A. Grammatchikov	Н.И. Скрыдлов	N.I. Skrydlov
С.И. Григорьев	S.I. Grigor'ev	В.В. Смирнов	V.V. Smirnov
О.Ф.К. Гриппенберг	O.F.K. Grippenberg	О. В. Старк	O.V Stark
К.П. Иессен	K.P. Iessen	В.А. Степанов	W.A. Stepanov
В.В. Игнациус	V.V Ignatsius	А.М. Стессель	A.M Stessel'
М.К. Истомин	M.K. Istomin	Е.А. Трусов	E.A. Trusov
Н.М. Иванов	N.M. Ivanov	П.П. Ухтомский	P.P. Ukhtomskiy
П.Ф. Иванов	P.F. Ivanov	И.П. Успенский	I.P. Uspenskiy
А.В. Каульбарс	A.V. Kaul'bars	Р.Н. Вирен	R.N. Viren
Ф.Э. Кельлер	G.K. Kel'ler	В.К. Витгефт	V.K. Vitgeft
К.К. Клапье де Колонг	K.K. Klap'e de Kolong	Н.М. Яковлев	N.M. Yakovlev
А.Н. Куропаткин	A.N. Kuropatkin	Н.В. Юнг	N.V. Yung
В.М. Ламздорф	V.M. Lamzdorf	В.К. Залесский	V.K. Zalesskiy
И.Н. Лебедев	I. N Lebedev	М.И. Засулич	M.I. Zasulich
П.П. Левицкий	P.P. Levitskiy	В.М. Зацаренный	V.M. Zatsarennyy
Н.П. Линевич	N.P. Linevich		

PIOTR OLENDER

RUSSO-JAPANESE NAVAL WAR 1904-1905

VOL. 2 BATTLE OF TSUSHIMA

STRATUS

Published in Poland in 2010
by STRATUS s.c.
Po. Box 123,
27-600 Sandomierz 1, Poland
e-mail: office@mmpbooks.biz
for
Mushroom Model Publications,
3 Gloucester Close,
Petersfield
Hampshire GU32 3AX, UK
e-mail: rogerw@mmpbooks.biz

ISBN
978-83-61421-02-3

Editor in chief
Roger Wallsgrove

Editorial Team
Bartłomiej Belcarz
Robert Pęczkowski
Artur Juszczak
Matthew Willis

Scale plans
Robert Panek

Maps concept
Piotr Olender

Maps drawing
Robert Panek

Cover
© Grzegorz Nawrocki
"Japanese Battleship Mikasa in the battle of the Yellow Sea"

Translation
Jacek Grochowski
Kazimierz Zygadło

Proofreading
Roger Wallsgrove

DTP
Artur Bukowski
Bartłomiej Belcarz

Printed by
Drukarnia Diecezjalna,
ul. Żeromskiego 4,
27-600 Sandomierz
tel. +48 (15) 832 31 92
fax +48 (15) 832 77 87
www.wds.pl
marketing@wds.pl

PRINTED IN POLAND

Table of contents

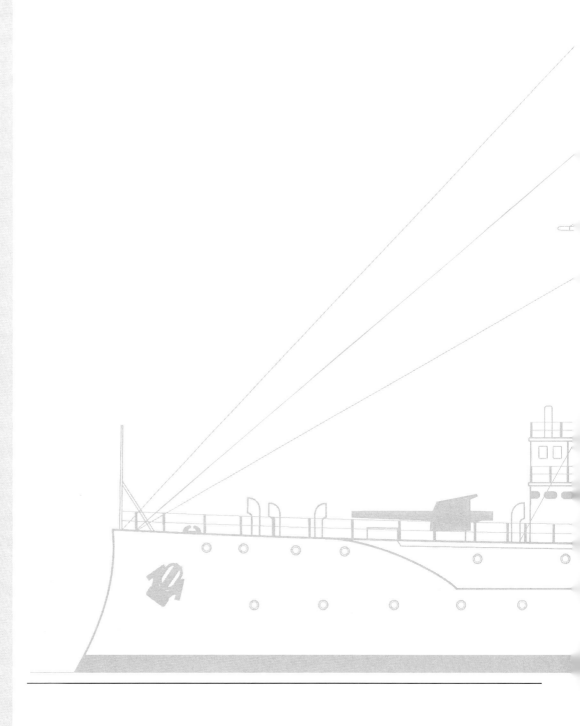

VLADIVOSTOK

30 | The first raids by Vladivostok cruisers

Cruiser Rossiya.

Cruiser Ryurik. *The photo was taken at Port Arthur a couple of months before the beginning of the war.*

The main task of the Vladivostok-based first squadron of cruisers was to attack Japanese vessels, distracting the stronger Japanese forces from their operations at Port Arthur, thus maintaining a favourable proportion of strength in that area. As a result, immediately on receiving information about the outbreak of war, Commander Reytsenshteyn gave his warships the order to leave harbour, and on the morning of 9th February the cruisers *Rossiya*, *Gromoboy*, *Ryurik*, and *Bogatyr'* set out for the coast of Honshu island. On reaching their destination on 11th February, the warships encountered and sank a Japanese ship, *Naganoura Maru* (1084 BRT), and then turned towards the northern coast of Korea. Stormy weather finally made the Russian commander abort the operation and on 14th February the Russians returned to Vladivostok[1].

Reytsenshteyn's squadron spent only 10 days in harbour, the time necessary to re-stock coal and carry out essential repairs. On 24th February the cruisers *Rossiya*, *Gromoboy*, *Ryurik* and *Bogatyr'* set out to sea again, this time bound for the Korean port of Gensan, controlled by the Japanese. The Russian cruisers reached their destination on the morning of 26th February, but despite cruising in the area until the evening of 28th February, encountered no enemy ships. Further searches were interrupted by a heavy storm on the night of 28th/29th February, which made the Russian cruisers turn back to Vladivostok, where they arrived on 1st March[2]

---

1 Egor'ev V.E., Operatsii vladivostokskikh kreyserov ... op.cit., pp. 67-69.
2 ibidem, p. 76.

31 The bombardment of Vladivostok by Vice Admiral Kamimura's squadron on 6th March, 1904

Both raids by the Vladivostok cruisers, though not entirely successful, disturbed the Japanese Command, particularly regarding the safety of the port of Gensan on the eastern coast of Korea[3]. After relocating the twelfth division to Korea, further transports of the second division and the guards' division were awaiting the order to set out, and their escort constituted the most important task for the fleet now. Therefore, Vice-Admiral Togo received new orders, placing Vice Admiral Kataoka's III Squadron under his direct command. In return, Vice Admiral Kamimura's II Division was formed (*Idzumo*, *Yakumo*, *Asama*, *Adzuma* and *Iwate*, backed up by cruisers *Kasagi* and *Yoshin*, which were replaced in the III Division by the armoured cruiser *Tokiwa*) to carry out a direct assault on Vladivostok. This was to distract the Russians from the transport of troops on their way to Korea, which the Japanese were unable to cover fully[4].

On 2nd March, Kamimura's detachment left the roadstead of Mokpho and four days later reached the area of Askol'd Island. From here they set out to the entrance of Vladivostok port. After entering Ussurian Bay, Kamimura left the cruisers *Kasagi* and *Yoshino* at its entrance, whilst approaching the coast with the other five armoured cruisers. The ice layer on the bay (up to 45 cm thick) made it impossible for the Japanese warships to get any closer to the shore than 45-50 cables, so they began

Cruiser Adzuma.

shelling from that distance between 13.53 and 14.20 (Japanese time), firing a total of 200 203-152 mm shells. Given the great distance from which the shelling was carried out, not a single Japanese shell reached the western part of the port, where the Russians ships were anchored. Several buildings on the shore were damaged, one civilian killed, and five more wounded[5].

After the shelling of Vladivostok, the armoured cruisers joined *Kasagi* and *Yoshino*, and together set out into the open sea. They returned to Vladivostok on 7th March, but this time Kamimura decided not to attack, and after performing several manoeuvres gave the order to sail to the coast of Korea. On 9th March, the Japanese force reached Gensan, and after a short stay there set out for Sasebo. On 16th March, they finally joined the main forces in Korean waters.

---

3   Corbett J.S., op.cit., vol. I, pp. 137-138.
4   ibidem, p. 143; Lacroix E., op.cit., part 5, TBS No 3/1968, p.221

5   Egor'ev V.E., Operatsii vladivostokskikh kreyserov ... op.cit., p. 78; Opisanie..., op.cit., vol.III, p.9; Russko-yaponskaya voyna... Rabota..., op.cit., vol. IX, p. 153.

Cruiser Kasagi.

32 | The third raid of Russian cruisers and the sinking of the transport *Kinshu Maru*

After taking over command of the First Pacific Fleet, Vice Admiral Makarov slightly modified the tasks of the Vladivostok squadron, placing a special emphasis on intercepting transports sailing from Japan to Gensan.

At the same time, the commander of the cruiser squadron, Reytsenshteyn, was called back to Port Arthur. He was replaced by Rear Admiral K.P. Iessen[6], who was recommended by Makarov himself. The new commander needed some time to get acquainted with his squadron. Therefore, the cruisers of the Vladivostok squadron left port only on 23rd April. Their destination was Gensan.

Meanwhile, after *Petropavlovsk's* sinking and Makarov's death, along with the damage to the battleship *Pobeda*, the range of the Port Arthur fleet's operations was seriously limited. Due to this, and taking into consideration the fact that transfer of the troops of the II

Army to Manchuria was still in progress, Vice Admiral Togo decided to detach Vice Admiral Kamimura's II Squadron and send it against the Vladivostok cruisers, to obstruct their potential attacks on Japanese units on the Japanese Sea and in the Korea Strait. Kamimura's ships were to be replaced on the Yellow Sea by Vice Admiral Kataoka's III Squadron, whose main task now was to provide direct escort for the Japanese transports. Kamimura, in turn, following his orders of 16th April, set out for Mokpho a day later. From there, on restocking, he sailed out towards the Korea Strait on 21st April, leading the II Division (*Idzumo, Adzuma, Kasuga, Tokiwa* and *Iwate*), the IV Division (*Naniwa, Takachiho, Tsushima* and *Niitaka*), the small cruiser *Chihaya*, the 1st Destroyer Division, auxiliary cruiser *Nikko Maru*, and the transport *Kinshu Maru*. On location, he was also joined by the cruiser *Idzumi*, and the 11th and 15th Torpedo Boat Divisions. On 22nd April, they reached Gensan. There, the Japanese admiral

6 He took over command on 16th March., Lacroix E., op.cit., part 5, TBS No 3/1968, p.228.

received a message that Russian advanced units of cavalry at Kyongsong and Songjin had been spotted, about 150 – 200 km from Gensan. This was disturbing, so he decided to send his torpedo boats and *Kinshu Maru* on a reconnaissance mission, whilst himself departing with his main force towards Vladivostok[7]. Therefore on 23rd April Kamimura's squadron left Gensan, heading north, but the following day dense fog made the Japanese admiral abandon his plan and turn back to Gensan, which he reached in the afternoon of 26th April. It was only then that he learnt about Iessen's attack on Gensan.

Meanwhile, on the morning of 23rd April, after extensive preparations the Russian cruiser squadron left Vladivostok (*Rossiya*, *Gromoboy* and *Bogatyr'*, initially accompanied by *Ryurik*, which, however, had to return to port for repairs). This time the squadron was strengthened by torpedo boats *205* and *206*. Sailing in thick fog, the Russians passed Kamimura's northbound detachment and reached Gensan around 10.00 on 25th April[8]. In the port they found only a small steamer, *Goyo Maru* (601 BRT), which was sunk by the torpedo boats. Next, the Russian squadron headed north towards Simpo. On the way they encountered and sank a small Japanese steamer, *Haginoura Maru* (219 BRT). Then the two torpedo boats turned

back to Vladivostok and the cruisers continued northwards along the shore. Around 22.20, some 10 sea miles from Simpo, they encountered a solitary transport, *Kinshu Maru* (3854 BRT), which was on its way back from the reconnaissance mission in Pallada Bay, north of Regin. After the Japanese crew was transferred to the Russian cruisers, the transport was sunk. Then Rejcenshejn's ships headed north and on 27th April returned to Vladivostok.

A day later, Kamimura's squadron also arrived at Vladivostok, after wasting two days looking for *Kinshu Maru*. Unable to attack the Russian cruisers harboured in the port, the Japanese auxiliary cruiser *Nikko Maru* laid three small mine-fields during the night of 28th/29th April: one near Skryplev Island, by the eastern entrance canal (12 mines), the second at the entrance to Ussurian Bay, 5 sea miles south of Wjatlina Island (39 mines), and the third 6.5 sea miles south of Cyvolka Island (24 mines), a total of 75 mines[9]. On completing the task, on 29th April Kamimura's squadron turned towards Gensan. From Gensan they headed for the Korea Strait, arriving there on 2nd May. After sending the armoured cruiser *Kasuga* away to join Togo's main force, the other ships went on to patrol the strait area, taking over the protection of Japanese shipping there from Vice Admiral Kataoka's III Squadron.

---

7   Opisanie..., op.cit., vol.III, p.13.
8   The two detachment passed each other probably in the morning of 24th April – that was when the radio operators on *Gromoboy* are said to have accidentally intercepted a message from *Idzumo*. As the theoretical radio range on the Russian cruiser was up to 24 sea miles (in practice it was up to 30 sea miles), it may be assumed that the teams passed each other at the distance of 24-25 sea miles. Egor'ev V.E., Operatsii vladivostokskikh kreyserov op.cit., p.96.

9   On 16th June, Russian torpedo boat *208* sank on these mines, as did German steamer *China* (1741 BRT), on 16th July. After the war they inflicted damage upon the German steamer *Slivia* (6506 BRT) on 30th January, 1906, and the Russian *Gorchakov* (3287BRT) on 31st May, 1906. Denisov B., Minnaya voyna u Vladivostoka..., op.cit., pp. 28-29.

33 | The June raid of Russian cruisers in the Korea Strait

Vice Admiral Nikolai Illarionovich Skrydlov leaving the Winter Palace after being nominated the commander of the Second Pacific Squadron. In fact, he never made it to Port Arthur and he took command of the Vladivostok squadron only.

On 22nd May Vice Admiral N.I. Skrydlov, accompanied by Rear Admiral P.A. Bezobrazov and the entire staff[10], arrived in Vladivostok. After Makarov's death, Skrydlov was nominated as commander of the I Pacific Squadron. After taking over command, he ordered another raid by the cruisers on Japanese shipping in the Korea Strait[11]. As a result, on 12th June *Rossiya*, *Gromoboy* and *Ryurik* left Vladivostok under Rear Admiral Bezobrazov's command and headed south[12].

10 Both admirals left Petersburg with the intention of visiting Port Arthur, but didn't make it before the Japanese captured Kinchou and cut off the fortress from Mukden. Consequently, they went to Vladivostok.

11 On transferring the II Army to Manchuria, and the commencement of the Port Arthur blockade, the demand of the troops fighting on the land and the Elliot Archipelago based fleet for supplies and reinforcements increased. Thus, the importance of the transport routes between the ports in southern Japan and Manchuria, through the Korea Bay increased as well.

12 The cruiser *Bogatyr'* did not join the squadron, as it had suffered damage on underwater rocks during a reconnaissance in Slavonic Bay, near Brius Cape, 20 sea

They reached the war zone on the morning of 15th June. They were spotted immediately by the Japanese cruiser *Tsushima*, which was on patrol there. However, *Tsushima* was unable to obstruct the enemy. The commander of the Japanese ship managed to warn the nearby cargo ships *Fuio Maru*, *Maiko Maru* and *Ugo Maru*, which turned back to the port of Takeshiki at once. He also managed to notify Kamimura's main forces in Ozaki Bay.

In the meantime, the Russians spotted another two Japanese steamers. One of them managed to escape, the other one, Ujina-bound *Idzumi Maru* (3229 BRT), was sunk. After this success, two more Japanese ships, *Hitach Maru* (6175 BRT) and *Sado Maru* (6225 BRT) sailing from Simonoseki, were spotted. They tried to turn back to port, but the Russians caught up with them. The former was sunk by the cruiser *Gromoboy*, the latter was torpedoed by the cruiser *Ryurik*. Despite two direct hits, and the serious damaged caused by them, the Japanese transport managed to stay afloat and thanks to an immediate rescue operation, on 18th June, was towed to shore. After provisional repairs, she

miles south-west of Vladivostok on 15th May. Severely damaged, it left dock as late as 15th June, yet due to the scale of repairs and objective difficulties, it was excluded from war operations practically until the end of the war. Egor'ev V.E., *Operatsii vladivostokskikh kreyserov* op.cit., p.112.

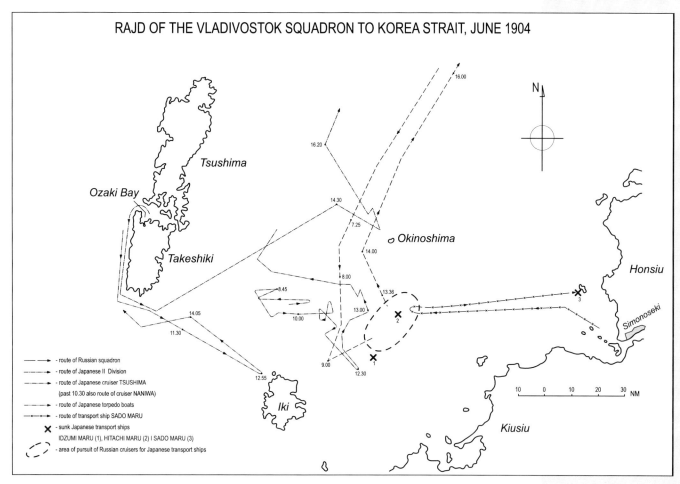

RAJD OF THE VLADIVOSTOK SQUADRON TO KOREA STRAIT, JUNE 1904

Tsushima

Ozaki Bay

Takeshiki

Okinoshima

Honsiu

Simonoseki

Iki

Kiusiu

— route of Russian squadron
— route of Japanese II Division
— route of Japanese cruiser TSUSHIMA
   (past 10.30 also route of cruiser NANIWA)
— route of Japanese torpedo boats
—x— route of transport ship SADO MARU
✕ — sunk Japanese transport ships
   IDZUMI MARU (1), HITACHI MARU (2) I SADO MARU (3)
- - - — area of pursuit of Russian cruisers for Japanese transport ships

was escorted to Nagasaki for general overhaul on 2nd July. This happened because the Russians were afraid of the arrival of Kamimura's main force, and did not wait for *Sado Maru* to sink but left immediately after the torpedoing[13].

Meanwhile, Vice-Admiral Kamimura assumed a position near Okinoshima Island, hoping to intercept the Russian flotilla on their shortest way back. However, the latter chose to sail north-east along the Honshu shore, and left the Korean Strait undisturbed. Next day, on 16th June, the Russians reached the vicinity of the port of Maizuru, where at around 09.00 (local time) they apprehended the British steamer *Allanton* (4252 BRT) with a load of coal, which was assumed to be war materiel. Sailing on north, on the morning of 18th June the Russian cruisers approached the entrance to Tsugaru Bay, and on 19th June they returned to Vladivostok.

Cruiser Bogatyr' *on the rocks. The damages it suffered then excluded it from further war operations.*

A rescue operation of the transport Sado Maru *after it was torpedoed by Russian battleships.*

13 Ibidem, s.130.

34 | The raid by Russian torpedo boats on the shores of Hokkaido

The same day that Bezobrazov's squadron of cruisers sank two Japanese transports in the Korea Strait (15th June), torpedo boats *203, 205* and *206* left Vladivostok on a mission to disrupt Japanese shipping off Hokkaido. Despite foul weather, the Russian units reached the shores of Japan on the morning of 16th June and soon intercepted and sank two small Japanese sailing vessels, transferring the crews to a third ship which was allowed to sail off.

After this success, at around 19.00 (Russian time) the torpedo boats headed south, though encountering only fishing boats on their way. Considering their limited fuel supply, on reaching the vicinity of Esashi port during the night of 16th/17th June the commander resolved to return to Vladivostok. Before they sailed away from the shores of Japan they encountered three more enemy schooners. The first of them was boarded and escorted to Vladivostok, the

second one was sunk and the third one set free, as it carried passengers, including women and children[14].

In the meantime, during the night of 17th/18th June the weather conditions deteriorated rapidly. The storm reached six on the Beaufort scale, and became a serious threat for small torpedo boats. As a result, when the Russian detachment entered the harbour in St. Olga Bay around noon on 18th June they had almost no coal left in their bunkers. However, they found only 30 tons of fuel in the harbour, which was not enough to take them back to Vladivostok. Therefore they had to wait until 19th June, when the auxiliary cruiser *Lena* and five torpedo boats arrived at St. Olga Bay. On refuelling, on 20th June, the entire group headed for Vladivostok, reaching their destination in the evening.

Russian torpedo boat 206.

---

14 Egor'ev V.E., Pervyy pokhod vladivostokskikh kreyserov v koreyskiy proliv i russkikh minonostsev k o-vu Khokkaydo v iyune 1904 g, MS No 7/1937, p. 141.

35 | The second raid by the Vladivostok cruisers in the Korea Strait

Soon after the return to Vladivostok from the raid on the Korea Strait, Vice Admiral Skrydlov received an order from Viceroy Alekseev to take to sea again. The order was connected with Rear Admiral Vitgeft's attempt to break the Port Arthur blockade and get through to Vladivostok, first planned for 21st June, and then put off until 23rd June. In these circumstances, the squadron of cruisers harboured in Vladivostok was to set out to meet with the main force, with the mission of distracting Vice Admiral Kamimura's II Squadron of cruisers on the waters of the strait.

Numerous defects in the Russian ships caused by their operations delayed the execution of this task. Finally the Vladivostok squadron, consisting of three armoured cruisers, the auxiliary cruiser *Lena* and eight torpedo boats, set out for Gensan on 28th June, five days after the attempt to break the blockade by the Port Arthur fleet (the result of the attempt was still unknown to the Russian command at that time). On the night of 29th/30th June, the Russian squadron reached their destination and in the roadstead they burnt a small Japanese steamer and a schooner. However, during this operation torpedo boat *204* damaged its rudder on underwater rocks and was sunk by the Russians to prevent slowing down the pace[15].

Before sinking *204*, in order to save time, Rear Admiral Bezobrazov commanded the return of the torpedo boats and the auxiliary cruiser *Lena* to Vladivostok. They turned back immediately after sinking *204* and reached the port on 2nd July. Around 15.00 (local time) Bezobrazov and his cruisers headed for the Korea Strait. Initially, the Russians were lucky. On the morning of 1st July thick fog limited visibility so much that the Japanese were unable to spot the Russians. Soon, however, Bezobrazov made a mistake by ordering interference of the Japanese radio messages intercepted by his crews, assuming wrongly that they conveyed information about the detection of his ships. This informed the enemy that the Russians were approaching the Korea Strait[16]. As a result, when the Russian ships entered the strait at around 18.20/18.40 they encountered Kamimura's main force south-east of Okinoshima. By that time the fog had cleared and the visibility was very good – the distance between the opposing ships was about 12.5 sea miles[17].

Right after spotting the enemy, aware of their advantage, Rear Admiral Bezobrazov ordered a change of course to the north-east and set out on his way back to Vladivostok. The Japanese pursued them, but soon it became dark and visual contact was lost. Kamimura's squadron gave up the pursuit on the morning of 2nd July. Then the Russian cruisers headed for Vladivostok, apprehending on the way the British steamer *Cheltenham* (3740 BRT) carrying contraband. After being taken over by a prize crew, it reached Vladivostok on 3rd July along with the cruisers.

15 Egor'ev V.E., Operatsii vladivostokskikh kreyserov..., op.cit., p.155. This decision was later severely criticized by the Russian command (ibidem, pp. 164-165).

16 Ibidem, p. 156. His information is confirmed by Japanese sources: Opisanie..., op.cit., vol.III, s.43.

17 At that time, Kamimura's squadron consled of armoured cruisers *Idzumo*, *Iwate*, *Adzuma* and *Tokiwa*, cruisers *Tsushima* and *Takachiho*, a small cruiser *Chihaya*, auxiliary cruiser *Kasuga Maru* plus the 17th and 18th squadron of torpedo boats., Lacroix E., op.cit., Part 7, TBS No 5/1968, p.422..

36 | The ocean raid of the Vladivostok cruisers

Soon after their arrival from the Korea Strait, there was an idea to send the Vladivostok cruisers to disrupt Japanese communication lines in the Pacific, between the ports on the eastern and southern coasts and the United States, Australia, and the Philippines. Though this plan required the Russian warships to venture far from their base and was risky, yet it was not impossible to carry out (the Russians counted on the element of surprise). If it worked out, Japanese losses would be huge. After making sure the Port Arthur fleet did not plan another attempt to beat the blockade (in which case a support operation in the Korea Strait would be the priority), on 17th July Vice Admiral Skrydlov decided to send the cruisers to the Pacific under Rear Admiral Iessen's command.

The very same day the Russian cruisers left Vladivostok and headed for the coast of Japan. On 19th July they reached the entrance to the Tsugaru Strait. At night they crossed it and sailed out into the Pacific. However, the Japanese spotted Iessen's squadron as it was crossing the strait and the element of surprise was lost. A warning message was radioed to most of the ships at sea and they managed to reach nearby ports safely[18].

In the meantime, on reaching the Pacific the Russian squadron turned to the south and started searching for Japanese vessels. On 20th July the Russians managed to sink only one small steamer and two schooners. They also apprehended a British steamer, *Samar,* but found no contraband on it. Further searches produced no desired effects, yet consumed a lot of precious time. By midnight on 20th/21st July, the cruisers were only 50 sea miles south of Shiriyasaki Cape. As a result, most of the ships off the eastern coast of Japan managed to receive the warning about the appearance of enemy units and find shelter in ports. Despite that, Iessen continued his mission and in the morning of 22nd

July managed to apprehend the German steamer *Arabia* in the area of the port of Hitachi. It had sailed from the United States with contraband on board. After placing a prize crew on board, it was sent to Vladivostok through the Soya Strait[19].

Sailing on along the eastern shores of Honshu, during the night of 22nd/23rd July the Russian squadron reached the area of Oshima Island, at the entrance to Tokyo Bay. Finding no ships there, during the night of 23rd/24th July Iessen's cruisers sailed between the islands of Kazushima and Miyakejima. Only then did they manage to intercept a British steamer, *Knight Commander* (4306 BRT), with war contraband, which was sunk after the search. After this success, the Russian squadron continued east, sinking within the next couple of two Japanese schooners. Around 15.00, the Russians intercepted British steamer *Hunan* (1862 BRT) with some contraband on board. It was released due to the fact that it carried several dozen civilian passengers, including women and children. Next, Rear Admiral Iessen decided to turn back east, as he was afraid the supplies of coal would not suffice for a further escapade westwards. Around midnight on 24th/25th July the Russian cruisers passed Oshima Island at the entrance to Tokyo Bay and in the early morning, 17 sea miles south-west of the Nojimazaki Cape, they encountered the German steamer *Thea.* After it was found to carry contraband, it was sunk[20]. Soon after sinking *Thea*, the Russians intercepted another ship, the British *Calhas* (6748 BRT), carrying machinery and food from Canada to Yokohama. As these goods were considered contraband, it was taken over and included in the squadron.

---

18 At that time the Tsugaru Strait was patrolled by small cruisers *Takao* and *Musashi*, and the 3rd Torpedo Boat Division – both cruisers acquired visual contact with the enemy. Opisanie..., op.cit., vol.III, p.53.

19 The goods assumed to be contraband were confiscated in Vladivostok, and the ship was set free at a later date. Lacroix E., op.cit., part.7, TBS No 5/1968, p.425.
20 Later it turned out *Thea* did not carry contraband (it carried fish oil and meal, and not fish and oil, as the Russians thought) and it should have been allowed to sail free. The mIake was made because of a poor knowledge of German on the part of the Russian officers who inspected the bill of loading., Egor'ev V.E., Operatsii vladivostokskikh kreyserov..., op.cit., pp.181-182.

About noon on 25th July the Russian squadron set out on a course to Hokkaido. Initially, Iessen intended to reach the Japanese Sea through Kunashir Strait and Soya Strait, but this was made impossible by thick fog (he reached his destination on 28th July). Therefore, afraid the supplies of coal might not last long enough, he decided to turn back and pass through Tsugaru Strait. He accomplished that on 30th July and on the afternoon of 1st August he arrived back at Vladivostok.

The ocean raid of the cruisers, although long (the distance covered by the Russian ships amounted to 3,100 sea miles), brought none of the expected losses to Japanese shipping. This was due mainly to the early spotting of the enemy ships by the Japanese. On the other hand, Iessen's operation brought about a lot of confusion, causing freight prices to go up considerably and disrupting the shipping of goods to Japanese ports. In August the delivery of goods to Japanese ports decreased by almost 20%[21], so it is hard to deny that the mission of the cruisers did have some effect. However, this was insufficient to influence the situation significantly.

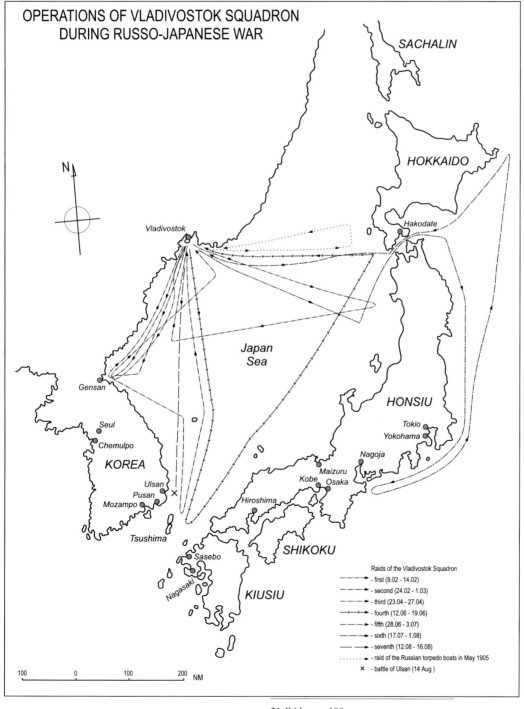

OPERATIONS OF VLADIVOSTOK SQUADRON
DURING RUSSO-JAPANESE WAR

Raids of the Vladivostok Squadron
- first (9.02 - 14.02)
- second (24.02 - 1.03)
- third (23.04 - 27.04)
- fourth (12.06 - 19.06)
- fifth (28.06 - 3.07)
- sixth (17.07 - 1.08)
- seventh (12.08 - 16.08)
- raid of the Russian torpedo boats in May 1905
× - battle of Ulsan (14 Aug)

21 Ibidem, p.190.

37 | The battle of Ulsan[22]

The commander of the II Squadron, Vice Admiral Kamimura Hikonojo, the victor in the battle of Ulsan.

Soon after returning from the Pacific sortie, Rear Admiral Iessen received an order to get his ships ready as soon as possible for another mission, this time in the area of the Korea Strait. Its purpose was to support Rear Admiral Vitgeft's squadron in his planned attempt to break the Port Arthur blockade. In the early morning of 12th August, when the outcome of the battle on the Yellow Sea was still unknown to the staff in Vladivostok or in Alekseev's headquarters in Mukden, the cruisers *Rossiya*, *Gromoboy* and *Ryurik* left port under Iessen's command and headed for the Korea Strait[23].

Heading south, the Russian cruisers reached the area of Pusan at the entrance to the Korea Strait at 04.30 . They turned west, planning to cruise between the coasts of Korea and Japan until 16.00, waiting for Vitgeft's squadron to arrive. However, ten minutes later, Vice Admiral Kamimura's division of armoured cruisers was spotted. To make things worse, they were approaching from the north, cutting the Russians off from their retreat route to Vladivostok. In these circumstances battle was inevitable.

Meanwhile, on the morning of 11th August Kamimura received news of the battle on the Yellow Sea the day before and that several

Russians ships had made it through the blockade. He left the Korea Strait leading the second squadron (only Vice Admiral Uriu's IV Division of cruisers remained on location) and headed for the island of Quelpart. There he had a rendezvous with Rear Admiral Togo's VI Division, who were searching for Reytsenshteyn's cruisers. It was Togo who informed Kamimura of the details of the battle and a potential attempt by some Russian cruisers to break through to Vladivostok across the Korea Strait. In these circumstances, the Japanese admiral decided to turn back, and returned to the area of Tsushima in the early morning of 13th August. There he received Togo's orders, warning him against a potential arrival at the Korea Strait of both the Vladivostok cruisers and the warships from the dispersed Port Arthur fleet. Executing his commander's orders, Kamimura immediately directed his squadron north, leaving the IV Division of cruisers and the 9th and 19th Torpedo Boat Divisions in the strait. Probably at about 01.00 (Tokyo time), the Japanese II division passed Iessen's squadron in the dark. At about 04.00, Kamimura turned south-west, and less than an hour later the Japanese warships spotted the enemy. At that moment, Iessen's squadron was 42 sea miles off Pusan, and the distance between the two squadrons, more or less on parallel courses towards the shores of Korea, was about 80 cable-lengths (14.5 km).

Initially, Rear Admiral Iessen hoped that he had encountered Vitgeft's squadron. After he discovered they were in fact Japanese ships, at 04.35/04.55 he turned to the east and headed for the open sea in an attempt to make his way to Vladivostok. However, Kamimura stayed alert and immediately turned his ships southeast, assuming a course parallel to the enemy's. At 04.50/05.10, when the distance between the two squadrons decreased to 51 cable-lengths (9.2 km), the Japanese warships were the first to open fire[24].

---

22 Also called the battle of the Japanese Sea, or the battle of Urusan.

23 Intensely used cruisers required repairs, though. They were to have been carried out on their return from the Pacific. However, Vitgeft's urgent call made it impossible to perform the extensive repairs as planned. Consequently, the cruisers *Rossiya* and *Ryurik* took to sea with their boilers not fully operative, which reduced their maximum speed by 1.5 – 2.0 knots., Egor'ev V.E., Operatsii vladivostokskikh kreyserov..., op.cit., pp.196, 198-199.

Vice Admiral Kamimura's flagship - cruiser Idzumo.

---

24 According to the Japanese, the distance then was below 47 cable-lengths (8.4 km). Opisanie..., op.cit., vol. III, p.60.

From the very beginning the Japanese seemed to be in control of the situation. Their greater firepower and better armoured ships soon allowed them to gain the advantage over the enemy. The first success for the Japanese came ten minutes into the battle, when they hit *Rjiurik's* fore area several times, starting a fire. Although several Russian shells also reached their target, at about 05.03/05.23 a Japanese shell damaged three boilers on *Rossiya*. With four other boilers not fully operational even before the battle had commenced, Iessen's flagship's speed dropped considerably, causing confusion amongst the other Russian cruisers. In order to avoid a collision with *Rossiya*, *Gromoboy* had to turn to port abeam *Rossiya*, whilst *Ryurik* was forced to turn to starboard. At that very moment, *Ryurik* received a hit to its side from a Japanese 203 mm shell, which crashed through the hull and damaged the rudder. At first, it seemed that the damage to *Ryurik* was not that serious, but when at 05.16/05.36 *Rossiya* and *Gromoboy* made a 20 degrees turn starboard, in order to chase off the cruiser *Naniwa* that was approaching from the east (at that moment it was about 40 cable-lengths away from *Rossiya*, and had just opened fire on the Russian warship), it was clear that *Ryurik* had serious problems manoeuvring.

Soon afterwards, the main damage to *Rossiya* was fixed, and the flagship managed to rejoin the formation. At about 05.40/06.00 the

Cruiser Gromoboy.

Russian ships took advantage of the fact that Kamimura's ships had sailed too much to the east and made a sharp turn north-west, in order to head for Vladivostok behind the sterns of the Japanese warships. However, the Japanese commander was alert and in the next five minutes repeated the manoeuvre, and soon assumed a parallel course to the Russians. During this manoeuvre, the Japanese ships intensified their shelling of the last in line, *Ryurik*. It received further hits at the stern, which ultimately incapacitated its rudder. To make things worse it lost speed and at about 06.05/06.25 dropped out of the formation. Due to the fact that its rudder was stuck it was turning to starboard, getting dangerously close to the enemy. In these circumstances, Iessen turned towards *Ryurik* in order to cover it, but his effort brought no results[25].

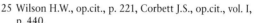

25 Wilson H.W., op.cit., p. 221, Corbett J.S., op.cit., vol. I, p. 440.

Cruiser Ryurik.

171

Table No. 1: The battle of Ulsan

Name of ship	Commander	Hits	Casualties		
		203-152mm	Killed	Wounded	Total
Russian					
Rossiya	Rear Adm. K.P. Iessen Captain A.P. Andreev	31	47	153	200
Gromoboy	Captain N.D. Dabich	27	93	166	259
Ryurik	Captain E.A. Trusov	about 150	192	216	408
Japananese					
Idzumo	Vice Adm. Kamimura H. Captain Ijichi S.	20	3	16	19
Adzuma	Captain Fujii K.	10	-	8	8
Tokiwa	Captain Yoshimatsu M.	3	-	3	3
Iwate	Rear Adm. Mizu S. Captain Taketomi K.	23	40	37	77
Naniwa	Vice Adm. Uriu S. Captain Wada K.	1	2	4	6
Takachiho	Captain Mori I.	1	-	13	13

Unable to rescue the heavily damaged *Ryurik*, the Russian commander finally gave up and, at 08.05/08.25, set course for Vladivostok, getting away from the battle area at a speed of about 17 knots[26]. The Russian ships were followed by four Japanese armoured cruisers, which continued shelling from a parallel course at a distance of about 35-40 cable-lengths (6.3 – 7.2 km). The exchange lasted until 09.40/10.00, when the Japanese admiral suddenly decided to stop the battle and turned south. Meanwhile, the heavily

damaged *Ryurik* was challenged by the newly arrived cruisers *Naniwa* (from the east, joining the battle at about 05.25/05.45) and *Takachiho* (from the south-west, joined *Naniwa* at 07.30/07.50). The Russian ship tried to defend itself, but it was already sinking. Bombarded by a hail of shells, at 10.00/10.20 it was abandoned by the crew, who speeded up its sinking by opening the kingstons. It sank at 10.22/10.42 [27].

After the battle the Japanese ships returned to patrolling the Korea Strait, except for *Idzumo*, *Adzuma* and *Iwate*, which were docked for repairs in Japanese shipyards. The Russian ships arrived back in Vladivostok on 16th August.

During the battle the Japanese fired a total of 958 203 mm shells, and 4,528 152 mm shells (761 from *Naniwa* and *Takachiho*), achieving over 200 hits. However, 140-150 of the hits were inflicted upon *Ryurik*, which was damaged half way through the battle and could not resist effectively. Moreover, at the end of the battle it was fired at from a very close distance. In practice, considering the actual battle, the Japanese achieved no more than 75 – 80 hits, which is about 1.5 percent of all the shells fired (all the hits constituted 3.6 percent). The Russians, in turn, fired a total of about 2,000-2,300 203-152 mm shells, achieving 58 hits, which constitutes 2.5 percent[28]. Despite a slightly higher efficiency of fire at long and medium distance, the Russians were defeated, which can

26 After the battle the Russian commander justified the abandonment of *Ryurik* by his intention to drag the main forces away from it, hoping that the Russian ship would somehow handle the cruisers *Naniwa* and *Takachicho*. *Rossiya's* and *Gromoboy's* damage also came into play – their surface damage was considerable and they suffered great human losses. What was even worse, most guns were destroyed or damaged, which made any further involvement in the battle practically impossible. Thus Iessen's decision was fully justified.

The stern 152mm cannon on the cruiser Gromoboy.

27 PRO, ADM 231/44, Reports..., vol. III, p. 190.
28 Otryad vladivostokskikh kreyserov v boyu 1 avgusta 1904 goda., „Gangut" No. 55 (2009), p. 58.

be accounted for by the fact that the Japanese ships had much better armour. Consequently, Iessen's cruisers were much more vulnerable to damage. To make things worse, their guns had almost no armour protection, and were easily damaged. The losses among the crews were also considerable. As a result, the Russians fired almost 2.5 times fewer shells than the Japanese, which ultimately determined the outcome of the battle.

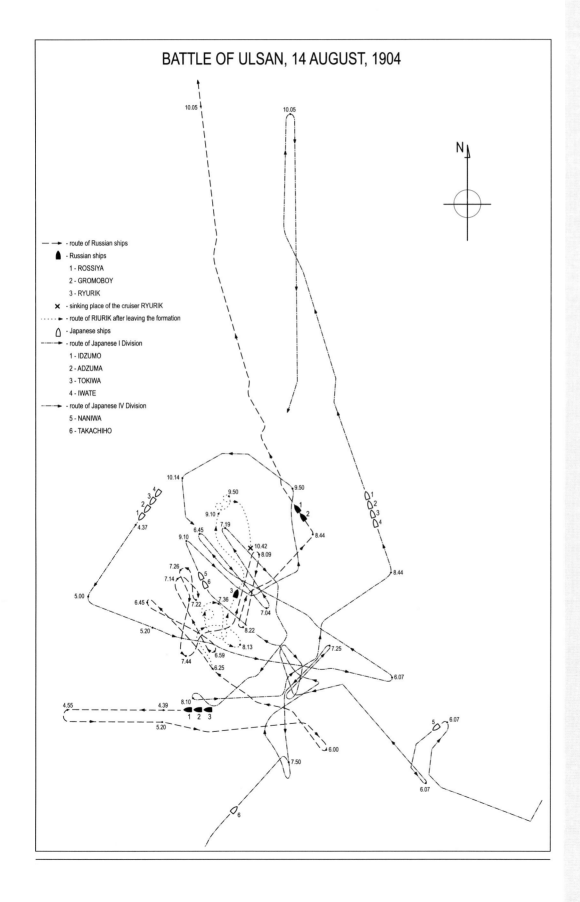

BATTLE OF ULSAN, 14 AUGUST, 1904

- → - route of Russian ships
- ▲ - Russian ships
  - 1 - ROSSIYA
  - 2 - GROMOBOY
  - 3 - RYURIK
- ✕ - sinking place of the cruiser RYURIK
- ⋯► - route of RIURIK after leaving the formation
- ◌ - Japanese ships
- —·—► - route of Japanese I Division
  - 1 - IDZUMO
  - 2 - ADZUMA
  - 3 - TOKIWA
  - 4 - IWATE
- —·—► - route of Japanese IV Division
  - 5 - NANIWA
  - 6 - TAKACHIHO

30 The Vladivostok's squadron operations after 14th August 1904

Russian submarine Del'fin.

Russian cruiser Rossiya. A photo taken after the modernisation and re-arming of the warship at the turn of 1904 and 1905.

After the battle of Ulsan, the activity of the Vladivostok cruisers was limited. First of all, the warships needed immediate repair of the damage suffered in battle, which took 2-3 months. To make things worse, *Gromoboy* damaged its hull on an underwater rock during acceptance tests on 13th October. This excluded the ship from war operations until the end of the year. Further inactivity of the Vladivostok squadron was determined in December, 1904 by the Ministry of the Navy, who ordered Vice Admiral Skrydlov to cease any operations that might expose the cruisers to any sort of danger. It was considered that the entire squadron should be ready for battle once the II Pacific

Fleet, sailing from Europe to the Far East, required their support[29]. Soon afterwards, following the annihilation of the Port Arthur fleet, Vice Admiral Skrydlov (official commander of the entire I Pacific Fleet, including the vessels stationed in Port Arthur) was recalled along with Rear Admiral Bezobrazov to Petersburg. Command was transferred to Iessen. However, the Ministry's orders remained binding. It was only in May, 1905 that Iessen was permitted to carry out a raid on the shores of Japan. As a result, between 8th and 11th May, *Gromoboy* and *Rossiya* made a sortie towards the area of the Tsugaru Strait. However, they managed to sink only two small schooners. A similar sortie to the shores of Hokkaido was made between 1st and 10th May by torpedo boats *201, 203, 205* and *206*, which sank one small Japanese sailing vessel and apprehended another[30].

Apart from those raids, right after the battle of Ulsan the auxiliary cruiser *Lena* also tried to undertake offensive action. It left Vladivostok on 11th August, 1904 and first headed towards the mouth of the river Amur with a cargo of supplies on board. From there she headed for the Pacific with the intention of intercepting

---

29 Egor'ev V.E., Operatsii vladivostokskikh kreyserov..., op.cit., p.250.
30 Ibidem, pp. 258-260

Japanese shipping. Before she reached the area of the most popular routes to Japanese ports, the failure of its machinery made it call into San Francisco on 12th September. Since the machinery required extensive repairs and the ship could not return to sea any time soon, it was disarmed and interned[31].

Another aspect of the operations of the Russian forces grouped in Vladivostok was the activity of submarines. This new type of weapon was of considerable interest to the Russians. They had built a couple of experimental boats before the war and ordered (after the war broke out) several of them from their own, as well as foreign, shipyards. Initially, they intended to deliver the boats to Port Arthur by railway, but due to the blockade of the fortress, only one small experimental unit of no combat value, dispatched as early as February, reached its destination. The rest of the boats were dispatched to Vladivostok starting August, 1904. By the end of December, seven boats had reached Vladivostok and on 1st January, 1905 were made into an independent squadron of torpedo boats – the very first independent operational fleet of submarines in history. Their first combat patrol took place on 14th February (carried out by *Som* and *Del'fin*). An average patrol lasted no longer then 24 hours. However, there were cases of three day patrols, and even one week patrols, though these were quite rare[32].

There was only one clash with Japanese ships during the patrols. It took place on 29th April, 1905, in the area of Povrotnyj Cape, 70 sea miles off Vladivostok. The submarine *Som* spotted Japanese torpedo boats, which fired several shots at it and then withdrew. On 1st July, in the Tartar Strait, the Nikoalevsk-upon-Amur based submarine *Keta* (included in the forces in June) also came into contact with the enemy. It encountered two Japanese torpedo boats, but it was spotted before it managed to submerge and thus failed to assume a proper firing position[33].

By the end of the war, the number of submarines in Vladivostok was 13, plus one more in

Russian submarine Kasatka.

Nikolaevsk. Not all of them managed, however, to achieve full combat readiness. There were no more encounters with enemy ships. The only loss suffered during operations was the sinking of the submarine *Del'fin*, which went down in port after an explosion of gasoline fumes[34].

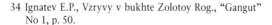

34 Ignatev E.P., Vzryvy v bukhte Zolotoy Rog., "Gangut" No 1, p. 50.

Russian submarine Kefal'.

31 Egor'ev V. E. claims, however (ibidem, p. 249) that the condition of *Lena's* machinery was not that bad and allowed further navigation. It is likely, then, that the internment was prompted by other factors, like the crew's low morale for example.
32 Bozhenko P., Podvodnye minonostsy: Russkie podvodnye lodki v voyne 1904-1905 g.g. Boevoy debyut., "Naval" No 1 (1991), p. 41
33 Ibidem, pp. 39, 41.

39 | Mine laying operations at Vladivostok

Mines on board the Russian mine transport.

Because the waters around Vladivostok froze in winter, mine laying operations, intended to protect of the port against a potential enemy assault, were commenced as late as April 1904. The mine transport *Aleut* was assigned for this task. The *Aleut* could take about 130 contact mines on board at a time. A huge drawback was that it was impossible to lay mines directly from the ship. A laborious technique of laying mines from special rafts (pontoons) had to be used. *Aleut* served only as the rafts' base and a carrier of mines during the operation. As a result, by the end of 1904 only 326 contact mines of different patterns were laid, which was not many considering the port's defensive requirements. One must also consider that a lot of mines became detached from their anchors during storms.

At the same time, numerous mine-fields were laid. They contained mines detonated electrically from the land. There were many of these in the Vladivostok depots. The task of laying them was delegated to the transport *Mongugay*, which was specially adapted for this purpose. It could take 150 mines on board at a time. Electrically detonated mines were laid up to 25-30 cable-lengths from the shore (usually it was less than that). They were laid in groups of five or six. By the end of 1904 about 500 of them had been laid in total[35].

Problems with mine laying by *Aleut* forced the Russian command to withdraw it and transfer this task to the transport *Mongugay*. The latter was modified to carry and lay contact mines. It could carry up to 180 of them. It performed relatively well and by the end of the war had laid a further 1,117 contact mines, and about 1,000 mines electrically detonated from the shore.

The total number of mines the Russians laid outside Vladivostok was 1,443 contact mines and 1,000–1,500 electrically detonated ones[36]. This was much more than around Port Arthur, but the effect was minimal. Electrically detonated were usually laid too close to the shore, where no Japanese ships ever appeared. Contact mines were potentially more dangerous to the enemy, but the fields were also located too close to the port. Besides, many mines were destroyed by the weather.

The Japanese, unable to use their naval forces to block Vladivostok port directly, made two attempts to deploy mines for that purpose.

---

35 Mines detonated electrically from the land, stored in the Vladivostok arsenal, were at the disposal of the

town land defence command, whilst contact mines belonged to the fleet command. Such a situation did not make their effective usage easier. Denisov B., Minnaya voyna u Vladivostoka v 1904-1905 gg., MS No 10/1935, pp.26, 29-30.

36 In his article "Minnaya voyna u Vladivostoka..." (op. cit., p. 27), Denisov B. gives the number of 1,500 electrically detonated mines. However, due to the removal of most of the 500 mines laid in the spring and summer of 1904, the number may be lower – some of them may have been laid again during the mine laying operations of 1905.

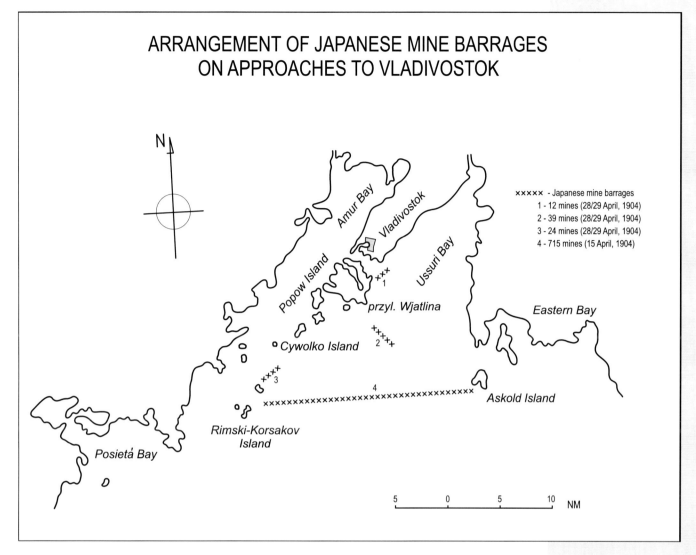

ARRANGEMENT OF JAPANESE MINE BARRAGES
ON APPROACHES TO VLADIVOSTOK

×××× - Japanese mine barrages
1 - 12 mines (28/29 April, 1904)
2 - 39 mines (28/29 April, 1904)
3 - 24 mines (28/29 April, 1904)
4 - 715 mines (15 April, 1904)

Initially this was done during Vice Admiral Kamimura's raid on Vladivostok on 28th April, when one of his auxiliary cruisers, used then as an auxiliary minelayer, laid three mine fields of 75 mines altogether. The Russians found out about them as late as July, when their torpedo boat *208* and a German ship, *China*, sank on them. All in all, these mines were not enough to hamper the operations of the Vladivostok squadron of cruisers in any significant way.

The second mine laying operation took place after the fall of Port Arthur. It was part of the Japanese scheme to "welcome" the Far East bound squadron led by Vice Admiral Rozhestvenski. Their intention was to block the passage into, and out of, Vladivostok for both the cruisers stationed there and Rozhestvenski's squadron, in case the latter broke through the Korea Strait. For that purpose, on 15th April, 1905 the auxiliary minelayer *Taihoku Maru* and the auxiliary cruisers adapted to carrying and laying mines, *Daichu Maru*, *Dainan Maru* and *Taichu Maru*, escorted by Kamimura's division,

laid a field of 715 mines, stretching over 35 sea miles from Askold Island in the east to Rimsky-Korsakov Island in the west[37]. It was, beyond doubt, the most extensive mine laying operation during this war. Yet possibly it was its great scale that prevented its success. Intending to cover the entire area, and having a limited number of mines, the Japanese made their barrier too thin (only three rows of mines), whilst the distance between individual mines was greater than usual. On the other hand, it could not be entirely ignored, as the example of the armoured cruiser *Gromoboy*, which was damaged on 23rd May, 1905, shows[38].

---

37 Ibidem, p. 28.
38 The encounter with the mines was due to Rear Admiral Iessen's negligence, who sent trawlers back to the port after sailing over only 6 sea miles, despite the fact that he knew about the Japanese barrier (though was not necessarily aware of its length – the encounter took place 23 sea miles in a straight line from the port). Egor'ev V.E., Operatsii vladivostokskikh kreyserov..., op.cit., pp.262-263.

40 Japanese fleet operations against Vladivostok-bound shipping

Small Japanese cruiser Musashi. Throughout the entire war it performed patrol operations in the Tsugaru Strait.

Preparing Vladivostok for the reception of the Second and Third Pacific Fleets, the Russian command decided to send additional supplies of ammunition and materiel, and most important of all, of coal. Dispatching the goods by trans-Siberian rail was practically impossible, as this was busy providing for the troops fighting in Manchuria (only top priority supplies, like ammunition, were transported by rail). It was decided to charter 80 ships from neutral countries, which were to deliver a total of over 400,000 tons of supplies (including 250,000 tons of coal). The first transports arrived in Vladivostok in July, 1904.

Russian preparations could not escape the attention of the Japanese. However, engaged in Port Arthur and protecting their own communication routes in the Korea Strait, they did not manage to intercept deliveries to Vladivostok. The situation changed after the fall of Port Arthur. The Japanese command immediately sent the forces at their disposal to patrol the routes along which the cargo ships tried to reach Vladivostok.

In December, 1904 the control of the Korea Strait was taken over by Vice Admiral Uriu. He was given five or six larger vessels (armoured cruisers, cruisers, and auxiliary cruisers), as well as the 11th, 17th, 18th, and 19th Torpedo Boat

Divisions. These ships continued patrolling the area until the spring, apprehending 10 vessels.

In January, 1905, the Tsugaru Strait was taken over by Rear Admiral Mizu's detachment. He was given two armoured cruisers, Hakodate-based small cruisers *Takao* (soon transferred to the VII Division) and *Musashi*, and the 3rd Torpedo Boat Division (he was additionally supported by the Ominato-based 13th Torpedo Boat Division, and later he was also reinforced by further units). Soon Mizu was promoted to the rank of Vice Admiral, and made the commander of the I Division. He was replaced by Rear Admiral Shimamura Hayao on 22nd January.

At the end of January, Shimamura's ships undertook the additional task of patrolling the Etorofu, Kunashir and Soya Straits, which had been frozen and inaccessible until then. In connection with that, his forces were strengthened by several other warships. By the beginning of April they had apprehended seven ships in the Tsugaru Strait, and eight in the Etorofu and Kunashir Straits.

At the beginning of April, the Japanese found out that Rozhestvenski's squadron had passed Singapore. As a result, Shimamura's ships were concentrated in the western part of the Tsugaru Strait and only the auxiliary cruiser *Kumano Maru* was left in the area of the Kuril Islands. In these circumstances, the patrol efficiency of Japanese ships was bound to deteriorate. After 18th April, most of Shimamura's ships were recalled from the northern waters to Sasebo, leaving only the auxiliary cruisers *Nippon Maru* and *Hongkong Maru*, the small cruiser *Musashi*, and the 3rd and 13th Torpedo Boat Divisions.

Out of 80 ships chartered by the Russians, 42 made it to Vladivostok, whilst 23 were intercepted by the Japanese.

41 | Japanese landing operations in Gensan and Songjin

In the summer of 1904 the Russian command came up with an idea to attack northeast Korea, which was under Japanese control. This would pose a threat to the communication routes in Manchuria and almost certainly pull part of the main enemy forces away from the war zone. Initially, the intention was to engage forces corresponding to the size of an infantry brigade with artillery and three Cossack regiments, with a possibility of further reinforcement[39]. Preparations for the operation commenced in July, with construction of a base on existing fortifications in Posiet Bay. At the same time a strong contingent of Cossacks, equipped with artillery, was dispatched by land to carry out a reconnaissance. They reported that due to the poor condition of the roads transfer of forces by land was impossible. In these circumstances the Russians decided to transfer the main force (originally a strengthened infantry division) and supplies by sea. For this purpose an operational base was set up in Songjin, south-west Korea, a town only 60 sea miles from Gensan, where supplies indispensable for the assault forces were to be stored[40]. Eventually, after the fall of Port Arthur, the Russian command gave up these plans, evacuating their contingent from Songjin on 13th January and destroying supplies gathered there. A military camp set up near the fortifications in Posiet' Bay was also abandoned and the forces stationed there were evacuated to Vladivostok by land (the last ones arrived on 1st February).

In the meantime, at the beginning of 1905, the Japanese decided to transfer additional forces to the north-west part of Korea. This came as a result of the development of the situation in Manchuria and their intention to strengthen their presence in Korea in response to the Russian plans, of which the Japanese must have been informed by espionage. First, on 10th February a strengthened infantry battalion was transferred to Gensan by transports escorted by the armoured cruisers *Idzumo, Tokiwa* and *Kasuga*, the cruiser *Suma*, and two destroyers. The second operation took place two weeks later during the battle of Mukden. This time an entire infantry division (2nd Reserve Division) was to be transferred by six transports to Songjin, 60 sea miles north of Gensan. On 24th February, the troops were embarked at Mozampo and sent off to Gensan, escorted by the battleship *Fuji* and armoured cruisers *Idzumo* and *Kasuga*, cruisers *Otowa, Akitsushima, Chiyoda* and *Suma*, the small cruiser *Chihaya*, and eight destroyers. The remaining units set out for Songjin on 28th February and arrived there on 1st March. The disembarkation of troops, setting up camp and a provisional harbour lasted until 4th March, and on 6th March the Japanese squadron returned to the Korea Strait[41].

The transfer of troops to Gensan and Songjin, only 200 miles from Vladivostok, disturbed the Russians greatly, since they rightly assumed them to be an indication of a later assault on Vladivostok. These, in fact, were the intentions of the Japanese command, never realised due to the ending of the war.

39 Istoriya..., op.cit. (edited by I.I. Rostunov), p. 352.
40 Ibidem, pp. 13-14.

41 Opisanie..., op.cit., vol.IV, pp.24-25.

Japanese troops landing in Korea.

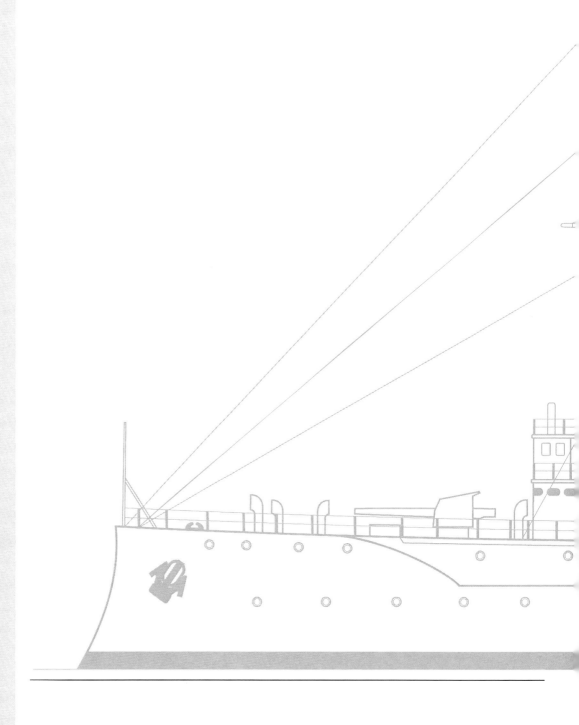

|TSUSHIMA

42 | The operations of Rear Admiral Virenjus' squadron

Russian battleship
Oslyabya.

In order to strengthen the fleet in the Far East, in autumn, 1903 the Russian command sent two battleships, two armoured cruisers, two cruisers, six destroyers, and four torpedo boats, as well as auxiliary units, from the Baltic Sea to Port Arthur. Of these, before the war broke out in December, 1903, only the battleship *Tsesarevich* and the armoured cruiser *Bayan* managed to reach their destination. The remaining units, most of which were dispatched in November, 1903 set out as late as on 8th February, 1904, commanded by Rear Admiral A.A. Virenjus. Due to the breakdown of the battleship *Oslyabya*, the problems the small torpedo boats had keeping pace with the rest of the detachment, and the delayed dispatch of the cruiser *Almaz*, the Russian units did not sail in one group. On the day the war broke out, the squadron consisting of the armoured cruiser *Dmitriy Donskoy*,

the cruiser *Avrora*, and the destroyers *Bodryy*, *Bystryy*, *Bedovyy* and *Bezuprechnyy* were in Aden. At the same time, in the north of the Red Sea, there was Virenjus' flagship, the battleship *Oslyabya*, accompanied by destroyers *Bravyy* and *Blestjaschchij* and torpedo boats *213* and *213*. Way behind, torpedo boats *221* and *222* were just passing Gibraltar, whilst *Almaz* was in the Atlantic close to the shores of Portugal[42].

After news of the outbreak of war had reached the Russians, all their warships, except *Alamaz*, and the torpedo boats *221* and *222*, gathered in Djibouti (a French colony) by 13th February. There Virenjus awaited further orders. On 18th February he received an order to bring the entire squadron back to Russia[43].

On their way back the Russian ships began to attack Japanese shipping. On February 19th they intercepted three steamers with coal for a Japanese consignee (two British and one Norwegian). The British government protested, however, as the ships had set out before the war was declared and, as a result, on reaching Suez on 28th February, the ships were released. In the face of war with Japan, the Russians could simply not afford a diplomatic crisis with Britain. By 29th February all the Russian ships had gathered in Suez, except *Almaz*, which had already turned back, and the torpedo boats *221* and *222*, which had set off for the area of Crete. Then the entire squadron passed through the Canal and sailed into the Mediterranean. There the Russian squadron was divided. Torpedo boats *212* and *213* were to set course for Greece and, on joining *221* and *222*, remain there (this decision had been made on 27th February). The remaining warships returned home in the first half of April (*Buynyy* on 10th May).

---

42 Corbett J.S., op.cit., vol. II, pp. 51, 54-55
43 Opinions concerning the return of the warships varied. Vice-Admiral Makarov opposed this plan. RGAVMF F.469, op.1 D.76.

43 | The operations of Russian auxiliary cruisers in the summer of 1904

The island location of Japan and the dependence of its economy on foreign trade gave Russian cruisers a number of opportunities to undermine Japanese shipping. The Russian command was well aware of this, yet no plan for such operations had been prepared before the war, except one limited to the Far East. Only as late as March, 1904 was the decision made to take action against the communication lines between Japan and Europe. The lines ran mainly through the Suez Canal and around the Cape of Good Hope. It was ruled that the forces indispensable for an efficient operation were to be six to eight auxiliary cruisers.

The required number of auxiliary cruisers was to be provided by the Voluntary Fleet[44]. It turned out, however, that out of their six units suitable for being turned into auxiliary cruisers, two were in the Far East, the other two were being used for other purposes and only two (*Petersburg* and *Smolensk*), harboured in ports on the Black Sea, could be used. In these circumstances, in the spring of 1904, the Russian authorities decided to purchase four more big passenger ships in Germany with the intention of turning them into auxiliary cruisers. Due to the necessity of carrying out conversion and crew training (the crews were made up mainly of reservist), along with the purchase of weapons and armour, the length of time before they could finally be engaged in military operations was considerable.

In these circumstances *Petersburg* and *Smolensk*, which were ready as early as June,

were engaged first. As non-military vessels (their weapons were hidden in their cargo bays), they crossed the Dardanelles and Bosporus at the beginning of July and then headed for the Red Sea, where they performed their military tasks for the rest of the month. They apprehended a total of five ships (three British and two German) and destroyed the cargo, assumed to be contraband, on a sixth one (German)[45].

The operations of the Russian auxiliary cruisers caused great resentment on the part of the British government. It issued a note of protest to the Russian government, demanding an immediate release of the ships. The British rightly justified their protest by the fact that the Russian ships left the Black Sea through the straits, which was prohibited for warships other than Turkish on the basis of the 1878 treaty. In this situation the Tsar's government, in order to avoid a diplomatic conflict, ordered the release of all the ships and sent the auxiliary cruisers to the Indian Ocean. However, due to the fact that the British insisted that the Russians withdraw their vessels operating in violation of the international law, both cruisers were eventually called back home, where they arrived at the beginning of October. (After their names were changed to *Rion* and *Dniepr*, they were later incorporated into the II Pacific Squadron).

Before these two cruisers were recalled, on 28th July two other units of the same class, *Don* and *Ural*, had been sent from Libawa to the Atlantic Ocean. The former headed for the north-west coast of Africa and the Canary Islands, and the latter for the Straits of Gibraltar. This time, however, there was no question of breaking international law. The Russians were unlucky, though. By 25th August, *Ural* had inspected 12 ships, but found no contraband and returned to Libawa on 5th September. The situation was even more unfortunate with *Don*, which had a breakdown of its boilers and also returned to Libawa on 5th September, having not inspected a single ship.

---

44 The Voluntary Fleet was set up upon the decision of the Russian government in April, 1878, after the war with Turkey. It was financed by government funds and donations. Initially, its only task was to provide the Russian fleet with warships and a sufficient number of auxiliary units. After the Congress of Berlin, and the stabilization of the international situation, the Voluntary Fleet was restructured to serve as a commercial fleet. The Russian government remained its main client (since the 1880s, the major task of the fleet was to maintain regular connections between Odessa on the Black Sea and the ports in the Far East) which, in practice, meant that it was subsidized by the state budget. In return, it maintained units that were not necessarily profitable, but useful for the navy. Yarovoy V.V., Kratkiy ocherk Iorii Dobrovolnogo flota., "Gangut" No 3 (1992)

45 Russian Auxiliary Cruisers in the Red Sea during 1904., WI No 2/1972, pp. 202-203; Bykov P.D., op.cit., p. 68.

Russian auxiliary cruiser Peterburg.

The auxiliary cruiser *Terek* was no more successful. It left Libawa on 25th August and headed for the Atlantic coast of Portugal. Between 5th and 18th September, it inspected 15 ships around Cape St. Vincent, but apprehended none. It returned on 26th September. The last of the cruisers, *Kuban'*, never made it to sea because of damage done in the Libawa dock. It was seaworthy as late as 2nd September, when the Russian command suspended all commerce raiding operations. Later all the auxiliary cruisers, apart from *Don* which required its boilers to be replaced, were incorporated into the Second Fleet, joining it off Madagascar.

Russian auxiliary cruiser Smolensk.

In case of war with Japan, the Russian strategic plan predicted shifting part of the Baltic Fleet to the Far East[46]. Immediately after war broke out, the Russian command considered this plan and finally, on April 30th, the Tsar's order was issued to establish the II Pacific Squadron (the forces based in the Far East were named the I Pacific Squadron)[47]. Rear Admiral Z. P. Rozhestvenski was appointed for this task. He had been head of the chief naval staff, a very controversial officer, undoubtedly brave and a good organizer, but with little tactical talent, very strict and overconfident about his abilities[48].

Rozhestvenski based the organization of the Second Fleet on ships from Virenjus' squadron, and four battleships of the *Imperator Aleksandr III* class (the fifth unit of this class, *Slava*, stood no chance of being launched before the spring of 1905). He also decided to include three older vessels (two battleships and armoured cruiser) which had returned from the Far East for repairs in Russia at the end of 1902, along with several additional destroyers. At the same time, talks with Argentina and Chile were undertaken regarding the purchase of several armoured cruisers that the two countries were ready to sell after settling their border problems. If the talks had been successful, the extra warships would have been manned by Black Sea Fleet crews and would have joined the main forces off Madagascar[49]. At the same time, efforts were made to purchase cargo and passenger ships abroad, with the intention of con-

verting them into auxiliary cruisers and transports. Several vessels of the Voluntary Fleet were deployed for the same purpose.

Efforts were also made to secure proper bases and supplies, mainly of coal, for the Far East bound squadron. The French, allies of Russia, were ready to solve the problem of anchorages, as there were many suitable harbours in its colonies. Maintaining coal supplies was a much more serious problem for the II Squadron. Despite all their support for the Russians, the French were reluctant to allow them to use their coal supplies, lest they were to be accused of violating their neutral status. As a result, the Tsar's government signed an agreement with the German Navigation Association HAPAG, concerning the delivery of coal along the II Squadron's route[50].

The commander of the Second Pacific Squadron, Vice Admiral Rozhestvenski.

50 PRO, AMD 231/44, Papers on Naval Subjects 1906, vol. I, pp. 9-10. The agreement regulated the provision of the total of 300,000 tons of coal, which made Germany delegate as many as 52 ships to this task (12 of their own large coal carriers and 40 chartered German and British vessels), which, sailing in groups of 7-8 were to secure a systematic coal delivery at prearranged locations along the entire Second Fleet route, including alterations caused by the development of the situation.

Battleship Knyaz' Suvorov – *Vice Admiral Rozhestvenski's flagship.*

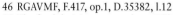

46 RGAVMF, F.417, op.1, D.35382, l.12
47 The final decision was made on 10th April, 1904, at the meeting of the government committee lead by the Tsar himself. Corbett J.S., op.cit., vol. II, p. 8; Dyskant J.W., Cuszima., Warsaw 1989, p. 29; Shirokorad A.B., op.cit., pp. 325-326.
48 Rozhestvenski received the nomination on May 2nd, 1904. Opisanie..., op.cit., vol.IV, p.46. Later analysis of Rozhestvenski's correspondence suggests the Russian Admiral treated the escapade of the II Pacific Squadron as a demonstration of military power, whose aim was to secure a better position for Russia in peace negotiations, rather than a purely military operation to gain advantage at sea!
49 The talks failed. PRO, FO 46/667; Dyskant J.W., Cuszima..., op.cit., pp. 33-34, Towle P., Battleship Sales During the Russo-Japanese War., WI No 4/1986.

Above: The Tsar inspecting the battleship Sisoy Velikiy.

Right: Tsar Nikolay I during an inspection of the ships of the Second Pacific Squadron, before they set out to the Far East – here on board of the cruiser Svetlana.

Certain doubts about sending the II Squadron to the Far East arose after the battle of the Yellow Sea. Eventually, the original decisions remained in place[51] and on 15th October the II Squadron, divided into four groups, left home waters heading for the Danish straits. It was made up of seven battleships (*Knyaz' Suvorov* – from 14th August Rozhestvenski's flagship, *Imperator Aleksandr III*, *Borodino*, *Orel'*, *Oslyabya*, *Sisoy Velikiy* and *Navarin*), two old armoured cruisers (*Admiral Nakhimov* and *Dmitriy Donskoy*), four cruisers (*Avrora*, *Svetlana*, *Zhemchug* and *Almaz*), seven destroyers (*Bodryy*, *Bedovyy*, *Bravyy*, *Bezuprechnyy*, *Bystryy*, *Blestyashchiy* and *Prozorlivyy*) and nine transports and auxiliary units[52].

On 17th October the Russian squadron reached the vicinity of Fakebjerg lighthouse at the entrance to Store Baelt, where Rozhestvenski received news of his promotion to the rank of a Vice-Admiral. On the morning of the following day the Russian warships restocked their coal supplies and entered the straits. On 20th October, at dawn, they anchored at Skagen, where they were joined by the transport *Anadyr"*. However, due to numerous breakdowns, the destroyer *Prozorlivyy* had to be towed back home by *Yermak*. After restocking coal from three Danish ships, Rozhestvenski divided the squadron into six groups and between 15.00 and 20.00 dispatched them one by one to the North Sea. The distance between consecutive groups was 16-20 sea miles. Tangier was their next destination.

51 Doubts were resolved at the conference of the government committee on August 23rd, 1904, by the same participants as in the one of April 10th. Bykov P.D., op.cit., p. 72; Russko-yaponskaya voyna... Rabota..., op.cit., vol. IX, p. 176; Zolotarev V.A., Kozlov I.A., Tri stoletya rossiyskovo flota, XIX-nachalo XX veka., Moskva-St. Peterburg 2004, p. 573.
52 The transport *Irtysh* remained in Libawa, as it broke down just before the planned departure (it joined the squadron later) and destroyers *Rezvyy* and *Pronzitelnyy*,

whose technical condition was unsatisfactory., Novikov, Russko-yaponskaya voyna 1904-1905 gg. Maaterialy dlya opisaniya deystviy Khronologicheskiy perechen' voennykh" deystviy flota v" 1904-5 g.g. Vypusk" II. Perechen' sobytiy pokhoda 2-oy eskadry Tikhago Okeana i eya otryadov" na Dalniy Vostok" i boy v" Tsusimskom" prolive., St. Peterburg 1912, pp.2-3; Opisanie..., op.cit., vol.IV, p.50.

The ships of the Second Squadron on the roadstead of Libawa shortly before departing to the Far East. The battleships anchored from the left: Suvorov, Aleksandr III, Borodino, Orel' *and* Oslyabya, *behind them the cruisers* Almaz *and* Zhemchug.

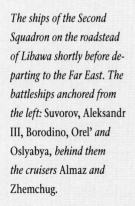

45 | The North Sea incident

Early in the preparations for sending the II Squadron to the Far East, the Russians were afraid that the Japanese might undertake sabotage operations to undermine the squadron's strength, or even send torpedo boats against them. Appropriate reconnaissance was performed, which resulted in inundation of the Ministry of the Navy with numerous messages about the movements of different suspicious units on the squadron's planned route[53]. All these messages, either made up or erroneous, press releases, and rumours led to a sense of constant threat among the commanders and crews of the II Squadron. In these circumstances, combat readiness was constantly maintained on the ships, wary of potential assault by fictitious Japanese torpedo boats. The search for Japanese mines was also in progress. Regular commercial ships and even fishing cutters were feared, due to intelligence warning that the Japanese were able to mount torpedo launchers on such units. For this reason, Rozhestvenski ordered the aiming of guns at all unidentified vessels passing the squadron, to open fire should they ignore

the warning against crossing the Russian fleet's course.

In such an atmosphere, unfortunate incidents were more than likely to happen. As early as 20th October the Swedish steamer *Aldebaran* was fired on (fortunately it was not hit), plus French sailing vessel *Guyane* and German trawler *Sonntag*. The night of 20th/21st October was calm, but in the morning the Russian warships entered an area of dense fog, which only increased the sense of threat. Moreover, the repair ship *Kamchatka* broke down and was lagging behind the last ship by about 17 sea miles. However, Rozhestvenski was not informed about this fact, so he was extremely surprised when at about 20.45 the commander of *Kamchatka* sent a radio message saying that he was being attacked by eight Japanese torpedo boats (he kept on sending further messages until 23.20)[54]. The alarm was immediately raised on all the Russian warships, as a torpedo attack from the rear was expected.

At 00.55, the Russians spotted unidentified small boats ahead of their ships. They had white numbers painted on their sides, whilst

Repair ship Kamchatka. *Its commander's false reports of an alleged Japanese torpedo boats assault became one of the causes of the North Sea incident.*

---

53 Novikov N.W., Gull'skiy intsident i tsarska okhranka., MS No 6/1935, pp. 101-102.

54 Ibidem, p. 105.

An English postcard depicting the North Sea incident.

the Dogger Bank[55]. They ceased fire (the shelling lasted about 12 minutes altogether) and, after re-establishing the proper formation, sailed away without providing any help for the British fishermen.

During the incident, the Russian warships sank the trawler *Crane* and damaged another five – *Mina*, *Moulimein*, *Snipe*, *Gull* and *Majestic*. Two fishermen were killed and six were seriously wounded[56]. Five light shells also hit the cruiser *Avrora*, which happened to be about 10-15 cable-lengths from the location.

The North Sea incident spurred an outburst of protests in Great Britain, whose government demanded an explanation and compensation. Even the European forces of the British Fleet were put on alert – on 25th October, ten armoured cruisers of the so-called 'Cruiser Squadron' were dispatched to follow and monitor the II Fleet Squadron. Thanks to the mediation of France, who as Russia's ally was anxious to maintain a newly-concluded agreement with Britain, on 25th November a British-Russian declaration was signed which transferred the investigation into the incident to a special commission made up of both Russian and British members plus representatives from neutral states. The commission conferred in Paris from December, 1904 until February, 1905. The statement made on 24th February announced that the Russians were responsible for the incident, although under wartime conditions such situations were likely. Thus Vice-Admiral Rozhestvenski and the warships' commanders were relieved of legal charges and only obliged to pay the fishermen's families a compensation of £65,000 sterling (about 600,000 roubles) and compensate the ship-owners' losses. The compensation was duly paid by the Russian government[57].

their silhouettes resembled those of torpedo boats. The Russians were convinced that they had just encountered the enemy and, after illuminating the alleged Japanese boats with floodlights, opened fire. Only after some ten minutes did they realise that these were not Japanese torpedo boats, but fishing boats on

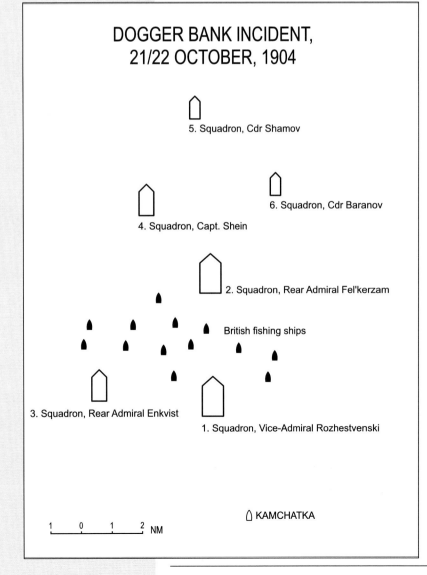

DOGGER BANK INCIDENT, 21/22 OCTOBER, 1904

5. Squadron, Cdr Shamov

6. Squadron, Cdr Baranov

4. Squadron, Capt. Shein

2. Squadron, Rear Admiral Fel'kerzam

British fishing ships

3. Squadron, Rear Admiral Enkvist

1. Squadron, Vice-Admiral Rozhestvenski

Ⓚ KAMCHATKA

1 0 1 2 NM

55 Later, when the causes of the incident were investigated, the Russians insisted that they opened fire after spotting two three-funnel torpedo boats among the fishing vessels. It is possible that British, or German destroyers, or torpedo boats were in the area at the moment of the incident (though Germans had no three-chimney units of this class) and their presence there was just kept secret. Dyskant J.W., Cuszima..., op.cit., p.62.

56 PRO, MT 9/801/M 7293, pp. 8-9.

57 Campbell J.P., The North Sea Incident of 1904., USNIP No 3/1974

46 | The II Pacific Squadron's passage to Madagascar

Right after the North Sea incident, Rozhestvenski's squadron headed for the port of Brest. Refueling on the roadstead of this port was made impossible by thick fog, so the Russian warships headed for Vigo, where they arrived on the morning of 26th October. The Russians stayed there until the North Sea incident was resolved. This peculiar internment lasted until 1st November, after the initial settlement of the controversial issues. After leaving Vigo, Rozhestvenski's detachment headed for Tangier, where they arrived in the afternoon of 3rd November. Here they joined most of the remaining warships of the Second Pacific Squadron.

In Tangier, the squadron was split into two groups, which were to sail to Madagascar along two routes: around Africa (Rozhestvenski's main forces), and through the Suez Canal (Fel'kerzam's group). The first detachment was made up of the battleships *Knyaz' Suvorov*, *Imperator Aleksandr III*, *Borodino*, *Orel'* and *Oslyabya*, armoured cruisers *Admiral Nakhimov* and *Dmitriy Donskoy*, the cruiser *Avrora*, transports *Meteor*, *Anadyr"*, *Malaja* and *Koreya*, repair ship *Kamchatka*, and the hospital ship *Orel'* (it joined the Second Fleet in Tangier)[58]. Fel'kerzam's detachment consisted of the battleships *Sisoy Velikiy* (flagship since 31st October) and *Navarin*, cruisers *Svetlana*, *Zhemchug* and *Almaz*, all of the seven destroyers, and transports *Kitay* and *Knyaz' Gorchakov'*[59].

Fel'kerzam's ships were first to leave Tangier, which they did in groups, the first one setting out on the evening of 30th October. They rendezvoused in Suda Bay in Crete, where they were joined by transports sent from the Black Sea, *Yaroslavl'*, *Voronezh*, *Vladimir*, *Tambov*, *Kijev*, *Yupiter* and *Merkuriy*. On 24th November the entire squadron arrived in Port Said, and passed through the Suez Canal between the morning of 25th November and the afternoon of 26th November. They left Suez the very next day, arriving in Djibouti on 3rd December. They stayed there longer than initially planned, since the French changed the stopping place for the II Pacific Squadron from Diego Suarez to Nossi Be, which the Russian admiral refused to accept at first. Finally, on 14th December, he left Djibouti and reached Nossi Be on 28th December.

Rozhestvenski's group left Tangier on the morning of 4th November, after refuelling. On 12th November the Russian squadron reached Dakar, where the warships refuelled again from ten German colliers that awaited them. On the morning of 16th November they sailed on. On 26th November Rozhestvenski's ships reached the mouth of the River Gabon in French Congo, where they restocked from German colliers that awaited them – each Russian warship had now so much coal on board that it could barely float. After a short stop, on 1st December the Russians moved on, and on 6th December they reached the Portuguese port of Mocamedes

58 Novikov, op.cit., p. 58
59 Ibidem, p.48

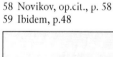

Battleships of the II Squadron on one of the Atlantic anchoring spots.

The Russian ships' crews' nightmare – restocking coal.

in Angola. As usual, they restocked with coal there. However, due to the protests of the Portuguese colonial authorities, they left the next day and headed for Angra Pequena Bay in German South-West Africa. This time, the German colonial authorities were favourable towards the Russian squadron, and after anchoring on 11th December they were granted permission to stay and reload coal from the accompanying transports. The Russians were held back by a violent storm and left the port as late as 17th December. Two days later the squadron passed the Cape of Good Hope and on 27th December reached the waters of southern Madagascar. After two more days they cast anchor in the strait between Madagascar and Saint Marie Island. There the squadron was joined by the hospital ship *Orel'* (it separated from the squadron in Angra Pequena to call at Capetown), which brought news of the annihilation of the Port Arthur Squadron and the ongoing formation of the III Pacific Squadron in the Baltic ports. Shocked by this news, Rozhestvenski decided to join Fel'kerzam's detachment immediately, which he did on 10th January in the roadstead of Nossi Be.

Before this, the Russian crews received news of the fall of Port Arthur. It was brought to them by the *Roland*, which was on its way from Tamatawa. In these circumstances the next destination for the II Pacific Squadron was, naturally, Vladivostok.

The battleship Navarin *of Rear Admiral Falkerzham's group in the Suez Canal.*

190

47 | The cruise of Captain Dobrotvorskiy's detachment

On 16th November, a group of warships that had not joined the II Pacific Squadron before 15th October left Libawa. They were late either due to prolonged quality tests, or various defects. Command over the detachment was assumed by the captain of the cruiser *Oleg*, Captain L.F. Dobrotvorskiy. Besides his ship, the group was made up of the cruiser *Izumrud*, auxiliary cruisers *Rion* and *Dniepr*, destroyers *Gromkiy*, *Groznyy*, *Prozorlivyy*, *Pronzitelnyy* and *Rezvyy*, and a transport, *Okyean*. A little earlier, at the end of October, three other auxiliary cruisers had left Libawa, the *Ural*, *Terek* and *Kuban'*. The first two sailed around Africa and joined the Second Fleet in mid January[60].

Somewhat delayed by the breakdowns of *Oleg*, *Dniepr*, and *Prozorlivyy*, the Russian ships crossed the Danish straits and on 24th November entered the North Sea. There they were caught in a storm, which resulted in further delays. On 26th November, the auxiliary cruiser *Dniepr* and the destroyer *Prozorlivyy* were sent to Cherbourg for repairs, whilst *Pronzitelnyy* ended up in Brest.

Another concentration of Dobrotvorskiy's group took place in Tangier. On 2nd December, *Rion*, *Prozorlivyy* and *Rezvyy* entered the port, joined the next day by *Dniepr*, *Gromkiy* and *Groznyy*, and on December 4th by *Oleg*, *Izumrud* and *Okyean*. *Pronzitelnyy* remained in Brest

---

60 Ibidem, p. 104

Cruiser Oleg.

The stern 152 mm turret on the cruiser Oleg.

longer and caught up with the squadron on 12th December in Algier. The next destination for the Russian detachment was Suda Bay in Crete. Only *Dniepr, Gromkiy* and *Groznyy* reached it on 12th December, as *Oleg* and *Izumrud* had to call at Malaga for quick repairs on 6th December, whilst *Rion, Prozorlivyy,* and *Rezvyy* called at Algier for the same reasons. As a result, Dobrotvorskiy's ships did not pass through the Suez Canal until 11th/12th January, and they did it without the destroyers *Prozorlivyy* and *Pronzitelnyy,* which were unable to continue. During the crossing, after colliding with a ferry, *Rezvyy* was also damaged and had to

be left behind in Suez. Dobrotvorskiy decided to wait for it in Djibouti, where he arrived on 18th January. The repairs to the destroyer, along with another breakdown in the boiler room of *Izumrud,* prolonged the stay in that port until the beginning of February. Finally, although *Rezvyy* made it to Djibouti, its condition was so poor that Dobrotvorskiy decided to send it back to Russia and continued with only two cruisers, two auxiliary cruisers, and two destroyers (*Okyean* was sent back to Russia after it left Algiers). On 14th February, Dobrotvorskiy's ships joined the II Squadron near Nossi Be.

Cruiser Izumrud.

192

40 | The voyage of the II Pacific Squadron across the Indian Ocean

The arrival of Dobrotvorskiy's detachment coincided with the preparations for sending the III Pacific Squadron from the Baltic Sea to the Far East under Rear Admiral Nebogatov's command. Due to this fact, Rozhestvenski initially received an order to wait for this squadron in the waters of Madagascar. An immediate departure turned out impossible due to the conflict with the HAPAG Company, which was to provide coal for the Russian squadron. Its management, concerned about the reaction of the Japanese, refused to deliver coal to the Russian warships on the Indian Ocean, justifying it vaguely by their obligation to respect neutrality laws. (In reality, they feared that clashes with the Japanese fleet might take place in the Indian Ocean, which constituted a threat for the German ships accompanying the squadron). Only a written intervention from Kaiser William II relieved the tension and resulted in HAPAG's declaration that the four largest transport ships with 30,000 tons of coal would sail with the II Squadron.

In the meantime, the II Squadron ships were anchored at Nossi Be awaiting further orders. The heat and problems with provisions connected with the preparation for such a long voyage had a very negative influence upon the crew's morale. Things became even worse on receiving the news of the outbreak of the revolution back home. As a result, incidents of insubordination and violation of regulations took place on many warships, though they did not, contrary to common opinion, have a political background. It forced the command to apply drastic measures (the detainees were sent back to Russia on the transport boat *Malaja*). The inactivity of the crews was broken by frequent reloading of coal (the boilers were on all the time, which on large warships consumed 20 – 25 tons of coal per day), minor repair works, and cleaning the underwater parts of the hulls. Also, at the end of January, training excercises were carried out in group manoeuvring, repelling torpedo assaults, and gunnery – the latter was limited, due to the lack of a sufficient surplus of ammunition. The training revealed certain deficiencies in the crew's preparation (which were nevertheless not as considerable as commonly believed), which did nothing to improve their morale, neither did the news of the defeat of Kuropatkin's army at Mukden which reached the II Squadron on 13th March.

Despite that, the orders remained unchanged (except for permission to join the III Squadron in Indochina). On 16th March the Russian ships left Nossi Be and headed across the Indian Ocean for the Malacca Strait. Afraid of Japanese espionage, Rozhestvenski kept the entire route secret and did not reveal it even to

Russian ships on the Wan Fong Bay.

his Government. Therefore, when on the morning of 5th April his warships turned up in the Malacca Strait, it caused a general surprise.

Contrary to what the Russians expected, the crossing of the strait produced no unexpected events and on 8th April the II Pacific Squadron passed Singapore and sailed into the South China Sea. Soon afterwards the Russian ships turned for Camranh Bay, 170 sea miles northeast of Saigon, which was to be their next stop. The Russians reached their destination on 13th April. Taking advantage of the benevolence of the French authorities, the Russian ships stayed in Camranh, waiting for Nebogatov's squadron until 22nd April. Only sharp protests by the Japanese, assuming this to be violation of neutrality laws, and the pressure imposed by Britain, which was Japan's (and until recently also France's) ally, forced the French authorities to 'expel' the Russians to Wan Fong Bay, 50 sea miles away. Wan Fong might have been a worse anchorage than Camranh, but due to its size it made it possible for the Russian warships to remain over three sea miles away from the shore, that is, beyond France's territorial waters. Although the Japanese protested again against this clear attempt to circumvent international law, this time they were far less effective. Only on 9th May, a day after the arrival of the French cruiser *Guichen* at Wan Fong with Rear Admiral de Jonquierès on board, did the II Squadron leave its anchorage and head for a new one in Kua Be Bay. This move was not, actually, prompted by the French, who were quite tolerant towards the Russians, but by the information that Nebogatov's III Squadron had reached Indochinese waters.

49 | The cruise of the III Pacific Squadron

The idea of sending reinforcements to Rozhestvenski's squadron came up in the Russian command as early as in October 1904. However, the decision to dispatch the III Pacific Squadron was finally made on 24th December[61]. The command of the squadron was vested in Rear Admiral N.I. Nebogatov. He was given the battleship *Imperator Nikolay I* (flagship), coast defence battleships *Admiral Ushakov*, *Admiral Senyavin*, and *General-Admiral Apraksin,* the old armoured cruiser *Vladimir Monomakh* and five transports and auxiliary units. Additionally, in the Mediterranean Nebogatov's squadron was to be joined by another two transports and the hospital ship *Kostroma* from the Black Sea[62].

Despite serious problems with the ships' equipment and crews (after Bloody Sunday, the political situation in Russia was extremely tense, which influenced the morale of the crews and shipyard workers)[63], on 15th February Nebogatov's squadron left Libawa, and headed for the Danish straits. Thick layers office on the eastern Baltic meant that the Russian warships did not reach Skagen until 20th February. The poor condition of her machinery made the

steamer *Rus* turn back to Russia. The remaining warships, after repairs, resumed their voyage on 23rd February and four days later reached Cherbourg. On the night of 3rd/4th March, after crossing the Bay of Biscay in a heavy storm, they arrived in the area of Gibraltar. After entering the Mediterranean the Russian took course for the waters of Crete and arrived at Suda Bay on 13th March. There, on 17th March the III Squadron was joined by *German Larkhe, Graf Stroganov* and *Kostroma* that had sailed from the Black Sea. After a longer stop, during which the machinery was inspected and necessary repairs made, the Russian warships resumed their voyage and between 24th and 26th March passed through the Suez Canal undisturbed. Crossing the Red Sea took another five days, and on 2nd April the III Squadron arrived at Djibouti. After another five days the Russian ships took to sea again, and after a short stop at Mirbat on 12th and 13th April, headed for the Malay peninsular. Nebogatov's squadron spent the Orthodox Easter at an anchorage in the area of the Nicobar Islands, and on 30th April entered the Malacca Strait. On 5th May, while in the area of Singapore, Nebogatov received information about the movements and the location of the II Pacific Squadron. After making radio contact the squadrons met on 9th May, 30 sea miles off Kua Be, and entered the bay together on the morning of the following day[64].

The commander of the III Squadron, Rear Admiral Nikolay I Nebogatov.

---

61 The initiative came from Vice-Admiral A.A. Birilev, who justified the idea by the fact that after the annihilation of the Port Arthur fleet, the Second Fleet would alone have to undertake the struggle to dominate at sea, and thus requires strengthening. RGAVMF, F.763, op.1, D.281, l.22-25; Russko-yaponskaya voyna…, op.cit., Documents. Otd. IV, Kn. 3, wyp. 5, pp. 313-314.
62 Novikov, op. cit., p.160.
63 Bloody Sunday was a massacre on 22 January 1905 in St. Petersburg, Russia, where unarmed, peaceful demonstrators marching to present a petition to Tsar Nicholas II were gunned down by the Imperial Guard.

64 Gribovskiy V.Yu., Krestnyy put' otryada Nebogatova. "Gangut" No 3 (1992), p. 25.

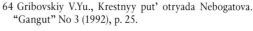

Rear Admiral Nebogatov's flag battleship Imperator Nikolay I.

Old cruiser Vladimir Monomakh.

Coast defence battleship Admiral Senyavin.

Rear Admiral Nebogatov's squadron in the Suez Canal.

Bringing the two squadrons together had a positive effect upon the morale of the Russian crews. Moreover, despite being made up of old vessels, or coastal units, the III Squadron covered the 11,000 sea miles from the Baltic Sea to Indochina in 83 days, without any serious breakdowns, or human losses, and was still in good condition (which testifies to Nebogatov's liberal command style, at least by Russian standards). Unfortunately Rozhestvenski, however cordial he was in welcoming Nebogatov, did not disclose to him to his plans, which would be particularly important in the light of Rear Admiral Fel'kerzam's critical health problems and his inability to continue with his command duties (he died on 24th May on board *Oslyabya*). From that moment on, Nebogatov became Rozhestvenski's actual deputy.

50 | The preparations of the Japanese to face the II and III Pacific Squadrons

Information about the Russian II Squadron going to sea caused great concern on the part of the Japanese command, which became even greater when espionage revealed the meticulous diplomatic and organisational preparation of the entire expedition. As a result, the Japanese calculated that the Russian squadron might reach the war theatre as soon as January 1905. Since Port Arthur was still putting up strong resistance in the autumn of 1904, and there was a likelihood that the fortress could hold out until the arrival of Rozhestvenski's forces, the situation was assumed to be serious, especially as the ships of the Combined Fleet were already fatigued by many months of struggle and most of them required extensive repairs. Thus, taking advantage of decreased activity by the Port Arthur fleet's main forces after the battle of the Yellow Sea, in autumn 1904 the Japanese began withdrawing single units from Port Arthur, sending them to shipyards for repairs. Initially, the Japanese were very cautious in doing this, as they were still afraid of another attempt to break the blockade of the Russian base, but when at the beginning of December the Port Arthur fleet was completely destroyed by Japanese siege artillery, in practice only light forces were left there, whilst most large warships were called back to Japan.

Soon the Japanese found out that Rozhestvenski's squadron had reached the waters off Madagascar. The reconnaissance activities did not confirm the presence of Russian forces in the Far East area, and the news from Russia was that the additional III Squadron under Nebogatov's command had been dispatched. In these circumstances the Japanese breathed a sigh of relief. They predicted that Rozhestvenski would wait for reinforcements, which gave them one precious additional month[65]. Therefore, not only could the Japanese command afford extensive repairs to their warships, but also use some of them to combat Vladivostok shipping.

Another reconnaissance carried out at the end of February and in March on the South China Sea also confirmed the absence of Russian forces. However on 8th March came the news of the Russian main forces crossing the Malacca Strait and the III Squadron leaving Djibouti a day before[66]. For the Japanese, this information confirmed the determination of the Russians to break through to Vladivostok. However the prolonged stay of Rozhestvenski's squadron in Indochinese waters, while waiting for the III Squadron, allowed the Japanese to complete the repair of all their warships before the end of April and gather them in the Korea Strait, where they awaited the arrival of the enemy.

66 Ibidem, pp. 6-7, 42-44.

Admiral Togo (on the right) on board the flag battleship Mikasa.

Main artillery of the Japanese battleship Asahi.

65 Opisanie..., op. cit., vol IV, pp. 4 – 5,

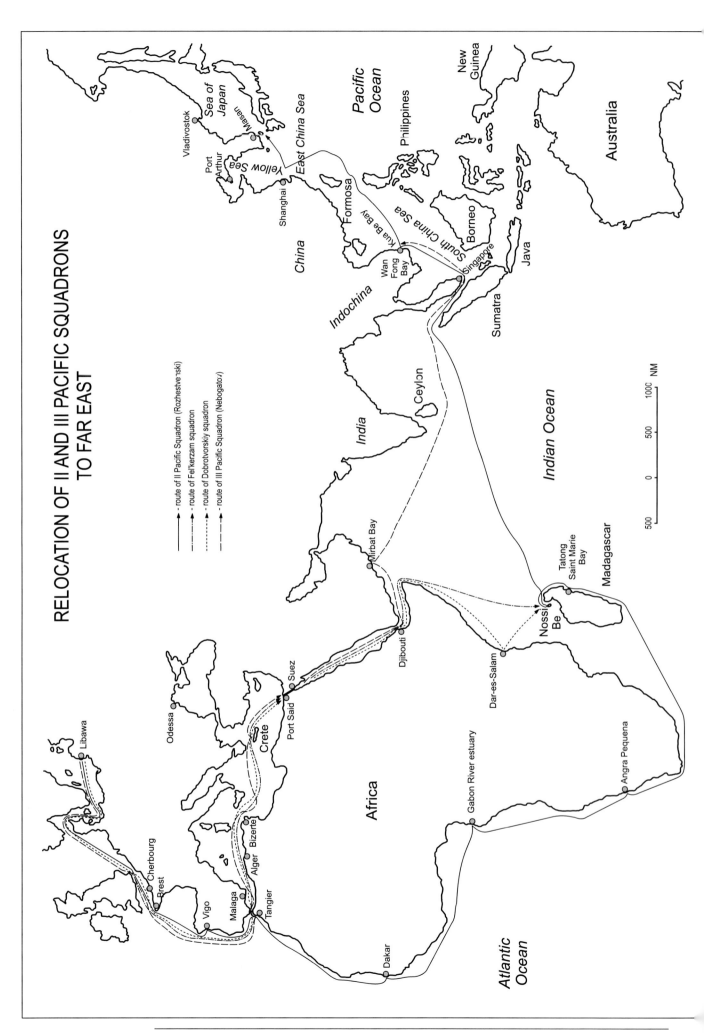

RELOCATION OF II AND III PACIFIC SQUADRONS
TO FAR EAST

- route of II Pacific Squadron (Rozhestvenski)
- route of Fel'kerzam squadron
- route of Dobrotvorskiy squadron
- route of III Pacific Squadron (Nebogatov)

Table No. 2: The organisation of the Japanese fleet as on 1st May, 1905

Squadron	Commander	Ships
First Squadron (Admiral. Togo H.) Despatch vessel: *Tatsuta*		
I Division	Vice Admiral Mizu S.	*Mikasa, Shikishima, Asahi, Fuji, Kasuga, Nisshin*
III Division	Vice Admiral Dewa S.	*Kasagi, Chitose, Niitaka, Otowa*
1 Division	Captain Fujimoto	*Harusame, Fubuki, Ariake, Arare, Akatsuki*
2 Division	Captain Yajima	*Oboro, Ikazuchi, Inazuma, Akebono*
3 Division	Captain Iosijima	*Shinonome, Usugumo, Sazanami, Kasumi*
14 Division	Lt. Commander Seki	*Chidori, Hayabusa, Manazuru, Kasasagi*
Second Squadron (Vice Admiral Kamimura H.) Despatch vessel: *Chihaya*		
II Division	Rear Admiral Shimamura H	*Idzumo, Adzuma, Asama, Yakumo, Tokiwa, Iwate*
IV Division	Vice Admiral Uriu S.	*Naniwa, Takachiho, Akashi, Tsushima*
4 Division	Commander Suzuki	*Asagiri, Murasame, Asashio, Shirakumo*
5 Division	Commander Hirose	*Shiranui, Kagero, Murakumo, Yugiri,*
9 Division	Commander Kawase	*Aotaka, Hato, Kari, Tsubame*
19 Division	Lt. Commander Matsuoka	*Kameom, Otoki, Kiji*
Third Squadron (Vice Admiral Kataoka S.) Despatch vessel: *Yaeyama*		
V Division	Rear Admiral Taketomi K.	*Itsukushima, Hashidate, Matsushima, Chin Yen*
VI Division	Rear Admiral Togo M.	*Suma, Idzumi, Akitsushima, Chiyoda*
VII Division	Rear Admiral Yamada H.	*Fuso, Takao, Tsukushi, Chokai, Maya, Uji,*
15 Division	Commander Kondo	*Hibari, Sagi, Hashitaka, Uzura*
1 Division	Lt. Commander Tukuba	*69, 67, 68, 70*
10 Division	Lt. Commander Otaki	*43, 40, 41, 39*
11 Division	Lt. Commander Fujimoto	*73, 72, 74, 75*
20 Division	Lt. Commander Kubo	*65, 62, 63, 64*
Auxiliary Squadron (Rear Admiral Ogura B.)		
Division of auxiliary cruisers	Rear Admiral Ogura B.	*Taichu Maru, Ameryka Maru, Sado Maru, Shinano Maru, Manshu Maru, Yawata Maru, Kumano Maru, Nikko Maru, Kasuga Maru, Dainan Maru*, 8 auxiliary gunboats
16 Division	Lt. Commander Wakabayashi	*Shirataka, 66*
17 Division	Lt. Commander Aoyama	*34, 31, 32, 33*
18 Division	Lt. Commander Kawada	*36, 35, 60, 61*
Guard and patrol ships		
Without assignment		*Tenryu, Katsuragi, Yamato, Musashi, Banjo, Akagi, Hongkong Maru, Nippon Maru, Yobo*, 10 auxiliary gunboats
2 Division	Lt. Commander Jinguji	*37, 38, 45, 46*
3 Division		*15, 20, 9*
4 Division		*5, 6, 7, 8*
5 Division	Lt. Commander Ogawa	*Fukuryu, 25, 26, 27*
6 Division	Lt. Commander Tochida	*56, 57, 58, 59*
7 Division		*11, 12, 13, 14*
8 Division		*10, 17, 18, 19*
12 Division	Lt. Commander Yamada	*50, 52, 54, 55*
13 Division		*Kotaka, 21, 24, 29, 30*
21 Division	Lt. Commander Egoi	*44, 47, 49, 71*

The main Japanese forces, that is the I and II Division (four battleships and eight armoured cruisers altogether) and one division of cruisers (it was the IV Division on 27th May) were stationed in Mozampo, Chinkai Bay. They were accompanied by all five squadrons of destroyers, and 9th, 14th, and 19th Torpedo Boat Divisions. The outer surveillance line was about 110 sea miles off the island of Okinoshima, and stretched over 100 sea miles from Quelpart to the northern part of the Goto Archipelago. This was patrolled by at least four auxiliary cruisers from the squadron of special warships (on 27th May these were *Amerika Maru, Sado Maru, Shinano Maru* and *Manshu Maru*), covered on the flanks by two cruisers from the VI squadron (on 27th May it was *Akitsushima* in the west and *Idzumi* in the east). In an emergency these units could count on support from the III or IV Divisions (on 27th May four cruisers from the III Division were on duty), which were located several sea miles north-east of the Goto Islands.

The second surveillance line was about 60-70 sea miles away from the first, and stretched along the Iki, Shimonoshima, and Oshima islands. This was patrolled by ships from the V squadron and the remaining cruisers from the VI squadron (on 27th May these were *Suma* and *Chiyoda*), supported by the VII Squadron (an old coast defence battleship, two small cruisers, and four gunboats) and the 11th, 16th, 17th, and 20th Torpedo Boat Divisions. (On the night of 26th/27th May, due to stormy weather, the units from the VII Division were located near Kosaki Cape, while the remaining ships were in Ozaki base in the Tsushima Archipelago, so there was essentially no surveillance line). In Miura Bay on Tsushima waters, the 1st, 10th, 15th, and 18th Torpedo Boat Divisions were additionally stationed[67].

---

67 Lacroix E., op.cit., Part 13, TBS No 5-6/1969, pp.425-426

51 | The cruise of the combined Russian squadron to the Korea Strait

Battleship Sisoy Velikiy.

Battleship Imperator
Aleksandr III.

The combined force of the II and III Pacific Squadrons left Kua Be on 14th May. Thirty-four warships and 16 transports and auxiliary vessels headed for the Strait of Taiwan, whilst seven ships, redundant for the moment, were sent back to Saigon. The Russian commander had already decided that they would be breaking through to Vladivostok along the shortest route across the Korea Strait. In order to mislead the enemy, on the night of May 18th/19th the squadron suddenly changed course east, heading for the Luzon Strait. This might have indicated that the Russians were attempting to reach Vladivostok by sailing around the eastern shores of the Japanese Islands. Soon afterwards, the Russian admiral sent the auxiliary cruisers *Kuban'* (21st May) and *Terek* (22nd May) to the Pacific, whilst *Rion* and *Dniepr* were sent to the Yellow Sea (25th May) with the task of disrupting Japanese shipping. On 22nd May the squadron reached the area of Miyako Island. The very next day the ships restocked with coal from accompanying transports for the last time. Because of Rozhestvenski's obsession for maintaining sufficient fuel on his warships, each ship took the maximum amount of coal on board, This considerably increased their regular displacement and reduced their freeboard, later to prove significant to the outcome of the battle[68].

On the very same day, in the night of 23rd/24th May, long-suffering Rear Admiral Fel'kerzam died on board his flagship *Oslyabya*. The news of his death was withheld from the crews of the squadron, lest it disturbed the sailors' morale. As a result the actual command over the second battleship detachment was taken over by

---

68 The coal overload on the Russian battleships decreased their maximum speed, already influenced by seaweed and shell covered hulls, and reduced their stability. Besides, deeply submerged battleships had their armoured belts under water, thus becoming much more vulnerable to damage. RGAVMF. F 421 Op.1. D.1354, Gribovskiy V.Yu., Krestnyj put'..., op.cit., p. 25, Gribovskiy V.Yu., Eskadrennye bronenostsy tipa „Borodino" v Tsusimskom srazhenii., "Gangut" No 2 (1991), pp. 28-29.

the commander of *Oslyabya*, Captain V.I. Ber (Fel'kerzam's flag was still on the warship). Rear Admiral Nebogatov, actually Rozhestvenski's deputy, knew nothing of the fact[69].

On the morning of 25th May the Russian squadron reached the Saddle Archipelago, about 90 sea miles from Shanghai. Taking advantage of this situation, Rozhestvenski sent four empty colliers off to the Chinese port, as they would have been a burden for the squadron otherwise. This turned out to be quite an unfortunate decision, as it confirmed the suspicion of the Japanese that the Russians planned to break through to Vladivostok along the shortest route across the Korea Strait. Had they planned to sail round Japan, they would probably have taken the colliers with them.

On 26th May, the first wireless messages between Japanese ships were intercepted by the Russians. The enemy was close, but Rozhestvenski did not bother to inform his commanders of his battle plan. All he did at 18.00 was to order preparation for battle, and continued blindly towards the Korea Strait in a group of three columns. The right-hand column comprised seven battleships and an armoured cruiser of the 1st and 2nd battleship detachment; the left-hend was made up of the 3rd battleship detachment and Rear Admiral Enkvist's detachment of cruisers (one battleship, three coast defence battleships and four cruisers), while in the middle were the remaining transports and auxiliary units (six altogether). The reconnaissance detachment was sailing about 1-1.5 sea miles ahead of the squadron; the destroyers were located between the right and the middle column (1st Flotilla), and the left and middle one (2nd Flotilla). In order to hamper their detection by

Battleship Navarin

the Japanese, the Russian ships maintained radio silence and theoretically sailed in a blackout – this effect was spoiled by the fully illuminated hospital ships *Orel'* and *Kostroma* that were following the squadron at a distance, as well as frequent light signals exchange between ships.

The first to spot the Russian warships was the Japanese surveillance auxiliary cruiser *Shinano Maru*. At around 02.25 (Japanese time), its crew noticed the illuminated Russian hospital ship *Orel'* (identified only after a two hour observation) and then, at 04.25, the rest of the squadron. After they were identified as Rozhestvenski's main forces, *Shinano Maru* immediately turned back and plunged into the thick fog and darkness, at the same time sending a message to Togo. On receiving this information about the enemy forces and their coordinates and speed, Admiral Togo was finally certain that the Russians had chosen to reach Vladivostok through the Korea Strait. In these circumstances battle was inevitable.

Table No. 3: The organisation of the Russian fleet on 27th May 1905

Squadron	Commander	Ships
1 Battleship Detachment	Vice Admiral Z.P. Rozhestvenski	*Knyaz' Suvorov, Imperator Aleksandr III, Borodino, Orel'*
2 Battleship Detachment	Rear Admiral D.G. Fel'kerzam (nominally, really Captain V.I. Ber)	*Oslabya, Sisoy Velikiy, Navarin, Admiral Nakhimov*
3 Battleship Detachment	Rear Admiral N.I. Nebogatov	*Imperator Nikolay I, General-Admiral Apraksin, Admiral Senyavin, Admiral Ushakov*
Cruisier Detachment	Rear Admiral O.A. Enkvist	*Oleg, Avrora, Dmitriy Donskoy, Vladimir Monomakh*
Reconnaissance Detachment	Captain S.P. Shein	*Svetlana, Ural*
1 Torpedo Detachment	Commander P.P. Levitskiy	*Zhemchug, Izumrud, Bedovyy, Bystryy, Buynyy, Bravyy*
2 Torpedo Detachment	Commander G.F. Kern	*Gromkiy, Groznyy, Blestjashhij, Bezuprechnyy, Bodryy*
Transport Detachment	Captain O.L. Radlov	*Almaz,* transports and auxiliary vessels: *Kamchatka, Irtysh, Anadyr", Koreya, Rus, Svir"*
Hospital ships		*Orel', Kostroma*

69 Dyskant J.W., Cuszima..., op.cit., p. 129, Gribovskiy V.Yu., Krestnyj put'..., op.cit., p. 26.

52 | The battle of Tsushima

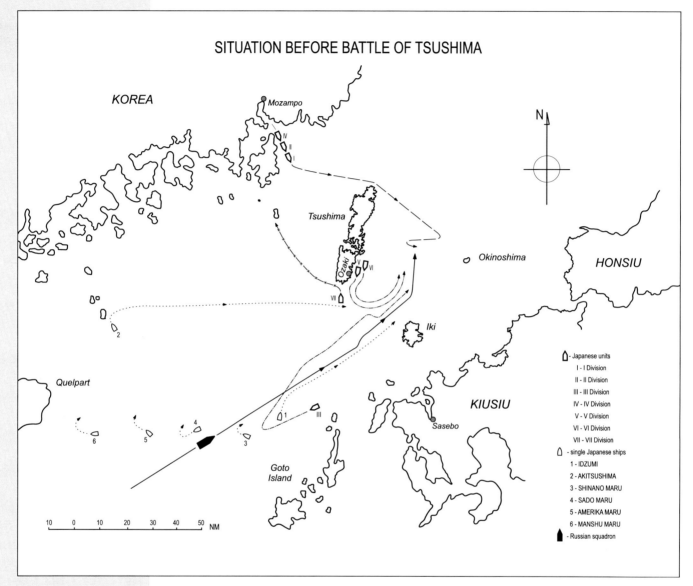

SITUATION BEFORE BATTLE OF TSUSHIMA

KOREA

Mozampo

Tsushima

Okinoshima

HONSIU

Ozaki

Iki

Quelpart

KIUSIU

Sasebo

Δ - Japanese units
   I - I Division
   II - II Division
   III - III Division
   IV - IV Division
   V - V Division
   VI - VI Division
   VII - VII Division
Δ - single Japanese ships
   1 - IDZUMI
   2 - AKITSUSHIMA
   3 - SHINANO MARU
   4 - SADO MARU
   5 - AMERIKA MARU
   6 - MANSHU MARU
◆ - Russian squadron

Goto Island

10 0 10 20 30 40 50 NM

When Rozhestvenski decided to go into battle with the Combined Fleet, it is reasonable to assume that the Admiral had a tactical plan. It will never be possible to say with certainty what shape the plan took as he did not share it with any of his subordinates. Even his immediate deputies, including Nebogatov, (whom he met personally only once, during the rendezvous of the II and III Squadrons) were unaware of Rozhestvenski's intentions! Judging by the orders he had given out during the last days before the battle, one may suppose that he had expected the battle to be a rather static gunnery confrontation on parallel courses[70]. For that mat-

ter, the Russian commander wanted to minimise the distance to the enemy and defeat them with direct fire[71]. This task was naturally to be executed by the main forces, made up of the 1st, 2nd and 3rd detachments of battleships (a total of eight battleships, three coast defence battleships, and an armoured cruiser). Meanwhile, Rear Admiral Enkvist's detachment of cruis-

---

70 In fact, there were only two documents preserved that could potentially reveal the Russian commander's plans: Order No 182 of April 16th, 1905, and Order

No 227 of May 8th (PRO, ADM 231/45, Reports..., vol. IV, pp. 236-237, 245). Besides these ones, there are two more orders that might shed some light on Rozhestvenski's plans: the order of January 23rd, regulating the rules of artillery combat (op. cit. pp. 215-216), and the order of March 27th, concerning the rules of providing support for endangered units (op. cit. p. 225). See also: Dyskant J.W., Cuszima..., op.cit., pp. 143-145; Kostenko V.P., op.cit., p. 496; Smirnov M., Srazhenie v Koreyskom prolive 14-go i 15-go maya 1905 g., MS No 4/1913, pp. 99-103.

71 Kostenko V. P., op. cit. p. 496

ers and a reconnaissance detachment (two old armoured cruisers, three cruisers and an auxiliary cruiser) were to provide cover for the transports. Fast cruisers *Zhemchug* and *Izumrud*, and all nine destroyers, were to serve as despatch units and to provide cover for the warships damaged in battle. In case the flagship broke out of the formation or sank, command was to be taken over by another warship, and so on. As a result, Rozhestvenski brought the centralisation of command to the level of absurd, and no one in the Russian squadron knew what to do in an unexpected situation. All they knew was that they should blindly push forward towards Vladivostok.

At the same time, Togo was in a situation totally different from the one during the battle of the Yellow Sea, when he had to save his strength for the encounter with the Russian reinforcements dispatched from the Baltic Sea to the Far East. Now the reinforcements were right before him and the Port Arthur fleet did not exist. Victory in the coming battle would give the Japanese unquestionable domination at sea, and thus influence dramatically the further development of the war. Considering the diminishing military and economic potential of the Japanese, this factor would ultimately determine the outcome of the entire conflict. Thus the Japanese admiral decided to achieve complete success and shatter the enemy, even at the cost of high losses of his own. For this reason it was not his intention to maintain a large distance, as his experience so far, and the gun training carried out in April indicated that, in the light of the deficiencies in the system of fire control, shelling over large distances was inefficient. Therefore a decision, as on 10th August, 1904 during the Battle of the Yellow Sea, to undertake a long distance shelling would have increased the chances of the enemy breaking through to Vladivostok

and would have been a strategic failure for the Japanese, even if they inflicted severe losses upon the enemy. Consequently Togo intended to engage in battle at a medium distance (about 40 cable-lengths), and shorten it during the battle down to 25-30 cable-lengths[72]. Besides, such tactics were forced upon him by the weather conditions in the Korea Strait on 27th May – it was cloudy, and foggy, with visibility limited to 2.5-3 sea miles in the morning, temporarily improving during the day but generally remaining below 5-6 sea miles[73].

Togo intended to fight the battle using 'L' tactics. Unlike Togo's situation at the battle of the Yellow Sea, he had the forces of the I and II Divisions at his disposal. The manoeuvring component of his fleet, Vice-Admiral Kamimura's II Division, had now sufficient potential to surround the enemy forces, or go round its leading units. Since the combat speed of the Russian squadron was relatively low (only 9-10 knots[74],

---

72 PRO, ADM 231/44, Reports..., op.cit., vol. III, p. 75.
73 Ibidem, p. 63; Smirnov M. op. cit., p. 105.
74 The main forces – the 1st, 2nd, and 3rd detachment – could sail at the speed of maximum 13 knots, but the

Japanese battleship Shikishima. *This battleship contributed greatly to the sinking of the Russian battleship* Oslyabya.

which gave the first division an advantage of about 6 knots and the second as much as 8-9 knots!), Togo chose the option in which the main forces were to carry out the 'L' manoeuvre. It seems likely, though, that he made this decision right before the battle, while facing the enemy[75]. The Japanese commander planned, at the same time, to concentrate fire on the leading warships and to eliminate the Russian flagship as soon as possible[76].

During the battle the I and II Divisions were to operate independently, yet in close co-operation with each other, while fighting the enemy's main forces. The remaining divisions of cruisers, also independent, were to attack the Russian transports and escorting cruisers. During the battle the main forces were to be accompanied by all the squadrons of destroyers and the larger torpedo boats. Togo's plan did not, however, include a torpedo assault on the Russian fleet in broad daylight. The destroyers were to maintain a certain distance from the battle area and attack only damaged ships, or possibly provide assistance for Japanese warships that needed help. A massive torpedo attack was scheduled for after sunset, and was also to be carried out by the squadrons of smaller torpedo boats stationed in Takeshiki in the Tsushima Archipelago, as rough seas prevented them from remaining at sea at all times.

Admiral Togo's battle plan was thus flexible. It gave a lot of independence to the commanders of particular squadrons. It was not chaotic, though, as the tasks were precisely delegated before the battle and constant contact with the chief commander was to be maintained.

After *Shinano Maru* lost visual contact with the enemy (it was regained once more at about 05.45/06.05, and lost again at 06.15/06.35) at around 06.10/06.30 the Russian squadron was spotted by the cruiser *Idzumi*, which from then on followed it persistently, providing the main forces with current information. Soon afterwards, at 06.30/06.50, the cruisers from Vice Admiral Dewa's III Division appeared near the Russian squadron (they came from the left) and at 08.45/09.05 Kataoka's V Division approached from ahead, and soon set on a parallel course. They maintained visual contact until 10.30/10.50 . Rear Admiral Togo's VI Division remained out of sight, in the fog, about 50-55 cable-lengths to port of the Russian fleet.

Rozhestvenski's squadron was sailing on surrounded by the Japanese cruisers, not reacting to their presence in any way. Only at 11.15/11.35 did a brief cannonade take place, as an accidental shot from a 152 mm gun on the battleship *Orel'* was fired towards the III Squadron cruisers and caused the other ships of the 1st and 3rd Russian squadrons to open fire too.

Around 09.10/09.30 Vice Admiral Rozhestvenski finally ordered a move into combat formation, which took the Russian warships about an hour. The 1st and 2nd battleship detachments increased their speed to 11 knots and moved ahead of Nebogatov's 3rd detachment, sailing at 9 knots to port, now forming a single column with it. At the same time *Zhemchug* and the destroyers *Bedovyy* and *Bystryy* assumed a position on the starboard beam of the flagship *Suvorov*, whilst the cruiser *Izumrud* and the destroyers *Buynyy* and *Bravyy* moved abeam of *Oslyabya*. The remaining destroyers of the 2nd torpedo detachment assumed their positions abeam of *Oleg*, (*Blestyashchiy* and *Bezuprechnyy*), *Svetlana*, (*Bodryy Gromkiy*, and *Groznyy*). As in this type of formation the transports, which were currently in the starboard column, were unprotected, Rozhestvenski ordered the armoured cruisers *Dmitriy Donskoy* and *Vladimir Monomakh* to assume a position abeam of them to starboard. However, for

speed of the entire Russian detachment was limited to the speed of the slowest unit, that is, the transport boat *Irtysh*, whose top speed was 9.5 knots. Smirnov M., op. cit. pp. 79, 81.

75 PRO, CAB 37/79/157.
76 The tactical assumptions concerning the battle are included in the instructions conveyed by Togo to the commanders of the Combined Fleet battleships on April 17th, 1905., Evans D.C., Peattie M.R., op.cit., pp. 112-114. See also: PRO, ADM 231/44, Reports..., op.cit., vol. III, pp. 58-60; Corbett J.S., op.cit., vol. II, pp.242-243.

reasons unknown, the order was executed only by the latter ship[77].

After regrouping, the Russian warships continued sailing into the Korea Strait at 9 knots. Around noon they turned 23° east, setting on the course straight to Vladivostok. At the same time Shein's reconnaissance detachment was given an order to cover the transports and consequently shifted its position from the rear to the port wing of the fleet.

At 12.20/12.40 Rozhestvenski decided to regroup once again. He ordered the warships of the 1st and 2nd battleship detachments to turn 90° to starboard at a speed of 11 knots. At the moment this order was given the Japanese forces were no further than 15 sea miles away from the Russians but were invisible due to fog, and the Russian admiral had no idea of their presence. Five minutes later the fog dispersed and, on spotting the enemy, Rozhestvenski suspended his order for the second detachment to make a turn. Consequently, at around 12.30/12.50 the main forces of the Russian fleet were sailing in two columns: four battleships from the 1st detachment with *Zhemchug* and two destroyers abeam on the right; the remaining eight ships of the 2nd and 3rd detachments with *Izumrud* and the other two destroyers 2,300 metres away from them on their left, abeam the leading ships. Behind the 3rd battleship detachment, to starboard, there were Enkvist's cruisers(*Oleg, Avrora* and *Dmitriy Donskoy*) with the destroyers of the 2nd torpedo detachment abeam, whilst

Captain Shein's cruisers were located behind the transports. Next to them, abeam the last one, *Vladimir Monomakh* was sailing alone.

It is hard to say why the Russian commander decided on such a formation[78]. It would have made sense, had the first detachment been to operate alone later, taking advantage of its considerable speed that matched that of the Japanese warships. As events would show, Rozhestvenski did not plan anything like that. After the fog dispersed again around 13.20/13.40, revealing the Japanese main forces sailing on a head-on course only seven sea miles away, he ordered the 1st Squadron to reassume position ahead of *Oslyabya*.

This manoeuvre was executed so poorly that only *Suvorov* and *Aleksandr III* assumed their proper positions in the formation, whilst *Borodino* and *Orel'*, sailing directly behind them, simply did not have enough room (Rozhestvenski ordered the 1st detachment units to reduce their speed too soon). This almost caused a collision with *Oslyabya* and forced the warship to abandon the formation, slow down, and finally disengage! Also the battleship *Sisoy*

---

77 Lacroix E., op.cit., part 14, TBS No 5-6/1969, p.427.

78 Rozhestvenski is said to have decided on a two-column formation as he was afraid of floating mines which the Japanese cruisers might have laid along the squadron's route – forming two columns 13 cable-lengths away from each other was supposed to force the Japanese to increase the distance and make it impossible for them to cross the Second Fleet's route (Semenov V., *Boy pri Tsusime.*, St. Peterburg 1911, p. 25; Smirnov M., op.cit., p. 108). Anyway, the Russian admiral's manoeuvers perplexed the commanders of the first squadron battleships (and not only them), who were totally unable to understand his intentions. *Russko-yaponskaya voyna...*, op.cit., Documents. Otd. IV, Kn. 3, wyp. 1, p. 56.

Velikiy, which was next in line, was made to turn to starboard. In this way the fatuous and unjustified manoeuvres in the face of the enemy triggered considerable confusion in the Russian squadron, which later contributed greatly to the outcome of the battle.

Meanwhile Admiral Togo, on receiving at 04.45/05.05 the first information from *Shinano Maru* about the enemy squadron, issued immediate sailing orders. He went to sea with his main forces (I, II and III Divisions) from Mozampo at 06.15/06.35. However, due to the bad weather conditions, and miscalculation of the Russian squadron's speed, they arrived at an expected rendezvous location too early. Around noon, after the Japanese squadron reached a position 15 sea miles north-west of Okinoshima, it made a turn west, and at 13.10/13.30 it turned south-west, thus assuming on a head-on course with the Russian warships approaching from the south.

Not knowing about the change in the Russian formation, Togo was convinced that they still sailed in two columns, with the transports in the middle. Therefore he intended to strike the weaker starboard column with all his forces and annihilate it quickly, thus making the enemy vulnerable before the decisive encounter with its main forces. At the same time all the cruiser units were to move to the starboard side of the Russian fleet and attack the enemy transports and escorting warships at a convenient moment. The destroyers were to remain by the main force.

Ten minutes after the turn, the Japanese admiral spotted Rozhestvenski's squadron 7-8 sea miles ahead of *Mikasa*, and soon realised that the enemy had altered its formation and was currently sailing in a single combat column. In these circumstances he decided to change his original plan and at 13.45/14.05 ordered his warships to make another turn north-east. Performing a loop in the face of the enemy, just 39-40 cable-lengths (7-7.2 km) away from the leading *Suvorov*, was an extremely risky manoeuvre, as it temporarily weakened the firing potential of the entire squadron, at the same time exposing the particular ships making a turn to enemy fire. However Togo expected Russian shelling over such a long distance to be quite inaccurate, and hoped to complete the manoeuvre before suffering any serious

losses. If, in turn, he managed to perform the loop, considering the advantage of higher speed, he would have been in a very convenient position to execute a T-crossing against the enemy's leading warships, which would have given him a huge advantage at the very beginning of the battle.

The first stage of the battle

Seeing the manoeuvre of the Japanese fleet, and realising how dangerous it could be, at 13.49/14.09 Rozhestvenski ordered his ships to open fire on the leading Japanese battleship *Mikasa*, without even waiting for his own formation to be completed. The distance between *Mikasa* and *Suvorov* at that time was below 39 cable-lengths (7 km), but the distance from *Oslyabya* was over 50 cable-lengths (9.2 km), from *Nikolay I* 64-65 cable-lengths (11.8-12 km), and from *Ushakov* 74 cable-lengths (13.6 km)[79].

The Russian warships concentrated fire mainly on *Mikasa*, but in reality Togo's flagship was being shelled by mainly by *Suvorov*, *Aleksandr III*, and *Borodino*. The remaining warships fired at it occasionally, generally focusing on other targets. Besides, considering the distance and their positions in the formation, only *Orel'* (which after several minutes managed finally to assume position in the formation) and *Oslyabya* (which, however, lost its fore 254 mm turret after only three shots) were able to carry out efficient shelling. *Sisoy Velikiy*, *Navarin*, *Nakhimov* and *Nikolaj I* participated in the shelling only to a limited extent, using exclusively their forward batteries. The coast defence battleships did not have any practical contribution at this stage of the battle. In this situation, despite the fact that the accuracy of

---

79 The minimum data according to the Japanese calculations (probably lowered regarding the boats of the Russian second and third team). Bykov P.D., op.cit., p. 87; Corbett J.S., op.cit., vol. II, p.246; Smirnov M., op.cit., p. 111. According to the contemporary operational battle maps, the distance from *Mikasa* to *Oslyabya* may be estimated to have been 65 cable-lengths, and even 82 cable-lengths to *Nikolay I*. According to the calculations by the Russians (also differing from each other), the moment fire was opened, the distance to *Mikasa* was only 32 cable-lengths (Russko-yaponskaya voyna..., op.cit., Documents. Otd. IV, Kn. 3, wyp. 1, p. 1, wyp. 3, p. 612), which should, however, be considered definitely underrated. In turn, on board of *Orel'*, the distance from *Mikasa* was estimated at 70 cable-lengths, while 10 minutes later at 57 cable-lengths – Russko-yaponskaya voyna..., op.cit., Documents. Otd. IV, Kn. 3, wyp. 1, pp. 58, 68.

BATTLE OF TSUSHIMA
SITUATION IN THE MOMENT OF OPENING FIRE
(13.49)

Ⓓ - Japanese ships

1 - MIKASA
2 - SHIKISHIMA
3 - FUJI
4 - ASAHI
5 - KASUGA
6 - NISSHIN
7 - IDZUMO
8 - YAKUMO
9 - TOKIWA
10 - ADZUMA
11 - ASAMA
12 - IWATE
13 - CHIHAYA
14 - TATSUTA

◆ - Russian ships

1 - KNYAZ' SUVOROV
2 - IMPERATOR ALEKSANDR II
3 - BORODINO
4 - OREL
5 - OSLYABYA
6 - SISOY VELIKIY
7 - NAVARIN
8 - ADMIRAL NAKHIMOV
9 - IMPERATOR NIKOLAY I
10 - GENERAL-ADM. APRAKSIN
11 - ADMIRAL SENYAVIN
12 - ADMIRAL USHAKOV
13 - ZHEMCHUG
14 - IZUMRUD

◣ - Russian destroyers

N

| 1 | 0 | 1 | 2 | 3 NM |

Japanese cruiser Tokiwa.

207

Russian fire was surprisingly high, amounting to 7-8% hits[80], it was much less powerful than that of their enemy and thus less effecive.

The Japanese opened fire only at 13.52/14.12, after the leading battleships *Mikasa* and *Shikishima* had already made their turn. *Mikasa* fired first, and according to its gunners' coordinates, it was followed by consecutive Japanese warships on the turn. At first, all four Japanese battleships targeted *Suvorov*, whilst *Kasuga* and *Nisshin* locked on to *Oslyabya*. *Oslyabya*, in turn, targeted most of the armoured cruisers from Kamimura's II Division[81]. *Adzuma* soon shifted fire and targeted *Suvorov*, whilst *Iwate*, last in the formation, made a turn and started shelling *Nikolay I*. After several minutes the targets were, however, changed. *Mikasa*, *Asahi*, *Fuji* and *Adzuma* started shelling *Suvorov*, *Shikishima*, *Kasuga*, *Niisshin*, *Idzuma*, *Tokiwa* and *Yakumo* (plus briefly also *Fuji*) targeted *Oslyabya*, whilst *Asama* and *Iwate*, which were last in the formation, targeted *Sisoy*.

The Japanese fire proved to be very effective from the very beginning of the battle, even though the Japanese gunners were not necessarily any more accurate than their Russian counterparts. Around 14.00/14.20 the distance between the leading warships of the opposing fleets – *Mikasa* and *Suvorov* – dropped down to 28 cable-lengths (5 km) and the Japanese warships started overtaking the enemy on an oblique course thanks to their higher speed (5-6 knots advantage over the Russian warships). In this way they managed to stay outside the range of the Russian stern guns, and at the same time managed to continue shelling the enemy warships with their side guns. In these circumstances the Russians were able to use only 12-16 heavy guns, mainly forward ones, against 17 Japanese 305-254 mm guns, and 30 203 mm guns. Therefore Admiral Togo assumed the crossed-T position just 15 minutes into the battle and, by doing this, determined the outcome of the confrontation.

The concentration of fire on two Russian battleships, *Suvorov* and *Oslyabya* (the latter was an accidental target, as it became an easy prey for the Japanese after it had turned to port and disengaged its engines in order to avoid colliding with *Borodino* and *Orel'*), soon caused heavy damage to them. Although *Suvorov* still managed to float, the very first hits made a huge hole on the waterline of *Oslyabya*'s bow area, and the warship started taking in masses of water. Consequently before the Russian ship could get underway again it started listing to port, and its bow was gradually submerging.

Unable to endure the Japanese bombardment, at 14.04/14.24, *Suvorov*, after having received multiple hits, turned 45° to starboard, causing the rest of the fleet to do the same. As a result the distance between the opposing sides stabilised and their courses became more or less parallel. However the Japanese were already well ahead of the Russian leading ships and were still able to fire at the first five or six warships, while Nebogatov's battleships, sailing far behind, could not effectively participate in the battle as they were firing from a very inconvenient position. At 14.20/14.40, after receiving further hits, *Oslyabya* dropped out of the formation and sank twenty minutes later. At the same time the third ship in the line, the battleship *Borodino*, also left formation. It had suffered damage to its rudder, but this was fixed within 15 minutes and soon the warship regained its position in the formation. Ten minutes later, at around 14.30/14.50, after receiving several more hits *Suvorov* dropped out of the formation. The Russian flagship, which had been the target for four to six enemy warships since the very beginning of the battle, was heavily damaged and practically unable to continue fighting. Although its engines were still operational, and there were no breaches on or below its waterline, all of its heavy guns, and most of the medium guns were destroyed, and there were severe fires on board.

In these circumstances the leadership of the squadron was taken over by *Imperator*

---

80 High efficiency of Russian fire in the first 15-20 minutes of the battle is confirmed by both Japanese and British observers' reports(PRO, ADM 231/44, Reports..., op.cit., vol. III, p. 64; CAB 37/78/104, p. 2; see also: Campbell N.J.M., The Battle of Tsushima., "Warship" vol.II (1978), p.129). The very first projectile fired from *Suvorov* landed only 20 metres behind *Mikasa*'s stern, and within the following 15 minutes the Japanese flagship received five 305 mm hits, and fourteen 152 mm hits (PRO, ADM 231/44, Reports..., op.cit., vol. III, p. 93, 120; Campbell N.J.M., op.cit., p. 130, 262).

81 The second squadron sailed behind, and a little left of the first one, and consequently made a turn about 1,500 metres north-west away from the spot where it had made a loop, and opened fire a little later, at 13.57/14.17., Campbell N.J.M., The battle of Tsushima., part 2, "Warship" vol.II (1978), p.128.

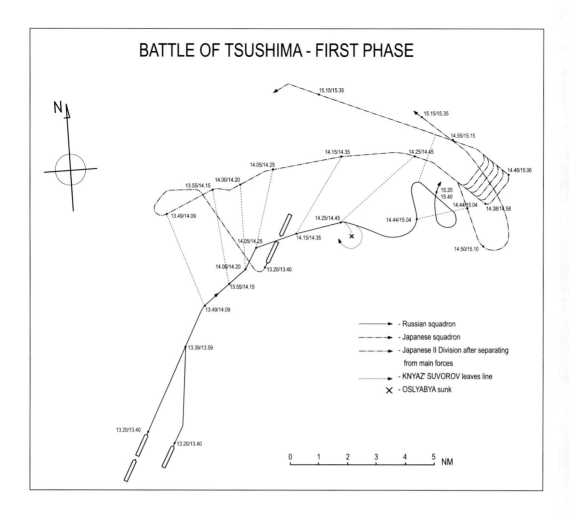

BATTLE OF TSUSHIMA - FIRST PHASE

Legend:
- → - Russian squadron
- ⟶ - Japanese squadron
- ⟶ - Japanese II Division after separating from main forces
- ⟶ - KNYAZ' SUVOROV leaves line
- ✕ - OSLYABYA sunk

0 1 2 3 4 5 NM

Aleksandr III. Its commander, Captain N.M. Bukhvostov, after noticing that the enemy was again trying cross the Russian 'T' by gradually 'bending' the course of its warships to starboard, at 14.50/15.10 made a sharp turn north in an attempt to charge Kamimura's armoured cruisers sailing at the end of the line. As a response to this manoeuvre, Togo ordered all the warships of the I Division to make a simultaneous turn by 180° and head north-west with Vice Admiral Mizu's flag armoured cruiser *Nisshin* in the lead. Thanks to this move the Japanese assumed a position close to T-crossing. However at 15.05/15.25 the vigilant Bukhvostov made a turn south-east, and both squadrons passed each other on opposing courses at a distance of 15-20 cable-lengths (2.7-3.6 km) and soon lost contact by plunging into fog. Fifteen minutes later Kamimura's squadron also lost contact with the Russian fleet. At 14.52/15.12 the former had made a turn north-west, following Togo's division and after a short exchange of fire over a distance of no more than 24-25 cable-lengths (4.3-4.5), departed from the battle area.

Soon afterwards, the second squadron encountered the heavily damaged and solitary battleship *Suvorov*. So as not to waste time, Kamimura dispatched against it the accompanying 5th Destroyer Division led by the small cruiser *Chihaya*, but the attack ended in failure.

The first stage of the battle ended in an unquestionable victory for the Japanese. Their success was determined in the first thirty minutes of the fighting, when Admiral Togo used his own advantages, as well as Rozhestvenski's mistakes, to the fullest. Consequently he managed to sink *Oslyabya* and eliminate *Suvorov*. These losses seriously undermined the position of the Russian squadron. What is more, due to the fact that Rozhestvenski had never bothered to discuss his plans with other commanders, after losing *Suvorov* the Russians automatically lost their chief commander, and the ensuing chaos made them unable to resist the enemy effectively any more. Although the Japanese suffered in the first stage of the battle – *Mikasa*, *Nisshin* and *Asama* were quite seriously damaged – all their ships, except the last one, remained in formation, preserving their combat potential.

The 305mm gun turret on the battleship Borodino.

Russian cruiser Admiral Nakhimov.

The second stage of the battle

Right after losing contact with the enemy, in compliance with Rozhestvenski's instructions given out before the battle, Bukhvostov again changed course to the north, heading for Vladivostok. Togo predicted that move and at 15.22/15.42 ordered a simultaneous turn of the I Division by 180° (thus *Mikasa* assumed the leading position), sailing north-west to intercept the enemy on its expected route. At 15.29/15.49

Kamimura also made a turn north-west and followed Togo.

Before the next clash between the main forces took place, at 15.35/15.55 Kamimura's II division of armoured cruisers, sailing north, once more encountered the heavily damaged battleship *Suvorov* and opened fire at it from a distance of only 10-15 cable-lengths (1.8-2.7 km). Togo's squadron also arrived at the scene soon after, and at 15.40/16.00 the main forces of the II Fleet, led now by the battleship *Borodino*, turned up (*Aleksandr III*, damaged at the end of the first stage of the battle, had to leave the formation for several minutes, and after provisional repairs and extinguishing fires, assumed position behind *Sisoy Velikiy*). At this time the opposing fleets were sailing on converging courses, while the distance between them, which amounted to 41-42 cable-lengths (7.5 km) between the leading ships at 15.40/16.00, dropped to 28 cable-lengths (5 km) 20 minutes later. Having a considerable speed advantage the Japanese managed to overtake the II Fleet warships, and concentrated fire mainly on the leading battleships *Borodino* and *Orel'*. After 16.00/16.20, the Japanese started to 'bend' their course to starboard in an attempt to perform a T-crossing, which made *Borodino* turn east, and

it was followed by the remaining warships. The ensuing confusion caused the Russian formation to fall apart. Fortunately for the Russians, they soon lost contact with the enemy. In the north they were cut off by Togo's I Division and in the east by Kamimura's II Division who, after taking the lead, at 16.10/16.30 started to 'bend' his course again, gradually achieving a T-crossing. Consequently, the Russian squadron turned south at 16.17/16.37 . This made it possible to rearrange its formation and resume combat capacity by the entire fleet.

Meanwhile the Japanese warships of the I Division turned north. Then, at 16.25/16.45, they resumed course eastwards and eight minutes later turned south to follow the Russian squadron. Kamimura's division also headed south, but after 16.24/16.44 had lost time performing various manoeuvres searching for the enemy. At 16.25/16.45 the armoured cruiser *Asama* rejoined the II Division and assumed the tail end position in the formation.

This stage of the battle was concluded by the 4th Division of destroyers' attack on *Suvorov*, ordered by Togo after 16.25/16.45 . This time the Japanese achieved one hit, but the Russian battleship remained afloat.

The second stage of the battle sealed the Japanese victory. Due to limited visibility the distance was not great and at times dropped below 20 cable-lengths. As a result the confrontation was particularly fierce. The Russians, disorganized and confused after the first stage, were clearly unable to pull themselves together and stand up to the enemy. Their fire turned out to be far less accurate than at the beginning of the battle, whilst the Japanese fired quickly and efficiently, achieving quite a high level of hits.

The third stage of the battle

Soon after losing contact with the Japanese main forces, the Russian main forces encountered Japanese cruisers fighting with Enkvist's ships. During a short 20 minute long confrontation the Russian battleships, quite fatigued but having a considerable advantage over the new enemy, forced them to turn back by inflicting severe damage upon its ships. Soon afterwards, at 16.42/17.02, contact with Togo's I Division was regained. Due to limited visibility (fog), it lasted only five minutes and there were no serious losses on either side. For the same reason

the clash with the division of armoured cruisers that turned up at 16.52/17.12 remained inconclusive. Without the I Division's support, Kamimura did not attack with sufficient determination (the distance was 36 cable-lengths/6.5 km, and later increased to 40 cable-lengths/7.2 km) and after 17.05/17.25, when the Russians made a turn north-west, the contact was lost.

In this manner the Russians managed to leave the enemy behind and set out on their way to Vladivostok. However, predicting the destination of the II Pacific Squadron, at 17.06/17.26 Togo, still having no contact with the enemy or any information about its movements, made an intuitive decision to direct the I Division north, finishing off the sinking auxiliary cruiser *Ural* on his way. Kamimura followed, after he made a large loop to port between 17.45/18.05 and 18.00/18.20 to search for the enemy.

The fourth stage of the battle

Meanwhile, after losing contact with the enemy the Russian fleet rearranged its formation in the fog. The lead was again taken over by the battleship *Borodino*, followed by *Orel'*, *Imperator Aleksandr III*, *Imperator Nikolay I*, *Admiral Ushakov*, *Admiral Senyavin*, *General-Admiral Apraksin* (Nebogatov's detachment filled the gap between *Aleksandr III* and *Navarin* that appeared in the third stage of the battle), *Navarin*, *Sisoy Velikiy* and *Admiral Nakhimov*. The cruiser *Izumrud* was sailing on the port beam of *Borodino*. Enkvist's detachment (with *Zhemchug*) were sailing about three sea miles west of the armoured units, followed by the damaged cruiser *Svetlana*, whilst the destroyers were sailing to port of the cruisers. The heavily damaged *Suvorov* was still cruising the battlefield. However, the Russian squadron lost contact with it after 17.30/17.50 . More or less at that time the incapacitated flagship was approached by the destroyer *Buynyy*, and despite the fact that it already had about 200 shipwrecked sailors from *Oslyabya* on board, it received the wounded Rozhestvenski, seven officers of his staff, and 15 other crew members[82].

At this time the Russian squadron was heading directly for Vladivostok, leaving both Togo's I Division and Kamimura's II Division behind. However in order to reach the shelter of the port,

82 Russko-yaponskaya voyna..., op.cit., Documents. Otd. IV, Kn. 3, wyp. 1, p. 6.

Russian coast defence battle-ship Admiral Senyavin.

the Russian warships would have had to sail at a speed at least matching the Japanese vessels, that is 15-16 knots. Unfortunately the seriously damaged warships of the Second Fleet could only sail at 11-12 knots. As a result the warships of the Combined Fleet started gaining on the Russians and at 17.39/17.59 the I Division came into visual contact with them.

This time the weather conditions were not favourable to the Japanese. The setting sun was dazzling the gunners, and when at 17.39/17.59 the Russians were first to open fire at a distance of 45 cable-lengths (8.1 km) they were in a very inconvenient position. Admiral Togo ordered a change of course to the north, and soon afterwards a course parallel to the Russian squadron, and at 17.42/18.02 ordered to his ships to open fire. Consequently a classic gunnery exchange on parallel courses took place. A first the Japanese were a little behind the Russians, but thanks to their speed advantage caught up with them quickly and came level with them at 18.17/18.37 . Then the distance dropped to 25 cable-lengths (4.5 km). Despite the fact that the II Fleet was facing only the I Division, and the

fighting had become quite static, the Japanese gained the advantage from the very beginning, as most Russian warships were already badly hit and their fire power was considerably decreased. The Japanese, on the other hand, fired as quickly and accurately as at the beginning of the battle. As a result, at 18.15/18.35 the battleship *Aleksandr III* left the formation, listing considerably to starboard. Soon afterwards, unable to endure the Japanese bombardment, *Borodino* deviated to port, pulling the remaining Russian units behind it. This manoeuvre increased the distance between the opposing ships by 3-5 cable-lengths, which gave the Russians some breathing space and, after a fire had been extinguished, made it possible for *Aleksandr III* to return to the formation between *Senyavin* and *Ushakov*. However the situation of the Russians became worse again at 18.32/18.52, after Kamimura's group of armoured cruisers arrived on the scene from the south and commenced shelling the Russian ships at the end of the formation.

In the meantime *Aleksandr III* was being systematically fired at by the Japanese and at 18.40/19.00 it left the formation, sinking ten minutes later. After *Aleksandr III* had left the formation, Togo's first squadron shifted fire to the Russian leading battleships *Borodino* and *Orel'* (the distance between them was then about 30-31 cable-lengths/5.4-5.5 km). Yet as it was already getting dark the Japanese admiral finally made a decision to cease fire. The I Division fired their last shots at 19.03/19.23, and at precisely this moment a 305 mm shell from *Fuji* hit *Borodino* on the waterline, below its aftermost starboard 152 mm turret, causing

Russian destroyer Buynyy, *which received wounded Vice Admiral Rozhestvensky on its board.*

the magazine to explode. As a result the warship capsized and sank within seven minutes, taking its entire crew with it[83]. Kamimura's division continued shelling the Russian warships until 19.10/19.30 and then like the I Division retreated north-east.

At the same time *Suvorov* met its doom. Since 18.20/18.40 it had been systematically fired at, along with the repair ship *Kamchatka* that had been accompanying it since 17.30/17.50, first by Vice Admiral Uriu's IV Division strengthened by cruisers *Niitaka* and *Otowa* from the III Division, and later also by the ships of the V and VI Divisions. *Kamchatka* sank as a result of fire from the V Division at 18.50/19.10. *Suvorov* in turn, which was impervious to the 152-120 mm shells, was soon attacked by the 11th Torpedo Boat Division, accompanying Vice Admiral Kataoka's V Division, which sank the Russian battleships with two accurate hits.

Thus the day of 27th May ended in a total defeat of the Russians. They lost four modern warships, whilst the remaining ones suffered severe damage and were unable to face the Japanese any more.

The battle of the cruisers

The confrontation between the light forces started fifteen minutes after the battle between the main forces had commenced. It was started by the cruiser *Idzumi*, which was sailing alone and at 14.05/14.25 attacked the column

83 PRO, ADM 231/44, Reports..., vol. III, p. 72; ADM 231/45, Reports..., vol. IV, p. 19; CAB 37/78/104, p. 8. According to Kostenko V. P. (op. cit. p. 439), the Russian battleship was hit by two shells at the same time, one of which caused the above mentioned explosion.

of transports. They were protected by *Vladimir Monomakh*, which although it received a hit itself managed to hit *Idzumi* too and after a short duel chased the Japanese cruiser away.

At 14.30/14.50, the cruisers of the Japanese III and IV Divisions joined the battle. The cruisers *Oleg* and *Avrora*, later followed by *Dmitriy Donskoy* and *Vladimir Monomakh* (after 15.10/15.30 they formed a line astern), hurried to rescue the shelled transports and the ships of Captain Shein's reconnaissance division that were trying to provide them with cover. Soon the battle turned into a gunnery duel on parallel courses at a distance of 35-40 cable-lengths (6.3-7.2 km). However the activity of the Russian cruisers was hampered by the behaviour of the transports, which panicked while under fire and were manoeuvring chaotically. In these circumstances the Japanese gradually started to gain the advantage and managed to inflict serious damages on the auxiliary cruiser *Ural* and the destroyer *Blestjaschchij*. Still the Russians were also successful to some extent. At 14.48/15.08 they hit Dewa's flag cruiser *Kasagi*, and at 15.37/15.57 the cruiser *Takachiho*, causing the former to leave the formation for several hours (it rejoined the IV squadron at about 18.00/18.20).

The intervention of Enkvist's cruisers turned out to be enough to pull Dewa's and Uriu's divisions away from the transports after 15.20/15.40. However at 15.25/15.45 Rear Admiral Togo's VI Division arrived from the south-west, joined at 15.50/16.10 by Vice Admiral Kataoka's V Division. Along with *Idzumi*, which rejoined its mother division, they attacked the transports again, now

BATTLE OF TSUSHIMA, 27 MAY, 1905

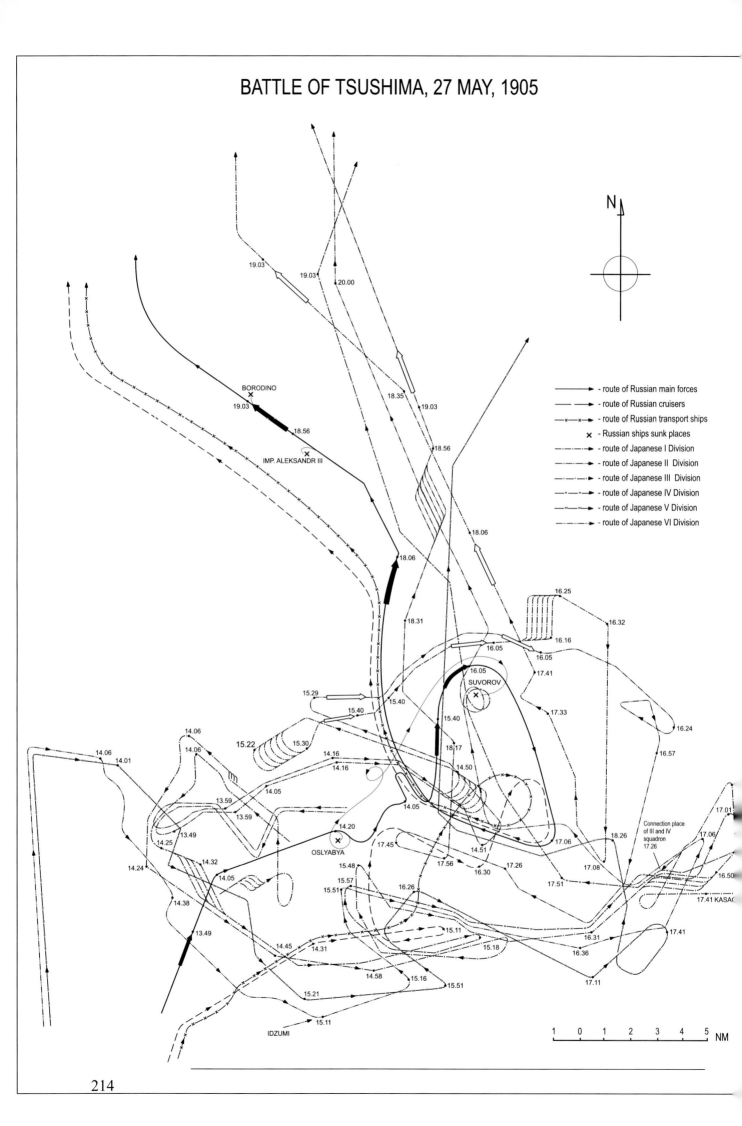

N

BORODINO
19.03

IMP. ALEKSANDR III
18.56

19.03
19.03
20.00
18.35
19.03
18.56
18.06
18.06
18.31
18.06

16.25
16.32
16.16
16.05
16.05
17.41
SUVOROV
16.05
17.33
16.24
15.29
15.40
16.57
15.40
15.40
14.06
18.17
14.06
15.22
15.30
14.16
14.50
14.06
14.16
14.01
14.05
14.05
13.59
13.59
14.20
14.05
17.45
Connection place
of III and IV
squadron
17.26
OSLYABYA
13.49
14.51
18.26
17.01
14.25
17.56
17.26
17.08
17.06
14.24
14.32
15.48
16.30
17.51
14.05
15.57
16.26
16.50
14.38
15.51
17.41 KASAG
13.49
15.11
14.45
14.31
16.31
17.41
15.18
16.36
14.58
15.16
17.11
15.21
15.51

IDZUMI
15.11

- route of Russian main forces
- route of Russian cruisers
- route of Russian transport ships
× Russian ships sunk places
- route of Japanese I Division
- route of Japanese II Division
- route of Japanese III Division
- route of Japanese IV Division
- route of Japanese V Division
- route of Japanese VI Division

1 0 1 2 3 4 5 NM

Vice Admiral Uriu's flagship – the cruiser Naniwa.

protected only by Shein's detachment. They put up fierce resistance against the Japanese, but facing four times stronger enemy forces could not do much. Consequently both *Svetlana* and *Ural* were seriously damaged. Again, Enkvist came to the rescue (at 16.00/16.20, his detachment was joined by *Zhemchug*, which had been sailing with the main forces so far). However Dewa's and Uriu's divisions returned along with it. Consequently the Japanese maintained their advantage, increased even more by the chaotic manoeuvring of the panic-stricken transports, which made it difficult for the cruisers to operate. In the overwhelming confusion, the heavily damaged *Ural* collided with *Zhemchug* (fortunately with no serious consequences to the latter), whilst *Anadyr"* rammed and sank the tug *Rus* while taking the crew of the sinking *Ural* aboard.

In the ensuing chaos it seemed that despite Enkvist's efforts the transports were doomed. However the situation was saved by the main forces of the II Fleet, which turned up unexpectedly at around 17.00/17.20. First came Nebogatov's detachment, and then the remaining Russian warships. After a short confrontation they forced the Japanese cruisers to withdraw by inflicting damage upon *Matsushima* and *Kasagi*, which ended the battle of the light forces. Although the Japanese cruisers returned after 18.00/18.20, they found no Russian forces there any more, except the damaged *Suvorov* and *Kamchatka* which they attacked.

Torpedo attacks on Russian warships by night

After the daylight battle had ended, and the Japanese main forces had withdrawn,

leadership of the Russian squadron was taken over by *Nikolay I*, commanded by Rear Admiral Nebogatov, who only now assumed actual command over the remnants of the II Fleet. He was followed by the heavily damaged *Orel'* and the still fully operational coast defence battleships *Apraksin* and *Senyavin*. At a certain distance behind the first four warships there sailed *Ushakov*, followed by *Navarin*, *Sisoy Velikiy* and *Nakhimov*. The virtually intact *Izumrud* sailed

Russian cruiser Zhemchug. *It initially accompanied the main forces, but joined Rear Admiral Enkvist's group soon after the battle had commenced and took part in the battle of cruisers.*

Japanese cruiser Akashi.

Japanese cruiser Chitose.

abeam the leading *Nikolay I*. Enkvist's cruisers sailed to port of the second group of warships. The transports and destroyers sailed together a little behind and west of the main forces.

After assuming command, Nebogatov considered turning south and giving up the attempt to break through to Vladivostok, which was now a mere 300 sea miles away. Eventually he resolved to continue sailing to the preset destination and, for that reason, at 20.20/20.40 he ordered a turn north-east, increasing speed to 12-13 knots. This manoeuvre caused the Russian squadron to disperse, as Rear Admiral Enkvist's cruisers lost contact with the main forces in the dark and, after increasing speed to 18 knots, sailed away southwards. Such a

high speed could be maintained only by *Oleg*, *Avrora*, and *Zemchug*. The remaining ships were unable to keep pace with the first three, so after some time they gave up and turned north-east with the intention of rejoining the main forces. Only *Vladimir Monomakh*, which assumed position on the right flank of the column of warships, next to the destroyer *Gromkiy*, managed to accomplish that before the torpedo attacks took place. *Dmitriy Donskoy*, in turn, along with the destroyers *Buynyy*, *Bedovyy*, and *Grozny*, assumed position a little behind Nebogatov's squadron. *Almaz* and severely damaged *Svetlana* were sailing alone a little further away. As regards the remaining units, the destroyers *Bodryy* and the heavily damaged

Russian battleship Navarin. *This battleship was sunk by the Japanese torpedo boats and destroyers in the night torpedo attacks of 27/28 May.*

Blestyashchiy followed Enkvist's cruisers, but *Bravyy* and *Bezuprechnyy* after 21.00/21.20 set course towards the shores of Japan. *Bystryy*, in turn, was alone heading north. The surviving transports, *Koreya, Anadyr"*, and *Svir"*, headed south-west towards the shores of Korea. The damaged *Irtysh* was sailing alone east towards Japan. Finally the remaining large Russian ships, sailing behind Nebogatov's four warships and unable to maintain 12-13 knots, were gradually falling behind and losing contact with the main group. These dispersed surviving units of the Second Fleet were attacked by the Japanese destroyers and torpedo boats.

Adm. Togo dispatched all five divisions of destroyers (21 ships altogether) and ten divisions of torpedo boats (1, 9, 10, 14, 15, 16, 17, 18, 19 and 20 – 37 ships altogether) to carry out torpedo assaults. Out of these, the 1st and 2nd Destroyer Divisions had accompanied Togo's I Division during the battle. Late in the afternoon they were also joined by the 9th Torpedo Boat Division, which had left Miura Bay at Tsushima a couple of earlier. After the battle those units managed to get a little ahead of the Russian squadron and were closing in on them from the north and north-east. The 3rd and 5th Destroyer Divisions had accompanied

Russian battleship Sisoy Velikiy. *It was damaged in the day artillery battle, and torpedoed in the night of 27/28 May by the Japanese destroyers, which ultimately decided its fate.*

Kamimura's II Division during the battle, and after it ended they were several miles east of the enemy's main forces. From this direction the 4th Destroyer Division, which operated independently after the attack on *Suvorov*, started on its torpedo mission. However, the distance to the Russian warships was much greater this time. The 15th Torpedo Boat Division had accompanied Togo's VI Division of cruisers in the battle (initially, also the 10th Division, but this was soon sent back to Miura Bay). The 11th and 20th Torpedo Boat Divisions had been with Kataoka's V Division (initially also the 17th and 18th Divisions, but they were sent back to Miura Bay before the battle commenced). After the battle ended they were sent to chase the

Japanese destroyer Shirakumo – *one of the ships that sunk the battleship* Navarin.

Japanese destroyer Asashio – *during the night torpedo attacks it managed to hit the battleship* Sisoy Velikiy.

Russian warships escaping north and attacked them, along with the 1st, 10th, 14th, 17th, 18th and 19th Torpedo Boat Divisions that arrived from the waters of Tsushima, from the south and the south-east. Their position was undoubtedly least convenient for the attack, therefore four of them (11th, 14th, 19th, and 20th) never managed to catch up with the enemy[84].

While dispatching his torpedo units, Togo did not ensure the coordination of their operations. Therefore individual divisions searched for and attacked the enemy on their own. The chaos was intensified even more by bad weather and falling darkness. As a result the Japanese attacks, which continued until dawn, produced only a partial success. Apart from the torpedo attacks carried out during the battle itself, during the night of 27th/28th May the Japanese destroyers launched 37 torpedoes (23 more torpedoes during the daylight battle on 27th May and a further five during the attacks on the armoured cruiser *Dmitriy Donskoy*), achieving six hits (plus a further three or four during the daytime attacks on 27th May)[85]. They succeeded in sinking the battleship *Navarin* (after three hits), the battleship *Sisoy Velikiy* (damaged earlier in the battle), and seriously damaging the armoured cruisers *Admiral Nakhimov* and *Vladimir Monomakh*. Moreover most Russian warships were dispersed. Consequently the II Fleet practically ceased to exist as an organized combat group. Only Rear Admiral Nebogatov's

squadron had some combat potential, two battleships (one seriously damaged), two coast defence battleships and a cruiser. Had he faced the Japanese main forces, though, he would not have stood a chance to break through to Vladivostok.

The capitulation of Nebogatov's squadron and the fate of the remaining Russian warships

Directly after the daytime battle and the dispatching the destroyers and torpedo boats, Admiral Togo decided to assume position between the islands of Dagelet and Liancourt in order to wait for the surviving units of the II Fleet if they tried to break through to Vladivostok. He gathered all available forces there. In the morning of 28th May it turned out that his intuition was correct again, as at around 06.00/06.20 Nebogatov's squadron was spotted by the ships of the V Division, at 09.10/09.30 also by the II Division and a little later by Togo's I Division. Both these divisions barred Nebogatov's way to Vladivostok. As at the same time the IV and V Divisions were approaching from the west, the VI from the south-east and the cruiser *Chitose* from the south, Nebogatov's warships were trapped. Under these circumstances, seeing no point in further fighting, the Russian admiral capitulated. The flag on *Nikolay I* was lowered at 10.18/10.38 [86].

Nebogatov's order was executed by all the remaining warships (*Orel'*, *Senyavin* and *Apraksin*) except *Izumrud*, whose commander, after an initial hesitation (he even pulled out a Japanese flag), increased speed and sneaked through the gap between the second and sixth squadrons. Sailing at 24 knots, the Russian cruiser headed east and soon escaped the pursuit by cruisers of the VI Division and *Chitose*. The remaining ships were boarded by the Japanese and escorted to Sasebo(*Nikolaj I*, *Senyavin* and *Apraksin*) and Maizuru (the heavily damaged *Orel'*)[87].

---

84 Lacroix E., op.cit., part 14, TBS No 1/1970, p.22; Opisanie..., op.cit., vol.IV, pp.129-130; The Japanese torpedo boats in the battle of Tsushima. WI No 2/1972, p. 198.

85 There is various data available. Dyskan J. W. (Cuszima, op.cit., p, 218) gives the number of 34-35 torpedoes launched in night attacks, Denisov B. (Ispolzovanije torpednogo oruzhija..., op.cit., pp. 15-16) claims that the Japanese launched the total of 30 torpedoes (5 hits) during the day, and 34 torpedoes (6 hits) in the night. The above data has been calculated by the Author.

86 Gribovskiy V.Yu., Krestnyj put'..., op.cit., p. 33.

87 After their return to the country from captivity, Nebogatov, and the commanders of *Nikolay I*, *Orel'*, *Senyavin*, and *Apraksin* were put on trial. Despite justifying his decision by humanitarian reasons, Nebogatov was sentenced to death by shooting. The commanders of *Nikolay I*, *Senyavin*, and *Apraksin* were also sentenced to death. Only Commander Shvede, who substituted fatally wounded commander of *Orel'*,Captain N.V. Yung, was exonerated, as his battleship was found unable to continue fighting after the damages it had suffered on May 27th. Eventually, the tsar pardoned the

Battleship Imperator Nikolay I, *Rear Admiral Nebogatov's flagship after the capitulation on May 28, 1905.*

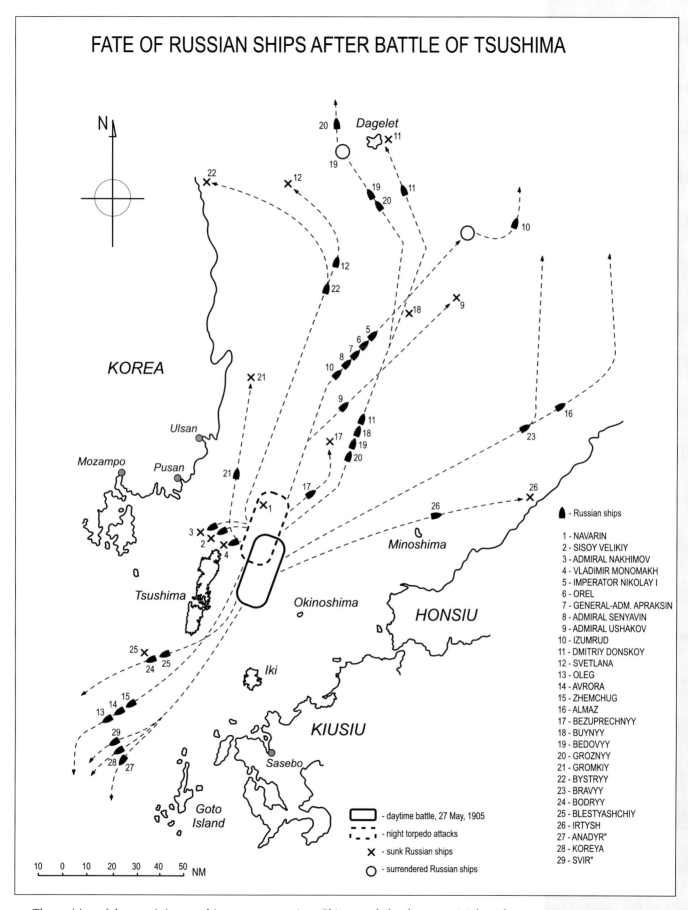

FATE OF RUSSIAN SHIPS AFTER BATTLE OF TSUSHIMA

- Russian ships

1 - NAVARIN
2 - SISOY VELIKIY
3 - ADMIRAL NAKHIMOV
4 - VLADIMIR MONOMAKH
5 - IMPERATOR NIKOLAY I
6 - OREL
7 - GENERAL-ADM. APRAKSIN
8 - ADMIRAL SENYAVIN
9 - ADMIRAL USHAKOV
10 - IZUMRUD
11 - DMITRIY DONSKOY
12 - SVETLANA
13 - OLEG
14 - AVRORA
15 - ZHEMCHUG
16 - ALMAZ
17 - BEZUPRECHNYY
18 - BUYNYY
19 - BEDOVYY
20 - GROZNYY
21 - GROMKIY
22 - BYSTRYY
23 - BRAVYY
24 - BODRYY
25 - BLESTYASHCHIY
26 - IRTYSH
27 - ANADYR"
28 - KOREYA
29 - SVIR"

◻ - daytime battle, 27 May, 1905
⋯ - night torpedo attacks
✕ - sunk Russian ships
○ - surrendered Russian ships

10 0 10 20 30 40 50 NM

The position of the remaining warships was no less pitiful. *Bezuprechnyy* was first to meet its doom. At dawn it encountered the north-west bound cruiser *Chitose* and the destroyer *Ariake*. After a short confrontation the Russian warship was literally shattered by the cruiser and at 05.07/05.27 it sank along with its entire crew.

convicts by changing the sentence to 10 years of imprisonment. All of them were freed in 1909.

Battleship Orel' *shortly after the capitulation. It bears clear signs of battle damage.*

The stern of the battleship Orel' *after the battle of Tsushima.*

Blestjashhij was next. Along with *Bodryy*, it turned south at night after its commander abandoned the plan to sail to Vladivostok, and sank at 06.00/06.20 due to the damage it had suffered during the battle.

Soon afterwards the armoured cruisers *Admiral Nakhimov* and *Vladimir Monomakh* sank after being heavily damaged in the night torpedo attacks. The former went down at around 09.00/09.20 north-east of Tsushima, the latter an hour later near the Kaminoshima islet, north of Tsushima. The battleship *Sisoy Velikiy* sank at 10.40/11.00 near Karazaki Cape in the Tsushima Archipelago.

The destroyer *Gromkiy*, which had been accompanying *Sisoy*, abandoned the sinking warship at 08.00/08.20 and alone tried to break through to Vladivostok, but was intercepted and sunk by the Japanese destroyer *Shiranui*

and the torpedo boat *63* at 12.23/12.43, 15 sea miles east of Ulsan.

Heavily damaged in the daytime battle, the cruiser *Svetlana* was sailing along with the destroyer *Bystryy* behind Nebogatov's squadron. At dawn it found itself between the ships of the Japanese V Division and the III and IV Divisions. After having been spotted by the enemy, it was attacked by the cruisers *Otowa* and *Niitaka* and sank at 10.45/11.05 .

The accompanying destroyer *Bystryy* abandoned the cruiser at about 10.20/10.40. However there was not enough coal on the Russian ship to reach Vladivostok. Therefore its commander turned towards the shores of Korea. Pursued by Japanese ships, it sailed onto a shoal, 350 metres off the shore, in the area of the River Chikuhen at 11.30/11.50 and was blown up there by its own crew.

The coast defence battleship *Ushakov* was following the main forces and at dawn encountered the Japanese ships of the V Division sailing on its left. However the distance between the Russian warship and the enemy was considerable and the latter ignored the solitary unit as it was engaged in the pursuit of Nebogatov's squadron. Eventually at 14.40/15.00, several miles south-east from the area of Nebogatov's capitulation, the Russian vessel was spotted by Kamimura's II Division. The armoured cruisers *Iwate* and *Yakumo*, under Rear Admiral Shimamura's command, undertook an immediate pursuit. Much faster, the Japanese warships soon caught up with the Russian ship, whose commander decided to fight regardless of the enemy's advantage. At 17.00/17.20, despite appeals for capitulation, he opened fire at a distance of almost 60 cable-lengths. In the face of the enemy strength *Ushakov* had no chance of success and was eventually sunk at 17.48/18.08, 60 sea miles west of the island of Oki.

The armoured cruiser *Dmitriy Donskoy*, along with the destroyers *Buynyy*, *Groznyy* and *Bedovyy*, tried to break through to Vladivostok by following Nebogatov's forces. Due to machinery breakdown, and the failure of one of the boilers on *Buynyy*, at dawn the wounded Rozhestvenski was moved to the destroyer *Bedovyy*. At 07.00/07.20 the latter, along with *Groznyy*, separated from the cruiser and headed north at top speed. However at 15.10/15.30, 40 sea miles south-west of Dagelet, the Russian ships were spotted by the Japanese destroyers *Sazanami* and *Kagero*, which were on their way back from patrol along the shores of Korea. For unknown reasons *Bedovyy* immediately lowered its flag and surrendered, whereas *Groznyy* put up a fierce fight and escaped from the enemy.

After the separation from *Bedovyy* and *Groznyy* the cruiser *Dmitriy Donskoy* and the destroyer *Buynyy* continued on course to Vladivostok. Another breakdown on *Buynyy*, however, forced the Russians to scuttle it at 11.30/11.50 . Continuing towards Vladivostok, *Dmitriy Donskoy* managed initially to avoid being spotted by the enemy, but at about 16.40/17.00, while passing the island of Dagelet to port, it was spotted by the cruisers of Vice Admiral Uriu's IV Division, accompanied by three destroyers of the II Division (*Oboro*, *Akebono* and *Inazuma*). Although *Donskoj* tried to perform an evasive manoeuvre, it was quickly caught up by the Japanese ships, soon joined by the cruisers *Otowa* and *Niitaka* and the destroyers *Asagiri*, *Shirakumo* and *Fubuki*. Despite its hopeless position, the Russian ship engaged the enemy. Heavily damaged, it found shelter near the shore of Dagelet after dark. At night the Japanese destroyers attempted to sink it with torpedoes, but achieved no success. Its own crew scuttled it at dawn.

The Russian ships that chose to sail to Vladivostok along the shores of Japan turned out to be the most fortunate. The only unit that failed was the transport *Irtysh* which, heavily damaged in the battle of 27th May, sank near

Hamada on the morning of 29th May. The ships that eventually made it to Vladivostok were the cruiser *Almaz* (reached Vladivostok on 29th May) and the destroyer *Bravyy* (despite a shortage of coal, it arrived at its destination in the evening of 30th May). It was preceded by the destroyer *Groznyy*, which had arrived several before.

The cruiser *Izumrud*, which had audaciously broken through the ring of Japanese warships surrounding Nebogatov's squadron, did not make it to Vladivostok. Its commander, Commander V.N. Ferzen, became a little carried away and, instead of heading directly for his destination, he sailed as far as St. Vladimir Bay, 180 sea miles north of Vladivostok, afraid that the Japanese might be blocking the port and awaiting the approaching Russian ships. During the night of 29th/30th May *Izumrud* sailed onto a rocky shoal and, unable to return

The sinking cruiser Admiral Nakhimov. *A photo taken early in the morning on May 28 from the Japanese auxiliary cruiser.*

Russian cruiser Svetlana. *Heavily damaged during the battle of 27 May. A day later, it undertook a heroic battle with the Japanese cruisers, during which it was sunk.*

Japanese cruiser Niitaka. *Along with the cruiser* Otowa, *it had the most contribution in sinking* Svetlana.

Japanese cruiser Otowa.

to deep waters, on the morning of 30th May was destroyed by its own crew[88].

Of the remaining Russian units that turned down south after the battle of 27th May, the transport *Koreya* and the tug *Svir"* reached the roadstead of Wusung on 29th May and were interned by the Chinese authorities the next day. The destroyer *Bodryy* ran out of fuel in the morning of 30th May and was drifting for the next four days until it was found by the British steamer *Kwei Lin*, which towed it to Shanghai, where it arrived on 4th June and, like the transports, was interned after 24 . Rear Admiral Enkvist's division of cruisers headed for Manila and reached it in the evening of 3rd June. The Americans allowed the Russians to restock coal there and remain in the port until 8th June. On 7th June, however, an order came from Petersburg to disarm the cruisers and have them interned. The transport *Anadyr"* avoided internment due to its huge range, which made it possible for it to reach Diego Suarez in Madagascar on 27th June. From there, after a short stay, it sailed home, arriving at Libawa at the beginning of August.

The outcome of the battle

The battle of Tsushima on 27th and 28th May 1905 ended with the overwhelming defeat of the Russian fleet. The Russians lost eight battleships (six sunk and two captured), three coast defence battleships (one sunk and two captured), three old armoured cruisers (sunk), one cruiser, one auxiliary cruiser (both sunk), and six destroyers (five sunk and one captured). Additionally, one cruiser was later destroyed by its own crew after it became stuck on the rocks, while three cruisers and one destroyer were interned in neutral ports. Out of the total number of transports and auxiliary units accompanying the II Fleet, three were sunk during the battle, or directly after it, and two hospital ships were apprehended by the Japanese[89]. About 5,000 Russian officers and sailors were killed, almost a thousand wounded, and 6,000 were taken prisoner (including many wounded)[90]. Only one cruiser and two destroyers made it to Vladivostok.

The losses seem even greater when compared to the Japanese ones. The Combined Fleet did not lose a single large ship during the battle, and after it ended all its battleships and armoured cruisers were operational and ready for battle. Only three torpedo boats were sunk during the night attacks. Casualties were a mere 118 killed and 565 wounded.

Several factors contributed to such an impressive victory[91]. During the battle, the twelve largest Japanese battleships from the first and second squadrons fired a total of 496 305-254 mm shells, 1,199 203 mm shells, and 9,464 152 mm shells (a further 89 203 mm shells and 278 152 mm shells were fired by *Iwate* and *Yakumo* during the clash with *Ushakov*), which is not many considering the result[92]. The number of Russian shells fired is unknown.

88 It is generally believed that the decision was too hasty, as the cruiser could still have been rescued., Alliluev A.A., Kreysery "Zhemchug" i "Izumrud". part 2, "Gangut" No 6 (1993), p. 29.

89 As a hospital ship *Kostroma* was released on July 14th, whilst *Orel'* was incorporated into the Japanese fleet, as the Japanese found the fact that it carried the crew of a previously sunk ship *Oldhamia* to be the violation of international conventions., Lacroix E., op.cit., part12, TBS No 4/1969, pp.323-324.

90 There are various figures concerning the Russian losses at Tsushima. According to the official Japanese sources, quoted by Corbett J. S. (op. cit., vol. II, p. 333), and after him by Wilson H.W. (op.cit., vol. I, p. 261) and Lacroix E. (op.cit., part 15, TBS No 2/1970, p. 137) 4,830 Russian officers and sailors were killed during the battle, 5,917 were taken prisoners of war (many of them wounded), and 1,862 were interned in neutral ports. However, quasi-official Russian data (Iorija..., op.cit., edited by I.I. Rostunov, p. 346) give the numbers of 5,045 killed, and over 800 wounded. Similar data is provided by Kostenko V. P. (op.cit., p. 490) – 5,044 killed, 5,982 POW's, and 2,110 interned in neutral ports.

91 Lacroix E., op.cit part 15, TBS No 2/1970, p. 138; Wilson H.W., op.cit., vol. I, pp. 254-255, 261

92 Campbell N.J.M., op.cit. Part 4, p. 260.

However, considering that the three surviving battleships from Nebogatov's squadron (*Nikolaj I*, *Apraksin* and *Senyavin*) fired during the entire battle 90 305 mm shells, 760 254-229 mm shells, 1,064 152 mm shells, and about 1,250 120 mm shells[93], one may estimate that Rozhestvenski's main forces fired at Tsushima a little over 1,000 305-254 mm shells, about 300 229-203 mm shells, and 7,500-8,000 152-120 mm shells. Thus the Russians fired a total of 9,000-9,500 heavy and medium shells, whilst the Japanese fired over 11,000 shells. The weight of the shells fired by the Russians was, however, 50 percent higher and it was precisely the shells of heavy

caliber (305-254 mm) that decided the outcome of the battle. There is no question, then, that it was not the weight of artillery that determined the outcome of the battle, because there was no real difference, and the strength of each side, though of different quality, was comparable.

Undoubtedly one of the factors that determined the success of Togo's squadron was the accuracy of the Japanese guns. They achieved about 4 percent hits, but for the number of 305-254 mm shells fired it was 14%, for 203 mm shells 9.5%, and for 152 mm shells about 2.7%[94]. Despite the fact that the general range

---

93 Gribovskiy V.Yu., Krestnyj put'..., op.cit., p. 32.

94 The Author's estimates, calculated on the basis of the duration of firing at particular Russian ships by specific Japanese ones, and the number of shells fired at them.

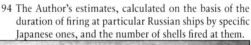

223

was 20-30 cable-lengths (3.6 – 5.2 km), that is shorter than during the battles of the Yellow Sea or the Japanese Sea, the percentage of hits was still impressive, as the Russians achieved about 3.5% hits with 305-203 mm shells and a little below 1% with 152-120 mm ones, so their accuracy was far from poor, especially during the initial stage of the battle when the percentage was even higher[95].

95 Kofman V., Tsusima: analiza protiv mitov., "Naval" No 1 (1991), p.11.

Cruiser Avrora *after the battle of Tsushima.*

The wreck of the cruiser Izumrud *destroyed by its own crew after getting stranded on the rocks.*

Destroyer Bedovyy, *on which wounded Vice Admiral Rozhestvenski was taken prisoner.*

Table No. 4: The battle of Tsushima

Name of ship	Commander	Hits				Casualities		
		305-254mm	229-203mm	152-120mm	Torpedos	Killed	Wounded	Total
Russia								
Knyaz' Suvorov	Vice Adm. Z.P. Rozhestvenskij Captain V.V. Ignatsius	20*	20*	65*	3	935	10	945
Imp. Aleksandr III	Captain N.M. Bukhvostov	12*	25*	40*	-	867	-	867
Borodino	Captain P.I. Serebrennikov	15*	15*	45*	-	865	-	865
Orel'	Captain N.V. Yung	7	9	39	-	43	87	130
Oslyabya	(Rear Adm. D.G. Fel'kerzham) Captain V.I. Ber	9-10*	20*	25*	-	531[1]	76[1]	607[1]
Sisoy Velikiy	Captain M.V. Ozerov	5	7	12	1	59	46	105
Navarin	Captain B.A. Fitingof	2*	5*	10*	3	700	3	703
Adm. Nakhimov	Captain A.A. Rodionov	2	3	13	1	25	69	94
Imp. Nikolay I	Rear Adm. N.I. Nebogatov Captain V.V. Smirnov	1	2	6	-	5	35	40
General-Admiral Apraksin	Captain N.G. Lishin	-	-	2	-	2	15	17
Adm. Senyavin	Captain S.N. Grigor'ev	-	-	-	-	-	3	3
Adm. Ushakov	Captain V.N. Miklukho-Maklay	-	5	3	-	87	11	98
Oleg	Rear Adm. O.A. Enkvist, Captain L.F. Dobrotvorskiy	-	1	5	-	13	43	56
Avrora	Captain E.R. Egor'ev	-	2	8	-	16	83	99
Dmitriy Donskoy	Captain I. N. Lebedev	-	-	25*	-	59	75	134
Vladimir Monomakh	Captain V.A. Popov	-	-	3	1	1	16	17
Svetlana	Captain S.P. Shein	-	1	15*	-	170	36	206
Zhemchug	Commander P.P. Levitskiy	-	-	5	-	13	30	43
Izumrud	Commander V.N. Ferzen	-	-	2	-	-	6	6
Almaz	Commander I.I. Chagin	-	-	2	-	6	13	19
Ural	Commander M.K. Istomin	2*	1*	20*	1?	22	6	28
9 destroyers		-	1	5	-	115[1]	75[1]	190[1]
6 transports and auxiliary vessels		3*	5*	15*	-	342	61	403
Japan								
Mikasa	Adm. Togo H. Rear Adm. Kato T. Captain Ijichi H.	10	-	22	-	8	105	113
Shikishima	Captain Teragaki I.	2	-	4	-	13	24	37
Fuji	Captain Matsumoto K.	2	-	3	-	8	22	30
Asahi	Captain Nomoto T.	-	-	2	-	8	23	31
Kasuga	Captain Kato S.	1	-	1	-	7	20	27
Nisshin	Vice Adm. Mizu S. Captain Takenouchi H.	6	1	2	-	6	89	95
Tatsuta	Commander Yamazumi	-	-	-	-	-	-	-
Idzumo	Vice Adm. Kamimura H., Captain Ijichi S.	6	-	3	-	4	26	30
Adzuma	Captain Murakami K.	7	-	4	-	11	29	40
Tokiwa	Captain Yoshimatsu M.	1	-	2	-	1	14	15
Yakumo	Captain Matsumoto A.	1	-	4	-	3	9	12
Asama	Captain Yoshiro R.	3	2	7	-	3	13	16
Iwate	Rear Adm. Shimamura H., Captain Kawashiro R.	2	3	3	-	-	14	14
Chihaya	Commander Eguchi R.	-	-	1?	-	-	4	4
Kasagi	Vice Adm. Dewa S. Captain Yamaya T.	1	-	2	-	1	9	10
Chitose	Captain Takagi S.	-	-	1	-	2	4	6
Niitaka	Captain Shoji Y.	-	-	1	-	1	3	4
Otowa	Captain Arima R.	-	-	3	-	6	24	30

Name of ship	Commander	Hits				Casualities		
		305-254mm	229-203mm	152-120mm	Torpedos	Killed	Wounded	Total
Naniwa	Vice Adm. Uriu S. Captain Wada K.	-	-	2	-	1	14	15
Takachiho	Captain Mori I.	-	-	1	-	-	4	4
Akashi	Captain Uchida J.	-	-	2	-	4	6	10
Tsushima	Captain Seyto T.	-	-	2	-	4	16	20
Itsukushima	Vice Adm. Kataoka S. Captain Tsuchiya T.	-	-	-	-	-	-	-
Chin Yen	Captain Imai K.	-	-	-	-	-	-	-
Matsushima	Captain Okumiya M.	-	-	1	-	-	1	1
Hashidate	Rear Adm. Taketomi K. Captain Fukui M.	-	-	2	-	-	7	7
Yaeyama	Commander Nishiyama S.	-	-	-	-	-	-	-
Suma	Rear Adm. Togo M. Captain Tochinai S.	-	-	1	-	-	3	3
Chiyoda	Captain Higashi F.	-	-	1	-	-	2	2
Akitsushima	Captain Hirose K.	-	-	1	-	-	2	2
Idzumi	Captain Ishida I.	-	-	3	-	3	7	10
21destroyers, 45 torpedo boats		1	-	2?	-	24	71	95

*   Author's evaluation data.

1   The losses of the armoured boat *Oslyabya* I and the destroyer *Buynyy* also include those officers and sailors who were killed on May 28th, on board of the heavy cruiser *Dmitriy Donskoy*: 22 killed and 7 wounded from *Oslabiai* and 3 killed and 12 wounded from *Buynyy*. The quoted losses of *Dmitri Donskoj* cover only its own crew.

Russian cruisers (from the right: Oleg, Zhemchug, Avrora) *after the battle of Tsushima on the roadstead of Manila port.*

Cruiser Alamz *in Vladyvostok after the battle of Tsushima.*

Such a high accuracy of Japanese fire was partly due to use of the new Stround Bar & Stround telescopic rangefinders, FA3 version, but first of all it was the superb preparation of the gunners. Their skill is also due to the fact that right after the campaign of 1904 Adm. Togo gathered the best gunners and placed them on his largest battleships. Consequently the percentage of hits achieved by the Japanese cruisers in combat with Enkvist's squadron was three times lower than that of the main forces.

Secondly the victory of the Japanese was achieved through the mistakes made by Rozhestvenski, mainly by wrong manoeuvres performed at the beginning of the battle. It made it possible for the Japanese to achieve an immediate local advantage which, along with their fire accuracy, determined the outcome of the battle. The Russian admiral himself made it easier for the enemy by putting fast and slow warships together in one group, let alone the fact that he went into battle with slow transport boats. Consequently he gave the Japanese the advantage of speed and manoeuvrability and thus enabled them to take the initiative and make best use of their assets from the very beginning[96].

Finally Vice Admiral Rozhestvenski made a huge mistake by overloading his warships with coal. As a result the displacement of the Russian ships was generally 15% greater than their nominal maximum, which obviously affected their speed, seaworthiness and stability. The extra weight also resulted in their main armour belts being under water. Consequently the sides of the Russian armoured ships were no longer protected, or were protected only partially. To make things worse the Japanese admiral accidentally demanded that his warships be equipped with high-explosive shells, filled with an agent far more powerful and generating much higher temperature than the explosives used before. These shells were capable of breaking through non-armoured or lightly armoured sides of warships and cause extensive damage. They made huge holes in the hull and caused fires. However they were much less efficient than other armour-piercing shells if they hit armoured sides. The use of the high-explosive shells against the overloaded Russian warships produced, therefore, an extraordinary effect[97].

All in all, it may be concluded that the Japanese owed their victory at Tsushima to Rozhestvenski's incompetence and their own superb skills. This should not, however, belittle Adm. Togo's merits, who managed to draw

conclusions from the mistakes he had made during the campaign of 1904 and skilfully turned the enemy's mistakes to his advantage.

The aftermath of Russian hits and premature explosion of shells in the gun barrels, – damage to the guns on the Japanese cruiser Nisshin.

96 Ibidem, pp. 7-8.
97 Campbell N.J.M., op.cit., Part 4, pp. 258, 265

The epilogue of the battle of Tsushima – the trial of Vice Admiral Rozhestwenski.

53 | The takeover of Sakhalin by the Japanese

Soon after the victory at Tsushima, the Japanese Combined Fleet was reorganised to perform new tasks and to incorporate the warships from Nebogatov's squadron. Consequently, two additional squadrons of large warships and the Fourth Fleet were formed. There were also changes in the command structure.

Table No. 5: The organisation of the Japanese fleet as of 15th June 1905.

	Commander	Ships
I Squadron (Admiral Togo H.) Despatch vessel: *Tatsuta*		
I Division	Vice Admiral Mizu S.	*Mikasa, Shikishima, Asahi, Fuji,*
IV Division	Rear Admiral Ogura B.	*Naniwa, Takachiho, Akashi, Tsushima*
1 Division	Captain Fujimoto	*Harusame, Fubuki, Ariake, Arare*
3 Division	Captain Iosijima	*Usugumo, Shinonome, Sazanami, Kasumi*
14 Division	Lt. commander Seki	*Chidori, Hayabusa, Manazuru, Kasasagi*
II Squadron (Vice Admiral Kamimura H.) Despatch vessel: *Chihaya*		
II Division	Rear Admiral Shimamura H.	*Idzumo, Asama, Tokiwa, Iwate*
III Division	Vice Admiral Uriu S.	*Chitose, Kasagi, Niitaka, Otowa*
2 Division	Captain Yajima	*Oboro, Ikazuchi, Inazuma, Akebono*
4 Division	Commander Suzuki	*Asagiri, Murasame, Asashio, Shirakumo*
9 Division	Commander Kawase	*Aotaka, Hato, Kari, Tsubame*
19 Division	Lt. Commander Matsuoka	*Kameom, Otoki, Kiji*
III Squadron (Vice Admiral Kataoka S.) Despatch vessel: *Yaeyama*		
V Division	Rear Admiral Yamada H.	*Yakumo, Adzuma, Kasuga, Nisshin*
VI Division	Rear Admiral Togo M.	*Suma, Idzumi, Akitsushima, Chiyoda*
5 Division	Commander Hirose	*Shiranui, Kagero, Murakumo, Yugiri,*
6 Division		*Satsuki*, Akatsuki*, Fumitsuki**
9 Division	Commander Kawase	*Aotaka, Hato, Kari, Tsubame*
15 Division	Commander Kondo	*Hibari, Sagi, Hashitaka, Uzura*
1 Division	Lt. Commander Tukuba	*69, 67, 68, 70*
10 Division	Lt. Commander Otaki	*43, 40, 41, 39*
11 Division	Lt. Commander Fujimoto	*73, 72, 74, 75*
20 Division	Lt. Commander Kubo	*65, 62, 63, 64*
Assigned units		*Yawata Maru, Hongkong Maru*
IV Squadron (Vice Admiral Dewa S.)		
VII Division	Vice Admiral Dewa S.	*Chin Yen, Iki*, Okinoshima*, Mishima**
VIII Division	Rear Admiral Taketomi K.	*Itsukushima, Hashidate, Matsushima*
IX Division	Rear Admiral Nakao Y.	*Chokai, Akagi, Maya, Uji*
15 Division	Commander Kondo	*Hibari, Sagi, Hashitaka, Uzura*
1 Division	Lt. Commander Tukuba	*67, 68, 70, 71*
10 Division	Lt. Commander Otaki	*41, 39, 40, 43*
11 Division	Lt. Commander Fujimoto	*73, 72, 74, 75*
20 Division	Lt. Commander Kubo	*65, 62, 63, 64*
Assigned units		*Manshu Maru, Tainan Maru*

* ex-Russian warships (not all of them were ready for service on June 15th)

Aiming at using their success so far to the fullest before the armistice (Russia agreed to peace talks on 10th May), at the beginning of July 1905 the Japanese command decided to take over Sakhalin. The island was not fortified and the garrison there was made up of only 7,000-7,200 soldiers: 1,100-1,200 in Korsakovsk area in the south and about 6,000 soldiers in Aleksandrovsk in the north. These units only had poor field artillery (coastal artillery was located only in Korsakovsk, and was made up of only 120 mm guns salvaged from the wreck of *Novik*). Japanese domination at sea guaranteed no reinforcements from the continent.

The newly formed 13th Division was assigned for this operation (after the fall of Port Arthur in the winter of 1905 the Japanese started forming four new infantry divisions, numbered 13-16), which consisted of over 16,000 soldiers. The operation was to be secured from the sea by Vice Admiral Kataoka's III Squadron (V and VI Divisions, 5th and 6th Destroyer Divisions, 9th Torpedo Boat Division, and auxiliary cruisers *Yawata Maru,* and *Honkkong Maru*), Vice Admiral Dewa's IV Squadron (the old battleship *Chin Yen* from the VII Division, the VIII and IX Divisions, 11th, 15th, and 20th Torpedo Boat Divisions and the auxiliary cruiser *Dainan Maru*) and the auxiliary cruisers *Kumano Maru* and *Kasuga Maru* from the auxiliary squadron. The concentration of the forces took place in Aomori, the port in the Mutsu Bay in the north of Honsiu.

The first troops (25th Brigade) left on ten transports on 4th July and three days later reached Sakhalin. On 8th July they took over Korsakovsk. On 10th July another regiment of the 25th Brigade landed on the shore of Aniwa Bay, a little west of Korsakovsk. The very next day the Japanese contingents moved inland and managed to defeat a Russian garrison outside the village of Dalnyy. Then the first phase of the Sakhalin operation was essentially complete[98].

Immediately after taking over Korsakovsk, Rear Admiral Yamada's squadron, made up of armoured cruisers *Nisshin* and *Kasuga* and the destroyers of the 1st Division, set out on a reconnaissance mission in the area of Vladivostok. Yamada penetrated the western shores of Primorsky Krai, from Olga Bay to St. Vladimir Bay (the Japanese discovered the wreck of *Izumrud* in the latter). After he found no trace of the enemy, Yamada returned to Hakodate on July 15th [99]. Other ships from Kataoka's fleet also headed there and only Dewa's IV Squadron remained off the shores of Sakhalin.

Soon afterwards, on 17th July, 22 transports with soldiers of the 26th Brigade of the 13th Division on board left Aomori, escorted by ships of the III Squadron. The Japanese forces reached Aleksandrovsk on 24th July. At the same time, in Korsakovsk, Dewa loaded the 49th Regiment of the 25th Brigade on board three transports and left Aniwa Bay with most of the ships of the IV

98 Istoriya russko-yaponskoy voyny 1904-1905 (edited by I.I. Rostunov)., Moscow 1977, pp. 355-356

99 Two days later the cruisers *Chitose* and *Chihaya* and two destroyers turned up in the area of Vladivostok. After they completed the reconnaissance, they returned to Rear Admiral Shimamura's squadron, made up of armoured cruisers *Iwate, Tokiwa,* and *Idzumo,* the cruiser *Niitaka* and two destroyers, which were cruising the shores of Korea. Earlier, this team had escorted 3 transports with reinforcements from Talien to Songchin in north-east Korea. Corbett J.S., op.cit., vol.II, p. 363.

Squadron on 21st July, also heading north. Two days later he reached Castries Bay, north-west of Aleksandrovsk. Kataoka's and Dewa's squadrons met on 24th July. Then the landing of the troops commenced, covered by the warships. The Russians tried to resist, but in the face of the enemy's superior forces they retreated inland on 25th July, and after a few days of fighting they capitulated on 1st August. About 4,000 Russian soldiers were taken prisoner, and the number of killed and wounded on each side amounted to about 500. The last Russian forces inland surrendered in the middle of August, and then Sakhalin became controlled entirely by the Japanese[100].

After the takeover of Sakhalin the Japanese fleet had achieved all the goals set by the chief command. Due to the peace talks in progress, activity was limited to a single raid on Kamchatka waters, carried out by the cruisers *Suma* and *Idzumi* between 10th and 21st August. The Japanese ships, under Rear Admiral Togo's command, shelled Russian positions several

times and apprehended two vessels with contraband. Besides that, light and auxiliary cruisers systematically patrolled the waters around Sakhalin and the Soya and Tsugaru straits. Before the end of the war they apprehended six ships (five steamers and one large sailing vessel) carrying goods to Vladivostok.

The last event of the Russian-Japanese war was the sinking of the flagship *Mikasa* in the port of Sasebo during the night of 10th/11th September, 1905, as a result of an explosion in its magazines. Later it was salvaged and, after renovation, it returned to service but did not take part in the celebration parade of the Combined Fleet, which was held on 23rd October in Yokohama. Before the Emperor and numerous spectators, 166 ships were on display including the recently converted ex-Russian armoured ships *Iki* (ex-*Nikolay I*), *Mishima* (ex-*Senyavin*), *Okinoshima* (ex-*Apraksin*) and *Peresvet* and *Poltava*, just salvaged from the bottom of Port Arthur and towed to Japan.

---

100   Istoriya russko-yaponskoy voyny..., op.cit., pp. 358-359.

A 120mm cannon dismounted from the wreck of the cruiser Novik *on location outside Korsakovsk, Sakhalin.*

54 | The end of the war

The defeat of the Russian fleet at Tsushima, as much as it entailed the total domination by the Japanese at sea and had a huge strategic significance, did not ultimately determine the outcome of the war. Nor did the previous victories at Port Arthur, or Mukden. In June, 1905, the Russians managed to gather 440,000 soldiers in Manchuria and a further 140,000-150,000 in Primorsky Krai, and their strength was growing every month, whilst the human and financial reserves of the empire were far from depletion. At the same time the Japanese had serious problems mustering 360,000 soldiers in Manchuria, plus over 150,000 in Korea and on the Liaotung Peninsula. Moreover, after more than 1,150,000 soldiers had already been drafted, the reserves of the empire were running out. In these circumstances it seems natural that after the success at Mukden, Marshal Oyama switched to defence, strengthening his current positions and getting reinforcements in place. These, however, were available much more slowly than the enemy reinforcements, and were of inferior quality. Therefore the victory at Tsushima should be perceived as the top military achievement of Japan.

Had Russia decided to continue a war of attrition, success might have been quite probable, but the Tsar's government wanted peace, as it was concerned by the revolutionary unrest in the country, which was intensifying and affecting even the army and the fleet. The suppression of the revolution was then a priority, a much more urgent problem than the Far East conflict. The continuation of the war was also against the European superpowers' interest. The British were aware of the exhaustion of their Japanese ally and wanted the war to be concluded at the moment of its triumph. The French, who were competing with the Germans in Morocco, wanted to draw their Russian ally's attention from the Far East as soon as possible. The Germans, in turn, wanted to gain Russia's support for the drafting of an anti-British pact. All this caused Russia and Japan to promptly accept American mediation, proposed on 8th June, 1905.

Peace talks commenced on 6th August, 1905, on board President Roosevelt's yacht *Mayflower*, anchored in the port of Portsmouth, New Hampshire. At the very beginning the Japanese proposed very tough conditions, including the payment of high reparations, the reduction of the Russian fleet in the Far East, turning in all the Russian warships interned in neutral ports, and permission to annex all of Sakhalin. The issues of removing Russian troops from Manchuria and accepting Korea under exclusive Japanese control were non-negotiable. These conditions were naturally unacceptable to the Russians, so long and tiresome negotiations commenced.

Eventually, a peace treaty was signed on 5th September, 1905, and all war operations were officially terminated. According to the final agreements, Japan was given exclusive control over Korea and the right to lease the Liaotung

The main figures at the peace conference in Portsmouth – from the left: Sergyush J. Witte, Roman R. Rosen, Theodore Roosevelt (as mediator), Komura Jutaro and Kagoro Takahiro.

A session of the peace conference in Portsmouth.

Peninsula from Russia, along with Port Arthur and Dalnyy (accepted by China in December, 1905) and the entire southern section of the East China Railway, with the right to maintain adequate military forces for its protection (the railway was to be used for peaceful purposes, though). Both countries, Russia and Japan, were to evacuate their troops from Manchuria, which was to return to Chinese authority. The Japanese were also granted the southern part of Sakhalin and 140 million roubles in reparations (officially as a compensation for maintaining POWs).

All in all, the Treaty of Portsmouth meant that Russia had to relinquish its plans for expansion in the Far East and left this right to Japan, which grew to be a new superpower – the first modern non-European one. It also led to changes in alliances in the Far East over the following years. Although the British-Japanese alliance was prolonged by the treaty of August, 1905, the relations between Japan and the United States deteriorated, as Japan was becoming a strong competitor in the intensifying struggle for the domination of the Chinese and Korean markets. In time, relations with Russia improved. After Russia had relinquished its previous Far East policy there were no more conflicting issues with Japan and in July, 1907 the two countries signed a pact maintaining the status quo in Asia, converted into a mutual cooperation agreement three years later. Sorting out the relations with Russia, and continuing good relations with Britain, made it possible for Japan to annex Korea in 1910, which was a fulfilment of Japanese ambitions since the war with China in 1894-1895.

55 | The Balance of losses

The Russo-Japanese war, the first great war of the 20th century, produced huge losses on both sides. They were much higher than those suffered in most 19th century wars. (No official reports have ever been released by either the Japanese or the Russians, and even the data published in official sources often differ considerably.) Losses on the Japanese side may be estimated at 88,000 killed (including 49,000 killed in combat, 14,500 dying from wounds, and 23,000 from disease, the rest lost in other circumstances). The aforementioned statistics include the losses of the Combined Fleet, which lost 1,883 killed and 1,809 wounded (along with the losses among the crews of the naval artillery engaged in the siege of Port Arthur)[101]. During the entire war 153,500 Japanese soldiers were wounded, although some of them recovered and returned to duty before it ended. Russian losses may be estimated at about 71,500 killed (53,000 killed in combat or dying from wounds and 18,500 dying from disease) among land troops and fewer than 10,000 sailors (including about 3,000 killed on land at Port Arthur). The number of wounded Russian soldiers and officers may be estimated at about 150,000 [102].

Moreover, during war operations 79,454 Russian soldiers were taken prisoner by the Japanese, including 16,211 officers and sailors of the Tsar's fleet. Of those POWs, 72,418 were placed in camps, whilst the rest died soon after being taken prisoner, or were released. As for the Japanese, 2,088 were taken prisoner, including 1,602 officers and soldiers of the ground forces, 24 sailors, and 462 civilians only indirectly engaged in combat (mainly sailors from ships mobilised for war purposes and sunk or apprehended by the Russians). Of these 44 were released soon after capture, 44 died in captivity, whilst the rest returned to their country before mid December, 1905. The Russian POWs

were, in turn, sent back to Russia in groups after the war ended. The last group left Japan in the second half of February 1906[103]. It should be noted that both sides made efforts to abide by international conventions regarding POWs, treating them well to say the least, even sometimes with a great deal of courtesy.

Despite an unquestionable victory for the Japanese, human losses were comparable on both sides, even slightly higher on the Japanese side (mainly due to the huge losses suffered by the III Army during the siege of Port Arthur). However, the balance of losses for the fleets of both countries was different. During the war the Japanese lost a total of two battleships (excluding the *Mikasa*, which was lost after the war), a small coast defence armoured ship, three cruisers, two small cruisers, two gunboats, two destroyers, seven torpedo boats, a small auxiliary cruiser and an auxiliary gunboat (excluding a certain number of mobilised ships). The Russian losses were much higher and amounted to the total of 14 battleships (12 sunk, and two captured), three coast defence battleships (one sunk, two captured), five armoured cruisers, six cruisers, three small cruisers, two torpedo gunboats, six gunboats, 20 destroyers (18 sunk, two captured), three torpedo boats, two mine layers and two auxiliary cruisers. However it must be added that a further Russian battleship, five cruisers, a gunboat, ten destroyers and an

The wreck of cruiser Varyag *being raised.*

103 Ibidem, p. 308.

101 Lacroix E., op.cit., cz. 16, TBS Nr 3/1970
102 Kowner R., HIorical Dictionary of the Russo-Japanese War, Lanham, Maryland, Toronto, Oxford 2006, pp. 80-81.

auxiliary cruiser were interned during the war in neutral ports (these warships returned after the war, though).

The Japanese lost most of their warships on mines during the operations at Port Arthur, whilst the Russians lost theirs during the bombardment of the fortress by the Japanese batteries, and in the battle of Tsushima as a result of the gunfire from enemy warships or torpedo attacks.

Table No. 6: The causes of the loss of warships in the Russo-Japanese war.

Class of warship	Cause of sinking* (Russian – Japanese warships)							Total
	Warship gunfire	Ground artillery	Warship gunfire and torpedoes	Torpedoes	Mines	Scuttled	Shipwreck	
Battleships	3 – 0	4 – 0	2 – 0	1 – 0	1 – 2	1 – 0	0 – 1	12 – 3
Coast defence battleships	1 – 0	0 – 0	0 – 0	0 – 0	0 – 1	0 – 0	0 – 0	1 – 1
Armoured cruisers	2 – 0	1 – 0	0 – 0	2 – 0	0 – 0	0 – 0	0 – 0	5 – 0
Cruisers	3 – 0	1 – 0	0 – 0	0 – 0	1 – 2	1 – 0	0 – 1	6 – 3
Small cruisers	0 – 0	1 – 0	0 – 0	0 – 0	0 – 2	2 – 0	0 – 0	3 – 2
Torpedo gunboats	0 – 0	1 – 0	0 – 0	0 – 0	0 – 0	1 – 0	0 – 0	2 – 0
Gunboats	0 – 0	2 – 0	0 – 0	0 – 0	1 – 0	3 – 0	0 – 2	6 – 2
Destroyers	6 – 0	0 – 0	0 – 0	2 – 0	1 – 2	8 – 0	1 – 0	18 – 2
Torpedo boats	0 – 3	0 – 0	0 – 1	0 – 0	1 – 1	1 – 0	1 – 2	3 – 7
Mine layers	0 – 0	1 – 0	0 – 0	0 – 0	1 – 0	0 – 0	0 – 0	2 – 0
Submarines	0 – 0	0 – 0	0 – 0	0 – 0	0 – 0	3 – 0	1 – 0	4 – 0
Auxiliary cruisers	1 – 0	1 – 0	0 – 0	0 – 0	0 – 0	0 – 0	0 – 1	2 – 1
Auxiliary gunboats	0 – 0	0 – 0	0 – 0	0 – 0	0 – 1	0 – 0	0 – 0	0 – 1

* Main cause that determined the sinking of the warship. In this light, the sinking of the cruiser *Varyag*, or *Novik* are ascribed to gunfire, as these were the damages incurred during the gunnery exchange that made the crews of those warships sink them later. The infliction of even serious damage that excluded a warship from further operations has not been recognized as the main cause, as long as its scuttling by its own crew took place at a later date and was not related to the inflicted damage (e.g. the sinking of the armoured boat *Sevastopol'*, or the Russian destroyers damaged on mines at Port Arthur).

It must be noted, however, that of all the sunk Russian warships the Japanese salvaged four battleships, an armoured cruiser, a cruiser, two torpedo gunboats and a destroyer at Port Arthur, as well as the cruiser *Varyag* in Chemulpo and *Novik* in Korsakovsk, which, after renovation, were incorporated into the Imperial fleet.

Table No. 7: Russian warships salvaged and brought back into service by the Japanese

Name of ship	Displacement	Date of salvage	Shipyard	Date renovation completed (month/year)	Japanese name
Retvizan	12,902 t	22.09.05	Sasebo	11/08	*Hizen*
Peresvet	13,810 t	3.07.05	Yokosuka	04/08	*Sagami*
Pobeda	13,220 t	17.10.05	Yokosuka	10/08	*Suwo*
Poltava	11,500 t	21.07.05	Maizuru	11/11	*Tango*
Bayan	7,802 t	24.06.05	Maizuru	/06	*Aso*
Pallada	6,823 t	11.08.05	Sasebo	05/10	*Tsugaru*
Vsadnik	432 t	23.10.05	Takeshiki	/06	*Makigumo*
Gaydamak	405 t	7.10.05	Takeshiki	/06	*Shikinami*
Sil'nyy	240 t	22.08.05	Takeshiki	/06	*Fumitsuki*
Varyag	7,022 t	8.08.05	Yokosuka	/07	*Soya*
Novik	3,080 t	16.07.05	Yokosuka	12/08	*Suzuya*

![A]ppendices

APPENDIX 1.
THE REGIER OF TORPEDO ATTACKS DURING THE RUSSO-JAPANESE WAR.

a) On the Japanese side:

Time (Japanese Time Zone)	Squadron	Name of ship	Number of torpedoes launched	Target	Hits	Remarks
Activity of the II Squadron in Korean Strait						
Second raid of the Vladivostok squadron onto the waters of Korean Strait, 1 July, 1904						
21.30	18 TBD	61	1	Ryurik	0	---
The battle of Tsushima						
Battle, Day One – May 2, 1905						
15.05	II	Chihaya	2	Borodino	-	---
15.15	II	Yakumo	1	Suvorov	-	---
	II	Adzuma	1	Suvorov	-	---
15.19	II	Chihaya	2	Suvorov	-	Heavily damaged
15.25	5 DD	Shiranui	1	Suvorov	-	Damaged
	5 DD	Kagero	1	Suvorov	-	---
	5 DD	Murakumo	1	Suvorov	-	---
	5 DD	Yugiri	1	Suvorov	-	---
16.25-16.30	4 DD	Asagiri	1	Suvorov	-	Damaged
	4 DD	Murasame	1	Suvorov	-	---
	4 DD	Asashio	2	Suvorov	-	---
	4 DD	Shirakumo	-	Suvorov	-	---
16.45	4 DD	Asagiri	1	Suvorov	-	Damaged
	4 DD	Murasame	1	Suvorov	1	---
17.32	I	Mikasa	1	Ural	-	---
	I	Shikishima	1	Ural	1(?)	---
19.00-19.10	11 TBD	73	1	Suvorov	-	---
	11 TBD	72	1	Svworov	1	---
	11 TBD	74	1	Suvorov	-	---
	11 TBD	75	1	Suvorov	1	---
Night torpedo attacks, 27/28 May, 1904, after day battle						
20.15-20.20	2 DD	Oboro	1	Nikolaj I	-	Damaged
	2 DD	Ikazuchi	1	Orel'	-	Heavily damaged
	2 DD	Inazuma	1	Orel'	-	Damaged
	2 DD	Akebono	1	Orel'	-	Damaged
20.30-20.40	5 DD	Shiranui	1	? (Nebogatov squadron)	-	---
	5 DD	Kagero	1	? as above	-	---
	5 DD	Yugiri	1	? as above	-	Dam. (collision)
	5 DD	Murakumo	-	? as above	-	Damaged
20.45-20.50	1 DD	Harusame	-	? (Nebogatov squadron)	-	Coll. w/ Yugiri
	1 DD	Fubuki	-	? as above	-	Enemy not found.
	1 DD	Arare	1	? as above	-	---
	1 DD	Ariake	1	? as above	-	---
	1 DD	Akatsuki	-	? as above	-	Dam. (collision)
21.02-21.05	3 DD	Shinonome	1	Nikolaj I	-	---
	3 DD	Usugumo	1	Nikolaj I	-	Damaged
	3 DD	Kasumi	1	Nikolaj I	-	Damaged
	3 D	Sazanami	1	Nikolaj I	-	---
21.10-21.20	9 TBD	Aotaka	1	Nakhimov	-	---
	9 TBD	Kari	1	Nakhimov	1	---
	9 TBD	Tsubame	1	Nakhimov	-	---
	9 TBD	Hato	1	Nakhimov	-	---
21.50-21.55	1 TBD	69	-	---	-	Sunk (collision)
	1 TBD	68	1	? (Nebogatov squadron)	-	Heavy. damaged
	1 TBD	70	-	? as above	-	Rudder failure
	1 TBD	67	1	? as above	-	---
21.10-21.30	17 TBD	34	1	Orel'	-	Sunk
			1	Apraksin	-	
	17 TBD	31	1	Orel' (?)	-	---
	17 TBD	32	1	Apraksin (?)	-	Heavily damaged
	17TBD	33	1	Apraksin (?)	-	---

Time (Japanese Time Zone)	Squadron	Name of ship	Number of torpedoes launched	Target	Hits	Remarks
21.15-21.25	18 TBD	36	1	Monomakh	-	---
	18 TBD	35	1	Monomakh	1	Sunk
	18 TBD	60	1	Monomakh	-	---
	18 TBD	61	-	---	-	Rudder failure
22.10-22.30	10 TBD	43	-	---	-	Dam. (collision)
	10 TBD	40	1	Navarin	1	---
	10 TBD	41	1	Navarin	-	---
	10 TBD	39	1	Navarin	-	---
21.10-22.20	15 TBD	Hibari	1	Navarin	-	---
	15 TBD	Uzura	-	---	-	Enemy not found.
	15 TBD	Hashitaka	-	---	-	Enemy not found.
	15 TBD	Sagi	-	---	-	Dam. (collision)
22.30	5 DD	Shiranui	1	Navarin	-	---
02.10-02.15	4 DD	Asagiri	1	Navarin	1	---
	4 DD	Asashio	1	Navarin	-	---
	4 DD	Shirakumo	1	Navarin	1	---
02.25	4 DD	Asagiri	-	Sisoy Velikiy	-	---
	4 DD	Asashio	1	Sisoy Velikiy	1	---
	4 DD	Shirakumo	1	Sisoy Velikiy	-	---
Attacks on the cruiser Dmitriy Donskoy, 28 May, 1905						
20.55-21.27	1 DD	Fubuki	2	Dmitriy Donskoy	-	---
	2 DD	Oboro	1	Dmitriy Donskoy	-	---
	2 DD	Akebono	1	Dmitriy Donskoy	-	---
	2 DD	Inazuma	1	Dmitriy Donskoy	-	---
	4 DD	Shirakumo	-	---	-	---
	4 DD	Asagiri	-	---	-	---

Together the Japanese fired 252 torpedos:

a)   during Port Arthur campaign – 187 torpedos

b)   during the II Squadron activity in Korean Strait – 1 torpedo

c)   during the battle of Tsushima – 64 torpedos

b) On the Russian side:

Time (local)	Name of ship	Number of torpedoes launched	Target	Hits	Remarks
Activity of the Vladivostock Squadron					
Third raid of the Russian squadron at Gensan, 25 April, 1904					
After 12.00	205	1	Goyo Maru	1	
	Rossiya	1	Kinshu Maru	1	
Raid of the Russian squadron onto the waters of Korean Strait, 15 June, 1904					
12.30	Gromoboy	2	Hitachi Maru	1	
	Riurik	2	Sado Maru	2	
Battle of Ulsan, 14 August, 1904					
about 09.00	Riurik	1	Naniwa	-	
The battle of Tsushima					
Battle, Day Two, 28 May, 1904					
11.10-11.20	Bystryy	2	Murakumo	-	
11.20	Gromkiy	2	Shiranui	-	

Together Russian fired 27 torpedos:

d)   During Port Arthur campaign – 16 torpedoes

e)   During the activity of the vladivostock squadron – 7 torpedoes

f)   During the battle of Tsushima – 4 torpedoes

APPENDIX 2.
Commercial vessels sunk or captured during the Russo-Japanese War.

Name of ship	Capacity (BRT)	Flag	Route	Cargo	Date	Location	Remarks
	**Vessels sunk or captured by the Japanese.**
s/s Ekaterinoslv	5627	Russia	Vladivostok - Odessa	varied	06.02.04	near Pusan	Cap. by *Sai Yen* →*Karasaki Maru*
s/s Mukden	1565	Russia	Nagasaki – Vladivostok	as above	as above	Pusan	Cap. → *Hoten Maru*
s/v Lesnik	87	Russia	Hakodate - Vladivostok	salt	as above	Hakodate	Cap. in port
s/v Bobrik	125	Russia	as above	as above	as above	as above	Cap. in port
s/v Nadezhda	68	Russia	as above	as above	as above	as above	Cap. in port
s/s Rossiya	2044	Russia	Dalnyy – Karatsu	as above	07.02.04	Bate Arch.	Cap. by *Tatsuta* → *Saishu Maru*
s/s Argun	2458	Russia	Dalnyy – Nagasaki	as above	as above	Near	Cap. by *Asama* (*Adzuma?*)
s/s Mandzhurja (i)	6193	Russia	Libawa – Port Arthur	war materials	08.02.04		Cap. by *Takasago* → *Kanto Maru*
s/s Hermes	1358	Norway	Moji – Port Arthur	coal	09.02.04	Near Port Arthur	Cap., released 09.03.04.
s/s Mandzhurja (ii)	2891	Russia	in port (repairs)	no cargo	10.02.04	Nagasaki	Cap. in port → *Manshu Maru*
s/s Kotik	400	Russia	as above (loading)	rails	as above	Yokohama	Cap. in port
s/s Aleksandr	261	Russia	on fishing grounds	no cargo	as above	Korea Bay	Cap. by V squadron
s/s Nikolaj	123	Russia	as above	as above	as above	as above	Cap. as above
s/s Mikhail	3461	Russia		rails	as above	as above	Cap. as above
s/s Sungari	2981	Russia		no cargo	as above	Chemulpo	s+, salvaged 08.05 → *Matsue Maru*
s/s Brisgravia	6477	Germany	Hamburg - Kiaochou	varied	28.03.04	Moji	Cap. in port, later released
s/v Talija	120	Russia		no cargo	13.04.04	Hakodate	Cap. in port
s/s Nagadan	599	Russia		as above	27.05.04	Dalnyy	s+, salvaged 08.04 → *Nagara Maru*
s/s Zeya	919	Russia		as above	as above	as above	s+, salvaged 08.05 → *Nikogawa Maru*
s/s Hsi Ping	1981	Great Britain	Shanghai - Newchwang	varied	14.07.04	Near Chefoo	Cap. by *Hongkong Maru*, released on confiscation of contraband
s/s Pei Ping	400	China	as above	varied	17.07.04	as above	as above
s/s Georges	179	France	Shanghai – Port Arthur	food	19.08.04	Near Port Arthur	Cap. →*Kotetsu Maru*
s/v Osaka	546	Great Britain	Shanghai - Vladivostok	ammo	26.09.04	near Etorufu	+b during cap.
s/s Si Shan	1351	Great Britain	Hongkong - Newchwang	food	07.10.04	Newchwang	Cap. in port, later released
s/s Fu Ping	1393	Germany	Shanghai – Port Arthur	weapons and ammo	12.10.04	near Newchwang	Cap. by *Shirataka*→ *Chozan Maru*
s/s Novik	338	Russia		no cargo	16.10.04	Port Arthur	+ Jap. art., salvaged 08.05 → ?
s/s Angara	7297	Russia		no cargo	30.10.04	as above	+ Jap. art., salvaged 05.05 → *Anegawa Maru*
s/s Veteran	1199	Germany	as above	food, clothes	19.11.04	near Chefoo	Cap. by *Tatsuta* → *Yaura Maru*
s/s King Arthur	1416	Great Britain	Port Arthur - Shanghai	no cargo	as above	as above	Cap. → *Otowa Maru*
s/s Nigretia	2368	Great Britain	Shanghai - Vladivostok	parafin oil	as above	Korea Bay	Cap. by *Tsushima* → *Urusan Maru*
s/s Bureya	919	Russia		no cargo	1-2.01.05	Port Arthur	s+, salvaged 08.05 → *Yuragawa Maru*
s/s Ninguta	990	Russia		as above	as above	as above	s+, salvaged 08.05 → *Ikuta Maru*
s/s Silach	578	Russia		as above	as above	as above	s+, salvaged 08.05 → *Sirachi Maru*
s/s Kazan'	6069	Russia		as above	as above	as above	s+, salvaged 08.05 → *Kasado Maru*
s/s Tsitsikar	1028	Russia		as above	as above	as above	s+, salvaged 08.05 → *Yumihari Maru*
s/s Evropa	2175	Russia		as above	as above	as above	s+, salvaged 08.05 → *Europa Maru*
s/s Amur	2415	Russia		as above	as above	as above	s+, salvaged 08.05 → *Amakusa Maru*
s/s Inkou	353	Russia		as above	as above	as above	s+, salvaged 08.05 → *Botkai Maru*
s/s Mongolja	2937	Russia		Hospital ship	2.01.05	Port Arthur	Cap. after fortress' capitulation, later released
s/s Roseley	4370	Great Britain	Cardiff - Vladivostok	coal	11.01.05	Korea Bay	Cap. by *Tokiwa* → *Takasaki Maru*
s/s Lethington	4421	Great Britain	as above	as above	12.01.05	as above	Cap. by 72 → *Wakamiya Maru*
s/s Wilhelmina	4295	Holland	Shanghai - Vladivostok	as above	16.01.05	as above	Cap. by *Naniwa* → *Kagoshima Maru*
s/s Bawtry	2407	Great Britain	Kiaochou - Vladivostok	food, battleship materials	17.01.05	as above	Cap. by *Tokiwa* → *Rokko Maru*
s/s Oakley	3798	Great Britain	Cardiff - Vladivostok	coal	18.01.05	as above	Cap. by *Tokiwa* → *Yeboshi Maru*
s/s Burma	3071	Austria	as above	as above	25.01.05	Bay of Tsugaru	Cap. by 30 → *Yesan Maru*
s/s M.S. Dollar	4121	Great Britain	San Francisco - Vladivostok	food and feed	27.01.05	As above	Cap. by *Asama* → Ryoki Maru
s/s Wyefield	3235	Great Britain	as above	feed	30.01.05	as above	Cap. by *Musashi* → *Shiyobuki Maru*
s/s Siam	3285	Austria	Cardiff - Vladivostok	coal	31.01.05	as above	Cap. by *Asama* → *Kinsho Maru*
s/s Eastry	2998	Great Britain	Muroran - Hongkong	coal	07.02.05	as above	Cap. by *Mieka* by *Matsushima*, later released

Name of ship	Capacity (BRT)	Flag	Route	Cargo	Date	Location	Remarks
s/s Paros	2578	Germany	Hamburg - Vladivostokv	food, shipyard materials	10.02.05	Bay of Etorofu	Cap. by *Hongkong Maru → Kasama Maru*
s/s Apollo	3829	Great Britain	Cardiff - Vladivostok	coal	14.02.05	Bay of Etorofu	Cap. by *Hongkong Maru → Kunashiri Maru*
s/s Scotsman	1677	Great Britain	Sajgon - Vladivostok	rice	as above	Bay of Tsugaru	Cap. by 30 → *Mori Maru*
s/s Powderham	3019	Great Britain	Cardiff - Vladivostok	coal	19.02.05	Korea Bay	Cap. by *Nikko Maru → Kaifuku Maru*
s/s Sylviana	4187	Great Britain	as above	as above	as above	as above	Cap. by *Nikko Maru → Goto Maru*
s/s Severus	3307	Germany	as above	as above	24.02.05	near w. Etorofu	Cap. by *Hongkong Maru → Shibetoro Maru*
s/s Romulus	2630	Germany	as above	as above	25.02.05	Bay of Tsugaru	Cap. by *Iwate*, sold later
s/s Easby Abbey	2963	Great Britain	as above	as above	27.02.05	near w. Etorofu	Cap. by *Nippon Maru → Isobe Maru*
s/s Vegga	2562	Sweden	as above	as above	03.03.05	Korea Bay	Cap. by *Nikko Maru → Kita Maru*
s/s Venus	3558	Great Britain	as above	as above	04.03.05	near w. Etorofu	Cap. by *Nippon Maru → Benten Maru*
s/s Aphrodite	3948	Great Britain	as above	as above	06.03.05	as above	Cap. by *Nippon Maru → Etorofu Maru*
s/s Saxon Prince	3471	Great Britain	Singapur - Muroran	railroad materials	09.03.05	Korea Bay	Cap. by mistake by *Kasuga*, released 16.03.05
s/s Tacoma	2812	USA	San Francisco - Vladivostok	Food, shipyard materials	14.03.05	Kunaszirska Bay	Cap. by *Takachiho → Shikotan Maru*
s/s Harbarton	3265	Great Britain	Cardiff - Vladivostok	coal	18.03.05	Bay of Etorofu	Cap. by *Akitsushima → Myoro Maru*
s/s Industrie	198	Germany		no cargo	27.03.05	near Pusan	Cap. by *Kasuga* for spying *Itahashi Maru*
s/s Henry Bolckov	1006	Norway	Shanghai - Korsakovsk	flour	07.04.05	Bay of Etorofu	Cap. by *Kumano Maru → Naka Maru*
s/s Lincluden	2764	Great Britain	Nikolaevsk - Kobc	corn	15.05.05	South of Yosu, Korea	Cap. by mistake, released 23.05.05
s/s Quang Nam	1431	France	Saigon - Shanghai	varied	18.05.05	near Pescadorow	Cap. by *Bingo Maru* for spying → *Kumano Maru*
Orioł	8175*	Russia	Libawa - Vladivostok	hospital ship	27.05.05	Korea Bay	Part of II Squadron, cap. for violation of regulations
Kostroma	3513	Russia	as above	Hospital ship	as above	Korea Bay	As above – later released
s/s Australia	2755	USA	at roadstead	flour, food	12.08.05	Petropavlovsk	Cap. by *Suma*
s/v Antiope	1468	Great Britain	to Nikolaevsk	salt	13.08.05	eastern coast of Sachalin	Cap. by *Tainan Maru*
s/s Lydia	1059	Germany	Hamburg - Nikolaevsk	tools, salt, oil	as above	near Luchu Island	Cap.
s/s Montara	2562	USA		no cargo (?)	18.08.05	near w. Beringa	Cap. for spying
s/s Barracouda	2152	USA	to Nikolaevsk	food	16.09.05	płd. wyb. Sachalinu	Cap. by *Fubuki*
s/s Hans Wagner	1594	Germany		building materials	10.10.05	Korea Bay	Cap. by mistake by *Otowa*, later released
s/s M. Struve	1582	Germany	to Vladivostok	food	as above	near Pusan	Cap. by *Akashi*, later released
Vessels captured or sunk by the Russians and Japanese vessels lost on mines or in shipwrecks.							
s/s Argo	1394	Norway			8.02.04	Port Arthur	Released mid March
s/s Brand	2003	Norway			As above	As above	As above
s/s Seirstad	995	Norway			As above	As above	As above
s/s Ras Bera	3837	Great Britain			As above	As above	Escaped from port 13.02.04
s/s Foxton Hall	4247	Great Britain		coal	As above	As above	Released mid March
s/s Fu Ping	1393	Great Britain			10.02.04	As above	Released 10.02.04
s/s Hsiping	1981	Great Britain	Chingwangtao - Shanghai		as above	near Port Arthur	Released 14.02.04
s/s Wenchou	898	Great Britain			11.02.04	Port Arthur	Released 18.02.04
s/s Naganoura Maru	1084	Japan			As above	Bay of Tsugaru	+ Sunk by Russian cruisers
s/s Etrickdale	3775	Great Britain	Barry - Sabang	coal	19.02.04	Red Sea	Cap. by *Oslyabya*, released 28.02.04
s/s Frankby	4182	Great Britain	Barry - Hongkong	coal	As above	As above	Cap. by *Oslyabya*, released 28.02.04
s/s Mathilda	3480	Norway	Penarth - Sasebo	coal	As above	As above	Cap. by *Oslyabya*, released 28.02.04
s/s Shinshu Maru	2905	Japan	to Chemulpo	supplies	9.03.04	Chemulpo	b+ Accident
s/s Nanyo Maru	3770	Japan			?.03.04	Quelpart Island	b+ Accident
s/v Hanyei Maru	76	Japan			26.03.04		+
s/s Fa Wan	?	Great Britain	Chemulpo - Newchwang		2.04.04	Newchwang	Released 3.04.04
s/s Goyo Maru	601	Japan		no cargo	25.04.04	Gensan	+ Russian torpedo boats
s/s Tajwan Maru	2392	Japan			?.06.04	Tokyo Bay	b+ Accident
s/s Haginoura Maru	219	Japan		food	As above	Japan Sea	+ Sunk by *Bogatyr'*
s/s Allanton	4253	Great Britain	Muroran - Singapore	coal	16.06.04	as above	Cap. by Russian cruisers, released 9.11.04
s/v Ansei Maru	148	Japan	Hakodate - Simonoseki	food	As above	as above, near Hokkaido	+Sunk by Russian torpedo boats

238

Name of ship	Capacity (BRT)	Flag	Route	Cargo	Date	Location	Remarks
s/v Seiyei Maru	99	Japan		As above	As above	As above	+ as above
s/v Hachiman Maru	136	Japan	Hakodate - Sasebo	As above	As above	As above	+ as above
s/v Hakatsu Maru	211	Japan		As above	18.06.04	As above	Cap. by Russian cruisers
s/v Seisho Maru	122	Japan			30.06.04	Gensan	+Sunk by Russian torpedo boats
s/s Koun Maru	36	Japan			As above	As above	+ as above
s/s Cheltenham	3741	Great Britain	Otaru - Pusan	railway sleepers	4.07.04	Japan Sea	Cap. by Russian cruisers
s/s Malacca	4045	Great Britain	Antwerp/London - Japan	varied, incl. explosives	13.07.04	Red Sea	Cap. by Pietierburg, released 27.07.04
s/s Fa Wan	?	Great Britain			15.07.04	Yellow Sea, near Port Arthur	Cap. by Russian battleships, later released
s/s Prinz Heinrich	6263	Germany	Hamburg - Yokohama	varied	16.07.04	Red Sea	Cap. by *Peterburg*, released on confiscation of mail
s/s Hipsang	1659	Great Britain	Newchwang - Chefoo	supplies	16.07.04	Yellow Sea, near Port Arthur	+ Sunk by *Rastoropnyy*.
s/s Ardova	3533	Great Britain	N. York - Manila	raili, explosives	17.07.04	M. Czerwone	Cap. by Smolensk, released 25.07.04
s/s Skandia	?	Germany	Hamburg -China	varied	18.07.04	As above	Cap. by Smolensk, released 25.07.04
s/v Okassima Maru		Japan			20.07.04	Japan Sea	+ Sunk by Russian cruisers
s/s Takashima Maru	319	Japan		varied, incl. explosives	As above	Tsugaru	+ as above
s/v Kiho Maru	140	Japan			As above	Pacific	+ as above
s/v Hokusei Maru	91	Japan			As above	As above	+ as above
s/s Arabia	4438	Germany	Portland - Hongkong	railroad materials, food	22.07.04	As above	Cap. by Russian cruisers., later released
s/s Knight Commander	4306	Great Britain	N. York - Chemulpo	railroad materials	24.07.04	As above	+ Sunk by Russian cruisers
s/v Jisai Maru	199	Japan			As above	As above	+ as above
s/v Fukushu Maru	121	Japan			As above	As above	+ as above
s/s Formosa	4045	Great Britain	London - Japan		As above	Red Sea	Cap. by Smolensk, released 27.07.04
s/s Holsatia	3349	Germany			As above	As above	Cap. by Smolensk, released 27.07.04
s/s Thea	1613	Germany	to Yokohama	fish meal	25.07.04	Pacific	+ Sunk by Russian cruisers
s/s Calhas	6748	Great Britain	Tacoma - Japan	food	As above	As above	Cap. by Russian cruisers, released 29.10.04
s/s Crane		Great Britain	During fishing	---	21.10.04	North Sea	+ Sunk by mistake by II Squadron battleships
s/s Musashino Maru	2978	Japan		supplies	6.02.05	Elliot Island	b+ Accident
s/v Idzumi Maru	?	Japan			9.05.05	Japan Sea	+ Sunk by Russian torpedo boats
s/v Yawata 3 Maru	100	Japan			As above	As above	Cap. by Russian torpedo boats, recaptured by Japanese transport while on the way toVladivostok
s/v Yaiya Maru	?	Japan			10.05.05	Bay of Tsugaru	+ Sunk by Russian cruisers
s/v Senrio Maru	?	Japan			As above	As above	+ as above
s/v Kiyo Maru	?	Japan			As above	As above	+ as above
s/v Hokuzei Maru	?	Japan			As above	As above	+ as above
s/s Hokuto Maru	2822	Japan			as above	Tsushima	b+ Accident
s/s Maiko Maru	1074	Japan			11.05.05	Elliot Island	+ Mincs
s/s Sobralense	1982	Great Britain	Newchwang - Kobe		12.05.05	Elliot Island	+ as above
s/s Oldhamia	3639	Great Britain	N. York - Hongkong	olive	19.05.05	near Taiwan	Cap. by II Squadron battleships, b+ Etorofu Island
s/s Tetartos	2409	Germany	Otaru - Tiensin	railway sleepers	30.05.05	East China Sea	+ Sunk by Rion
s/s Cilurnum	2123	Great Britain	Shanghai - Kobe	varied	2.06.05	As above	Cap. by Rion, released after destroying part of cargo
s/s Ikhona	5252	Great Britain	Rangun - Yokohama	food	5.06.05	South China Sea	+ Sunk by Terek
s/s St. Kilda	3518	Great Britain	Hongkong - Yokohama	food	As above	As above	+ Sunk by Dniepr
s/s Prinsesse Marie	5416	Denmark	Copenhagen - Yokohama		22.06.05	as above	+ Sunk by Terek
s/s Kinjo Maru	2081	Japan			23.08.05	near Moji	z+ Accident
s/s Idzumi Maru		Japan			24.08.05	Japan Sea	Cap. by Russian torpedo boats.
s/s Sanchiu Maru	1538	Japan			5.09.05	near Port Arthur	+ Mines
s/s Snochu Maru	1570	Japan			22.09.05	near Port Arthur	b+ Accident

APPENDIX 3.
THE STATUS OF JAPANESE AND RUSSIAN WAR FLEETS.

The II includes seaworthy battleships, as well as the ones completed or purchased during the war. It also includes some battleship classes for special purposes. The II omits the units which were completely out-of-date, and excluded for that purpose from war operations, but assigned to auxiliary tasks, or remaining in reserve.

Due to the fact that there are various classifications, it has been necessary to introduce unified criteria in this II. The II includes:
- battleships (displacement over 6000 t)
- coast defence battleships (also old ironclads, displacement under 6000 t)
- armoured cruisers (big cruisers with armoured belts)
- cruisers (displacement over 2000 ton)
- small cruisers (displacement under 2000 ton)
- torpedo gunboats
- gunboats
- destroyers
- torpedo boats
- small torpedo boats (displacement under 40 ton)
- minelayers
- auxiliary cruisers (steamers over 2000 tons, with medium-caliber artillery)
- auxiliary gunboats (small steamers with light guns)

Comparative Table of the official classification of battleships in the Japanese and Russian fleets.

	Fleet clasificacation	Official Japanese fleet clasification[1]	Official Russian fleet clasification[2]	Remarks regarding classification used in the paper
1.	Battleships	Senkan	Eskadrennye bronenoscy	
2.	Coast defence battleships	Kaibokan	Bronenoscy beregovoy oborony	The term *kaibokan* refers to a "coast defence ship" and in the Japanese navy it was also used for all the old units (including those without side armour) deployed for patrolling and guarding.
3.	Armoured cruisers	Junyokan (Soko junyokan)	Kreysera rank I (Bronenosnye kreysera)	*Junyokan* – cruiser *Soko junyokan* – armoured cruiser
4.	Cruisers	Junyokan Kaibojunyokan (Nito junyokan)	Kreysera rank II (Bronepalubnye kreysera)	*Kaibojunyokan* – coast defence cruiser, only Itsukushima class *Nito junyokan* – II class cruisier.
5.	Small cruisers	Junyokan (Santo junyokan) Isuchikan	Kreysera rank II	*Santo junyokan* – III class cruisier (not used in practice in 1904). *Isuchikan* – aviso
6.	Torpedo gunboats	Isuchikan	Minnye kreysera	
7.	Gunboats	Hokan	Morekhodnye kanonerskie lodki (larger), kanonierskie lodki beregovoj oborony (smaller)	
8.	Destroyers	(Kuchikukan)	(Eskadrennye minonoscy)	Classification used widely despite its omission in ordinances (at the moment the ordinances became effective, destroyers served in neither the Japanese nor Russian navy).
9.	Torpedo boats	Suiraitei (itto suiraitei, nito suiraitei)	Minonoscy	Itto suiraitei – large torpedo boats (displacement over 120 tons) Nito suiraitei – medium size torpedo boats (displacement below 120 tons). In 1904-1905 it was an unofficial, though quite popular classification.
10.	Small torpedo boats	Suiraitei (santo suiraitei)	Minonoski	
11.	Minelayers	(Fusetsukan)	Minnye transporty	
12.	Submarines	(Sensuitei)	(Podvodnye lodki)	Classification used widely despite its omission in ordinances (at the moment the ordinances became effective, submarines served in neither the Japanese nor Russian navy).

1. Classification according to the ordinance of the MinIer of the Navy of 21.03.1898, later amended by the ordinance of 12.12.1905. (in the amended version, amongst other changes, there was a division into ranks within a particular class, used unofficially before, and an official introduction of class suiraiteiand and sesuitei).
2. Classification according to the ordinance of the Morskoje Vedomstvo of 01.02.1892. The brackets contain the unofficial classification, though widely used, also in official documents (mainly for those battleship classes, which had not yet exIed on the day the official classifications were implemented)..

Within every class, the battleships were grouped according to types – from the oldest to the newest. The II has been presented in the form of tables. The tactical-technical data includes:

The name of the type – given first in a separate line. The same line includes the information concerning the armour of a particular battleship type. It contains the specification of the side armour (water-line belt, upper belt, in case of a belt of varied thickness - its maximum thickness fore, mid, and after; the brackets contain the length and width of the belt), the thickness of the lateral armoured bulkheads, the deck armour (in case of a convex deck – the numerator refers to the thickness of its horizontal part, and the denominator to its slanting parts), the armour of the artillery (main and medium), and of the command position. The thickness of the armour has been given in millimetres.

Below, particular columns contain:
- name of ship,
- name of shipyard, where the ship was built, and its location
- yearly dates of launching and completion of building, below them the dates of major modernisations if relevant
- displacement – normal, that is, with the equipment compliant with effective regulations in particular navies. For submarines, the numerator specifies the surface displacement, whilst the denominator the submersion displacement. The displacement for the Japanese ships has been given in English tons (1016 kg), whilst for the Russian ones in metric tons (1000 kg).
- dimensions – given in the following order: length between perpendiculars (if no info available, it is the full length), the maximum width of the hull, maximum submersion at normal displacement. Dimensions given in metres, ~10 cm.
- machines' induced power (planned, or possibly planned, and actually achieved),
- maximum speed (achieved during tests, and planned, or possibly only planned). For submarines, the numerator specifies the surface speed, whilst the denominator specifies the speed in submersion. The speed given in knots (sea miles per hour).
- artillery armament – given in formulas: number of cannons x calibre (the shell diameter) given in millimetres / barrel length in calibres.

- torpedo armament – given in a formula: number of torpedo launchers (tubes) and the torpedo calibre in millimetres. All calibres rounded to 1 mm. This rubric also contains an approximated number of carried mines.

Mark "?" by particular information stands for "probably", + - sunk, # - captured, = - heavy demaged.

Abbreviated names of shipyards:
- Ansaldo – Gio. Ansaldo & Co.
- Armstrong – W.G. Armstrong, Whitworth & Co.
- Balt. – Baltijskij Sudostroitelnyy i Miekhanicheskiy Zavod Morskogo Vedomstva
- Bergsund – Motala Gewerkschaft
- Brown – John Brown & Co. Shipbuilding & Engineering Works
- Burmeister – Burmeister & Wain
- CACL – Cociete des Atelier et Chantiers de La Loire
- Cramp – Wm. Cramp & Sons Ship & Engine Building Co.
- Crichton – Crichton & Co.
- CSE – Clydebank Shipbuilding & Engineering Co. Ltd.
- FCM – Forges et Chantiers de la Mediterranee
- FRZ – Franko-Russkij Sudostroitelnyj Zavod
- Galernyy – Zavod Galernyy Ostrovok
- Germania – Krupp-Germania
- Hawthorn, Leslie – R. & H. Hawthorn, Leslie & Co. Ltd.
- Ishikawajima – Ishikawajima Zosensho KK
- Izhora – Izhorskiy Zavod
- Kawasaki – Kawasaki Zosensho
- Kure – Kure Kosho
- Laird – Cammell Laird & Co.
- Lake – Simon Lake Works
- NAW – Arsenal Nikolaev
- N. Adm. – Nowoe Admiralteystvo
- Nevskiy – Nevskiy Zavod
- NNS – Newport News Shipbuilding & Dry Dock Co.
- Normand – Augustyn Normand & Cie.
- Onohama – Onohama Zosensho
- ROPiT – Russkoe Obshhestvo Parokhodstva i Torgovli
- Sasebo – Sasebo Kosho
- Schichau – F. Schichau
- Schneider – Schneider et Cie.
- Thornycroft – John I. Thornycroft & Co. Ltd.
- Union IW – Union Iron Works Co.
- Vulcan – Aktien-Gesellschaft "Vulcan"
- Yarrow – Yarrow & Co. Ltd.

Name	Builder	Year date (launched/in sernice)	Displacement (t)	Dimensions (m)	Machinery (ihp)	Speed (kn)	Artillery armament	Torpedo and mine amament	Remarks
Battleships									
"Yekatyerina II" class Water-line belt: 152-406-203 mm (complete x 2.45 m); belt/citadel: 305 mm (53.2/65.6x2.5/2.7 m); bulkheads (citadel): 254 mm (fore). 229 mm (aft); deck: 63+38-51 mm; main artillery: 76 mm (gun-houses). 305 mm (citadel); conning tower: 229 mm Georgiy Pobedonosec: water-line belt: 406 mm (53.3 x 2.1 m); belt/citadel 305 mm (53.3x4.9 m); conning tower: 305 mm; the rest – as above.									
Yekatyerina II	NAV Nikolaev	1886/88	11048 (9990)	97.5x21x8.5	9100 (9000)	15.3 (15)	6x305/30. 7x152/35. 8x47/23². 4x37/20²	7 tt 381	
Chesma	ROPiT Sevastopol'	1886/88	11396 (9990)	97.5x21x8.8	9060 (9000)	13.6 (15)			
Sinop		1887/89	11310 (9990)	97.5x21x8.6	8890 (9000)	15	6x305/35. 7x152/35. 8x47/23². 4x37/20²		
Georgiy Pobedonosets		1892/96	11940 (10280)	97.5x21x8.7	10600 (11000)	17 (16.5)	6x305/35. 7x152/35. 8x47/44. 10x37/23		
"Imperator Aleksandr II" class Water-line belt: 152-356-127 mm (complete x 2.45 m); bulkheads: 152 mm (fore and aft); deck: 63 mm; main artillery: 254 mm (turret – only Nikolaj I). 254 mm (barbette); secondary artillery: 76 mm (casemates); conning tower: 203 mm									
Imperator Aleksandr II	N. Adm. St. Peterburg	1887/89 05	9244 (8440)	99.3x20.4x7.9	8500	15.3 (16)	2x305/30. 5x203/45. 8x152/45. 10x47/44	5 tt 381	
Imperator Nikolay I	FRZ St. Peterburg	1889/91 00	9672 (8440)		7840 (8500)	14.8 (16)	2x305/30. 4x229/35. 0→1x152/45. 8x152/35. 16x47/44. 2x37/23	---	28.05.05. after the battle of Tsushima. capitulation
"Dvenadcat' Apostolov" class Water-line belt: 356 mm (66 x 1.7 m); bulkheads: 254 mm (fore). 229 mm (aft); deck: 51/63 mm; main artillery: 76 mm (hoods). 305 mm (barbettes); secondary artillery: 127 mm (casemates); conning tower: 203 mm									
Dvenadcat' Apostolov	NAW Nikolaev	1890/92	8433 (8113)	100.6x18.3x8.4	8760 (8500)	16.5 (16)	4x305/30. 4x152/35. 12x47/44. 10x37/23. 4x37/20²	6 tt 381	
"Navarin" class Water-line belt: 356-406-356 mm (67 x 2.15 m); upper belt: 305 mm (45.7x2.4 m); bulkheads: 305 mm (fore and aft); deck: 63/76 mm; main artillery: 305 mm (turrets). 305 mm (citadel); secondary artillery: 152 mm (casemates); conning tower: 254 mm									
Navarin	FRZ St. Peterburg	1891/96	10206 (9476)	103x20.4x8.4	9140 (9000)	15.9 (16)	4x305/35. 8x152/35. 18x47/44. 12x37/23	6 tt 381	+27/28.05.05. after the battle of Tsushima. torpedoes
"Tri Svyatitelya" class Water-line belt: 457 mm (88 x 2.45 m); upper belt: 406 mm; bulkheads: 406 mm (fore). 356 mm (aft); deck: 51/76 mm; main artillery: 406 mm (turrets and barbettes); secondary artillery: 127 mm (casemates); conning tower: 305 mm									
Tri Svyatitelya	NAV Nikolaev	1893/98	13318 (12480)	113.1x22.2x8.7	11310 (10600)	17.7 (16)	4x305/40. 8x152/45. 4x120/45. 10x47/44. 30x37/23. 10x37/20²	6 tt 381	
"Sisoy Velikiy" class Water-line belt: 305-406-305 mm (83.5 x 2.15 m); upper belt: 127 mm (51.5x2.1 m); bulkheads: 229 mm (fore and aft); deck: 51/76 mm; main artillery: 305 mm (turrets). 254 mm (barbettes); secondary artillery: 127 mm (casemates); conning tower: 229 mm									
Sisoy Velikiy	N. Adm. St. Peterburg	1894/96	10400 (8800)	103.8x20.7x7.8	8490 (8500)	15.7 (16)	4x305/40. 6x152/45. 12x47/44. 12x37/23. 4 MG	6 tt 381	+28.05.05. scuttled after the battle of Tsushima
"Poltava" class Water-line belt: 254-406 (Sevastopol' – 368)-254 mm (73.2 x 2.3 m); upper belt: 127 mm (50x2.3 m); bulkheads: 229 mm (fore). 203 (aft); deck: 51/76 mm; main artillery: 254 mm (turrets). 254 mm (barbettes); secondary artillery: 152 mm (turrets). 127 mm (barbettes). 76 mm (casemates); conning tower: 229 mm									
Poltava	N. Adm. St. Peterburg	1894/97	11500 (10960)	108.7x21.3x7.8m	11260 (11250)	16.3 (16.5)	4x305/40. 12x152/45. 12x47/44. 28x37/23	6 tt 381	+05.12.04. Port Arthur. Jap. land artillery
Petropavlovsk	Galernyy St. Peterburg	1894/97	11354 (10960)		11210 (11250)	16.9 (16.5)			+13.04.04. near Port Arthur. mined
Sevastopol'	Galernyy St. Peterburg	1895/99	11842 (10960)		9370 (11250)	15.4 (16.5)			+01/02.01.05. scuttled before the capitulation of Port Arthur
"Rostislav" Water-line belt: 368 mm (83.5 x 2.15 m); upper belt: 127 mm (83.5x2 m); bulkheads: 229 mm (fore). 127 mm (aft); deck: 51/76 mm; main artillery: 254 mm (turrets and barbettes); secondary artillery: 127 mm (turrets); conning tower: 152 mm									
Rostislav	NAV Nikolaev	1896/98	10140 (8880)	105.2x20.7x6.7	8700 (8500)	17.6 (16)	4x254/45. 8x152/45. 12x47/44. 14x37/23	6 tt 381	

Name	Builder	Year date (launched/ in sernice)	Displacement (t)	Dimensions (m)	Machinery (ihp)	Speed (kn)	Artillery armament	Torpedo and mine amament	Remarks
"Peresvet" class									
Water-line belt: 178-229-178 mm (95 x 2.4 m); upper belt: 102 mm (57.3x2.2 m); bulkheads: 178 mm (fore and aft); deck: 51/63 mm; main artillery: 229 mm (turrets). 229 mm (barbettes); secondary artillery: 127 mm (casemates); conning tower: 305 mm (Peresvet and Oslyabya). 229 mm (Pobeda)									
Peresvet	Balt. St. Peterburg	1898/01	13810 (12674)	122.3x21.8x7.9	15780 (14500)	18.5	4x254/45. 11x152/45. 20x75/50. 20x47/44. 8x37/23	5 tt 381	+07.12.04. Port Arthur. Jap. land artillery
Oslyabya	N. Adm. St. Peterburg	1898/01	13408 (12674)		15060 (14500)	18.3 (18.5)			+27.05.05. the battle of Tsushima. Jap. gunfire.
Pobeda	Balt. St. Peterburg	1900/02	13220 (12674)		15440 (14500)	18.5			+07.12.04. Port Arthur. Jap. land artillery
"Retvizan" class									
Water-line belt: 76-229-51mm (complete x 2.15 m); upper belt: 76-152-51 mm (complete x 2.3 m); bulkheads: 178 mm (fore and aft); deck: 51/76 mm; main artillery: 254 mm (turrets). 229 mm (barbettes); secondary artillery: 127 mm (casemates); conning tower: 254 mm									
Retvizan	Cramp Philadelphia	1900/01	12902 (12780)	114.6x22x7.9	16120 (16000)	18.8 (18)	4x305/40. 12x152/45. 20x75/50. 24x47/44. 8x37/23. 2 MG	6 tt 381	+06.12.04. Port Arthur. Jap. land artillery
"Knyaz' Potemkin-Tavricheskiy" class									
Water-line belt: 127-229-127 mm (72.2 x 2.3 m); upper belt: 152 mm; bulkheads: 178 mm (fore). 127 (aft); deck: 51/76 mm; main artillery: 254 mm (turrets and barbettes); secondary artillery: 152 mm (casemates); conning tower: 229 mm									
Knjaz' Poteomkin-Tavricheskiy	NAV Nikolaev	1900/03	12582 (12480)	113.1x22.3x8.3	11300 (10600)	16.7 (16)	4x305/40. 16x152/45. 14x75/50. 6x47/44. 2 MG	5 tt 381	
"Tsesarevich / Borodino" class									
"Tsesarevich": water-line belt: 160-250-170 mm (complete x 1.85 m); upper belt: 145-200-120 mm (complete x 1.85 m); deck: 40/50 mm; main artillery: 250 mm (turrets). 250 mm (barbettes); secondary artillery: 150 mm (turrets). 127 mm (barbettes); conning tower: 254 mm "Borodino": water-line belt: 127-194-127 mm (complete x 1.65 m); upper belt: 102-152-102 mm (complete x 1.7 m); deck: 32/51 mm; main artillery: 254 mm (turrets). 254 mm (barbettes); secondary artillery: 152 mm (turrets). 127 mm (barbettes); conning tower: 203 mm									
Tsesarevich	FCM La Seyne	1901/03	13120 (12912)	113.4x23.2x7.9	16500 (16300)	18.7 (18)	4x305/40. 12x152/45. 20x75/50. 20x47/44. 2x37/23. 8-10 MG	4 tt 381	15.08.04. interned in Tsingtao
Borodino	N. Adm. St. Peterburg	1901/04	14091 (13516)	114.8x23.2x8	15800	(18)			+27.05.05. the battle of Tsushima. Jap. gunfire
Imperator Aleksandr III	Balt. St. Peterburg	1901/03	14181 (13516)		16300	17.7 (18)			+27.05.05. the battle of Tsushima. Jap. gunfire
Orel'	Galernyy St. Peterburg	1902/04	14151 (13516)		15800	17.6 (18)			#28.05.05. after the battle of Tsushima. capitulation
Knyaz' Suvorov	Balt. St. Peterburg	1902/04	14200? (13516)		15800	17.6 (18)			+27.05.05. the battle of Tsushima. Jap. gunfire and torpedos
Slava		1903/05	13733 (13516)		16360 (15800)	17.7 (18)			
Coast defence battleships									
"Admiral Ushakov" class									
Water-line belt: 203-254-203 mm (53 x 2.15 m); bulkheads: 203 mm (fore). 152 mm (aft); deck: 25/51 mm; main artillery: 178 mm (turrets). 152 mm (barbettes); conning tower: 178 mm									
Admiral Ushakov	Balt. St. Peterburg	1893/96	4648 (4126)	81.9x15.9x5.9	5770 (5000)	16.1 (16)	4x254/45. 4x120/45. 6x47/44. 18x37/23	4 tt 381	+28.05.05. the battle of Tsushima. Jap. gunfire.
Admiral Senyavin	N. Adm. St. Peterburg	1894/96	4792 (4126)		5330 (5000)				#28.05.05. after the battle of Tsushima. capitulation
General-Admiral Apraksin		1896/99	4152 (4126)	81.9x15.9x5.2	5760 (5000)	15.1 (16)	3x254/45. 4x120/45. 10x47/44. 12x37/23		#28.05.05. after the battle of Tsushima. capitulation
Armoured cruisers									
"Vladimir Monomakh" class									
Water-line belt: 114-152-114 mm (complete x 2.4 m); conning tower: 152 mm									
Vladimir Monomakh	Balt. St. Peterburg	1882/85 97	5593	89.8x15.9x7.6	7040	15.8	5x152/45. 6x120/45. 18x47/44. 4x37/23	4 tt 381	+28.05.05. scuttled after the battle of Tsushima
"Dmitriy Donskoy" class									
Water-line belt: 114-152-114 mm (complete x 2.4 m); conning tower: 152 mm									
Dmitriy Donskoy	N. Adm. St. Peterburg	1883/85 95	6200	90.4¹x15.8x7.9	6610	16.5	6x152/45. 10x120/45. 6x47/44. 10x37/23. 12x37/20²	4 tt 381	s+29.05.05. scuttled after the battle of Tsushima

Name	Builder	Year date (launched/ in sernice)	Displacement (t)	Dimensions (m)	Machinery (ihp)	Speed (kn)	Artillery armament	Torpedo and mine amament	Remarks
"Admiral Nakhimov" class Water-line belt: 254 mm (45 x 2.45 m); bulkheads: 229 mm (fore and aft); deck: 51/76 mm; main artillery: 63 mm (hoods). 203 mm (barbettes); conning tower: 152 mm									
Admiral Nakhimov	Balt. St. Peterburg	1885/87	8524 (7782)	97.8x18.6x8.4	7780 (9000)	16.7 (17)	8x203/35. 10x152/35. 12x47/44. 6x37/23. 4 MG	3 tt 381	+28.05.05. scuttled after the battle of Tsushima
"Pamyat' Azova" class Water-line belt: 152 mm; bulkheads: 38/63 mm; conning tower: 38 mm									
Pamyat' Azova	Balt. St. Peterburg	1888/90	6734 (6230)	108x15.6x8.2	7520 (8500)	16.8 (17.5)	2x203/35. 13x152/35. 7x47/44. 8x37/23	3 tt 381	
Typ "Ryurik" Water-line belt: 203-254-203 mm (80.5 x 2.05 m); bulkheads: 102 mm (fore and aft); deck: 63/89 mm; conning tower: 152 mm									
Ryurik	Balt. St. Peterburg	1892/95	11690 (9957)	125.6x20.4x8.3	13590 (13500)	18.8 (19)	4x203/35. 16x152/45. 6x120/45. 10x47/44. 12x37/23	6 tt 381	+14.08.04. the battle of Ulsan. Jap. gunfire
"Rossiya/Gromoboy" class Rossiya: water-line belt: 152-203-127 mm (to aft 119.8 x 2.6 m); : bulkheads 178 mm (fore); deck: 51/89 mm; conning tower: 305 mm. Gromoboy: water-line belt: 152 mm (91.5 x 2.35 m); bulkheads: 152 mm (fore and aft); deck: 51/76 mm; main artillery: 127 mm (casamtes); secondary artillery: 80 mm (casamates); conning tower: 305 mm									
Rossiya	Balt. St. Peterburg	1896/97	13675 (12130)	141.3x20.9x8.5	18430 (17000)	20.2 (19)	4x203/45. 16x152/45. 12x75/50. 20x47/44. 16x37/23	5 tt 381	
Gromoboy		1899/00	13220 (12359)	144.2²x20.9x8.8	15490 (14500)	20.1 (19)	4x203/45. 16x152/45. 24x75/50. 12x47/44. 18x37/23. 4 MG	4 tt 381	
"Bayan" class Water-line belt: 100-200-100 mm (from prow 115 x 1.8 m); upper belt: 80 mm (from prow 105x1.7 m); bulkheads: 203 mm (aft); deck: 50 mm; main artillery: 150 mm (turrets). 170 mm (barbettes); secondary artillery: 80 mm (casemates); conning tower: 164 mm									
Bayan	FCM La Seyne	1900/03	7726	125x17.4x6.7	17400 (16500)	22 (21)	2x203/45. 8x152/45. 20x75/50. 8x47/44. 2x37/23	2 tt 381	+08.12.04. Port Arthur. Jap. land artillery
Cruisers									
"Pamyat' Merkuriya" class									
Pamyat' Merkuriya	FCM La Seyne	1880/82 94	2996 t	89x12.4x6	3005 (2950)	16.7 (15.5)	6x152/28. 4x47/44. 2x37/23. 2x37/20²	4 tt 381	
"Admiral Kornilov" class Deck: 38/63 mm; conning tower: 76 mm									
Admiral Kornilov	SACL St. Nazaire	1887/88 95. 05	5893 t (4940 t)	107x14.8x7.8	6580 (8260)	17.3 (18.5)	10x152/45. 6x47/44. 6x37/23	6 tt 381	
"Svetlana" class Deck: 37/63 mm; conning tower: 102 mm									
Svetlana	FCM. Granville	1896/98	3828 t → 3727 t	101¹x13x5.7	10100 (8500)	20.2 (20)	6x152/45. 0→ 4x75/50. 10→ 8x47/44. 2→0x37/23	2 tt 381	28.05.05. the Battle of Tsushima. Jap. gunfire
"Pallada" class Deck: 38/63 mm; conning tower: 152 mm									
Pallada	Galernyy St. Peterburg	1899/01	6731 (6630)	121.5x16.8x6.4	13100 (11610)	19.2 (20)	8x152/45. 24x75/50. 8x37/23	3 tt 381	+07.12.04. Port Arthur. Jap. land artillery
Diana		1899/01	6737 (6630)		12130 (11610)	19.3 (20)			28.08.04 interned in Saigon.
Avrora	N. Adm. St. Peterburg	1900/03	6740 (6630)		11910 (11610)	19.2 (20 w)			08.06.05 interned in Manila
"Varyag" class Deck: 38/76 mm; conning tower: 152 mm									
Varyag	Cramp Philadelphia	1899/01	7022 (6465)	121.9x15.9x6.3	20000	24.5 (23)	12x152/45. 12x75/50. 8x47/44. 2x37/23. 2 MG	6 tt 381	+09.02.04. hevily demaged during the battle of Chemulpo. then scuttled
"Askol'd" class Deck: 50/75 mm; conning tower: 152 mm									
Askol'd	Germania Kiel	1900/02	6096 (5959)	130x15.6x6.2	20420 (19000)	24.5 (23)	12x152/45. 12x75/50. 8x47/44. 2x37/23. 2 MG	6 tt 381	25.08.04 interned in Shanghaj
"Novik" class Deck: 32/51 mm; conning tower: 38 mm (Novik). 45 mm (Zhemchug. Izumrud)									
Novik	Schichau Gdańsk	1900/01	3080	106x12.2x5	19000 (17800)	25.6 (25)	6x120/45. 6x47/44. 2x37/23. 2 MG	5 tt 381	+20/21.08.04. Korsakovsk, Sachalin. after damage 20.08.04 by Niitaka.

244

Name	Builder	Year date (launched/ in sernice)	Displacement (t)	Dimensions (m)	Machinery (ihp)	Speed (kn)	Artillery armament	Torpedo and mine amament	Remarks
Zhemchug	Nevskiy St. Peterburg	1903/04	3153	106x12.8x5	17000	24	8x120/45. 6x47/44. 4 MG	3 tt 381	08.06.05 interned in Manila
Izumrud		1903/04	3106				6x120/45. 6x47/44. 2x37/23. 2 MG		+30.05.05. Sv. Vladimir Bay. grounded. then scuttled
"Boyarin" class Deck: 38/51 mm; conning tower: 76 mm									
Boyarin	Burmeister. Kobenhaven	1901/02	3274 (3200)	105.6x12.6x4.9	20420 (19000)	24.5 (23)	6x120/45. 8x47/44. 1x37/23. 2 MG	5 tt 381	13/14.02.04. Talien bay. mined
"Bogatyr'" class Deck: 34/70 mm; main artillery: 127 mm (turrets). 73 mm (barbettes). 80 mm (casemates); conning tower: 140 mm									
Bogatyr'	Vulcan. Szczecin	1901/02	6645 (6410)	126.1x16.6x6.3m	24270 (19500)	24.1 (23)	12x152/45. 12x75/50. 8x47/44. 2x37/23. 2 MG	6 tt 381	=15.05.04. Posiet' bay. grounded and hevily demaged
Oleg	N. Adm. St. Peterburg	1903/04	6675 (6440)		21000 (19500)	23.4 (23)		4 tt 381	08.06.05 interned in Manila
Kagul	NAV Nikolaev	1902/05	6645		19500	22.5 (23)			
Ochakov	Sevastopol'	1902/05			20400 (19500)	22.7 (23)			=28.11.05. Sevastopol'. hevily demaged during the boshevik mutiny
Small cruisers									
"Kreyser" class									
Kreyser	N. Adm. St. Peterburg	1875/76	1598	63.3'x10.1x4.4-5	1210 (1500)	11.4	2x152/28. 4x107/20. 2x47/25². 4x37/20²	1 tt 381	Iron-hulled.
Dzhigit	Galernyy St. Peterburg	1876/77	1380		1380 (1500)	12	2x152/23. 4x107/20. 2x47/25². 6x37/20²		Iron-hulled. 08.04 - disarmed. +01.01.05. scuttled in Port Arthur.
Razboynik	Nevskiy St. Peterburg	1878/79 81. 00	1350		1785 (1500)	13.3	2x152/28. 4x107/20. 4x47/44. 6x37/20²	---	Iron-hulled. 08.04 – disarmed. +01.01.05. scuttled In Port Arthur
Plastun	Balt. St. Peterburg	1879/79	1334		1535 (1500)	13	2x152/28. 4x107/20. 4x47/25². 4x37/20²		Iron-hulled. sheathed with wood.
Strelok	Balt. St. Peterburg	1879/79 99	1365		1530 (1500)	13	6x37/20²		Iron-hulled. Since 1899 become a training ship.
Vestnik	Nevskiy St. Peterburg	1880/81	1275		1530 (1500)	12.8	1x152/28. 2x152/23. 4x107/20. 4x47/25². 4x37/20²	1 tt 381	Composite hulled.
Oprichnik	Balt. St. Peterburg	1880/81 97	1511		1810 (1675)	12.9	2x107/20	---	Iron hulled. sheathed with wood. Since 1897 become a training ship.
"Zabiyaka" class									
Zabiyaka	Cramp Philadelphia	1878/79 00	1236	67.1x9.1x4	1430	14.2	4x107/20. 4x47/44. 6x37/20²	---	Since 1900 partialy disarmed → depot-ship for torpedo boats and destroyers. 04.04 – disarmed. +25.10.04. Port Arthur. Jap. land artillery.
Torpedo gunboats									
"Leytenant Il'in" class and similars									
Leytenant Il'in	Balt. St. Peterburg	1886/87 96	604	69.2x7.3x2.8	3280	19.3	5x47/44. 2x37/20²	7 tt 381	
Kapitan Saken	NAV Nikolaev	1889/89 97	620	64x7.3x2.8	2340	18.3	6x47/44. 4x37/20²	3 tt 381	

Name	Builder	Year date (launched/ in sernice)	Displacement (t)	Dimensions (m)	Machinery (ihp)	Speed (kn)	Artillery armament	Torpedo and mine amament	Remarks
"Kazarskiy" class									
Kazarskiy	Schichau Elbląg	1889/90	411 (395)	57.2x7.4x3-3.4	3500	21.2 (21)	6x47/44. 3x37/23	2 tt 381	
Voyevoda		1891/92	415 (395)		3840	22.2 (21)			
Posadnik		1892/92	394 (395)		3680	22.1 (21)			
Vsadnik	Kriejton Abo	1893/94	432 (395)		3350	21			+15.12.04. Port Arthur. Jap. land artillery
Gaydamak		1893/94	405 (395)		3500	20 (21)			+01.01.05. scuttled in Port Arthur
Griden'	NAV Nikolaev	1893/95	400 (395)			22.5 (21)			
"Abrek" class (enlarged "Kazarskiy" class)									
Abrek	Krejton Abö	1896/97	535	64.6x7.7x3.3	4480 (4500)	21.2 (21)	2x75/50. 4x47/44	2 tt 381	
Gunboats									
"Sivuch" class									
Sivuch	Krejton Abö	1884/84	1134 (950)	57.1x10.7x3.5	1130 (1150)	11.7 (11.5)	1x229/30. 1x152/28. 6x107/20. 4x37/20². 4 MG	---	+02.08.04. Liao river. near Sanchaho. scuttled
Bobr	Bergsund Stockholm	1885/85	1187 (950)	57.1x10.7x3.7	1140 (1150)	11.2 (11.5)			+26.12.04. Port Arthur. Jap. land artillery
"Koryets/Kubanets" class									
Koryets	Bergsund Stockholm	1886/87	1334 (1224)	64x10.7x3.5-3.8	1560 (1500)	13.5 (13)	2x203/35. 1x152/35. 4x107/20. 2x47/44. 4x37/20²	1 tt 381	+09.02.04. scuttled after the battle of Chemulpo
Mandzur	Burmeister Kobenhaven	1886/87	1418 (1224)		1960 (1500)	13.3 (13)			26.03.04 interned in Shanghaj
Kubanets	ROPiT Sevastopol'	1887/87	1284 (1224)		1520-1820 (1500)	13.3-13.5 (12)	2x203/35. 1x152/35. 6x47/23². 4-1x37/20²	2 tt 381	
Uralets		1887/88	1227 (1224)						
Tierek		1887/88	1284 (1224)						
Zaporozhets	NAV Nikolaev	1887/88	1224		1520–1820 (2000)	13.5-13.7 (14)			
Chernomorets		1887/89	1299 (1224)						
Donets		1887/89	1224						
"Grozyashchiy" class									
Water-line belt: 102-127-76 mm (from stern 55 x 1.5 m); bulkheads: 38 mm (fore); deck: 25/38 mm; conning tower: 25 mm									
Grozyashchiy	N. Adm. St. Peterburg	1890/92	1627 (1492)	68x12.7x4-4.4	2060 (2000)	13.3 (13)	1x229/35. 1x152/35. 4x47/44. 4x37/20²	2 tt 381	+19.08.04. near Port Arthura. mined
Gremyashchiy		1892/93	1700 (1492)		2070 (2000)	13.7 (13)	1x229/35. 1x152/35. 4x75/50. 6x47/44. 4x37/20²		
Otvazhnyy	Balt. St. Peterburg	1892/93	1717 (1492)		2470 (2000)	15.4 (13)			=08.11.04. Port Arthur. Jap. land artillery +02.02.05. scuttled before the capitulation of Port Arthur
"Khrabryy" class									
Khrabryy	N. Adm. St. Peterburg	1895/97 00	1763 (1492)	70.2x13.1x4.2	2640 (2000)	14.5 (14)	2x203/45. 1x152/45. 5x47/44. 7x37/23	1 tt 381	
"Gilyak" class									
Gilyak	N. Adm. St. Peterburg	1897/98	1251 (963)	61x11.3x3.3	935 (1000)	11.3 (12)	1x120/45. 5x75/50. 4x47/44. 4x37/23. 1 MG	1 tt 381	+08.12.04. Port Arthur. Jap. land artillery

Name	Builder	Year date (launched/ in sernice)	Displacement (t)	Dimensions (m)	Machinery (ihp)	Speed (kn)	Artillery armament	Torpedo and mine amament	Remarks
				Destroyers					
				"Prytkiy" class					
Prytkiy	Yarrow Poplar	1895/95	220	57.7x5.6x2.3	4490	30.2	1x75/50. 3x47/44	2 tt 381	
Pylkiy	Krejton Abö	1898/00	240		3800	25.7-27			
Poslushnyy		1898/00							
Prochnyy	Izhora St. Peterburg	1898/00							
Porazhayushchiy		1898/00							
Pronzitelnyy		1898/00							
Prozorlivyy	Nevskiy St. Peterburg	1899/01							
Rezvyy		1899/01							
Retivyy		1900/02							
R'yanyy		1900/01							
Podvizhnyy	Izhora St. Peterburg	1901/02							
Strogiy	Krejton Abö	1901/02							
Smetlivyy		1901/02							
Stroynyy	Nevskiy St. Peterburg	1901/02							
Svirepyy	Krejton Abö	1901/02							
Stremitelnyy		1901/02							
Serdityy	Nevskiy St. Peterburg	1901/03							02.01.05. interned in Chefoo
Smelyy		1902/02							03.01.05. interned in Tsingtao
Reshitel'nyy	Izhora St. Peterburg	1902/03							12.08.04. saized in Chefoo by Jap.
Storozhevoy	Nevskiy St. Peterburg	1902/03							=15/15.12.04. White Wolf Bay. Jap. torpedo; +01/02.01.05. scuttled in Port Arthur
Steregushchiy		1902/03							+10.03.04. near Port Arthurem. Jap. gunfire
Razyashchiy	Izhora St. Peterburg	1903/03							=24.08.04. near Port Arthura. minyed; +01/02.01.05. scuttled in Port Arthur
Rastoropnyy		1903/03							+15.11.04. scuttled in Chefoo
Skoryy	Nevskiy St. Peterburg	1903/03							02.01.05. interned in Chefoo
Sil'nyy		1903/03							=11.11.04. near Port Arthura. mined; +01/02.01.05. scuttled in Port Arthur
Strashnyy		1903/04							+13.04.04. koło Port Arthura. art. jap. NT
Statnyy		1903/04							02.02.05. int. w Chefoo
				"Leytenant Burakov" (eks Chinese "Hai Hua")					
Leytenant Burakov	Schichau Elbląg	1898/99 01	284	59.1¹x6.4x2.6	6000	33.6	6x47/44	1 tt 381	+25/26.07.04. scuttled In Tahe bay. after torpedoed 23/24.07.04
				"Boyevoy" class					
Boyevoy	Laird Birkenhead	1899/00	350	64.9²x6.6x1.9	6000	27.7 (27)	1x75/50. 5x47/44	2 tt 381	=23/24.07.04. Tahe bay. torpedoed; +01/02.01.05. scuttled in Port Arthur

Name	Builder	Year date (launched/ in sernice)	Displacement (t)	Dimensions (m)	Machinery (ihp)	Speed (kn)	Artillery armament	Torpedo and mine amament	Remarks
					"Bditelnyy" class				
Bditelnyy	Schichau Elbląg	1899/00	346	60x7x1.9	6000	27.1-27.4 (27)	1x75/50. 5x47/44	3 tt 381	=11.11.04. near Port Arthur. mined; +01/02.01.05. scuttled in Port Arthur
Besposhchadnyy		1899/00							15.08.04. internet in Tsingtao
Besstrashnyy		1899/00							15.08.04. Internet in Tsingtao
Besshumnyy		1900/00							15.08.04. Internet in Tsingtao
					"Vnimatel'nyy" class				
Vnimatel'nyy	Normand Le Havre	1900/01	312	55.8x6.3x2	5200	27-28.4 (26)	1x75/50. 5x47/44	2 tt 381	+27.05.04. Murchinson Island. grounded
Vnushitel'nyy	FCM Le Havre	1901/01							+25.02.04. Pigeon Bay. Jap. gunfire
Vynoslivyy	FCM Le Havre	1901/01							+24.08.04. near Port Arthur. mined
Vlastnyy	Normand Le Havre	1901/02							02.01.05. interned in Chefoo
Grozovoy		1901/02							24.08.04. Internet In Shanghaj
					"Boykiy" class				
Boykiy	Nevskiy St. Peterburg	1901/02	350	60.2x6.4x1.8	6000-5700	25-27.7 (26)	1x75/50. 5x47/44	3 tt 381	03.01.05. Internet in Tsingtao
Buynyy		1901/02							+28.05.05. scuttled after the battle of Tsushima
Bravyy		1901/02							
Burnyy		1901/02							+11.08.04. scuttled after driven ashore of Shantung
Blestyashchiy		1901/02							+28.05.05. sank after the battle of Tsushima
Bystryy		1901/02							+28.05.05. scuttled in Chikuhen bay. Korea. after the battle of Tsushima
Bodryy		1902/02							04.06.05. interned in Shanghaj
Bedovyy		1902/02							28.05.05. surrender after the battle of Tsushima
Bezuprechnyy		1902/02							+28.05.05. after the battle of Tsushima. Jap gunfire
Zavidnyy	NOMZ Nikolaev	1903/03						3 tt 457	
Zavetnyy		1902/03							
Zadornyy		1904/05							
Zvonkiy		1904/05							
Zorkiy		1904/05							
Groznyy	Nevskiy St. Peterburg	1904/04							
Gromkiy		1904/04							+28.05.05. after the battle of Tsushima. Jap. gunfire
Gromyashchiy		1904/04							
Zharkiy	NAV Nikolaev	1904/05							
Zhivoy		1903/05							
Zhivuchiy		1904/06							
Zhutkiy		1904/05							
Vidnyy	Nevskiy St. Peterburg	1904/05						3 tt 381	

Name	Builder	Year date (launched/ in sernice)	Displacement (t)	Dimensions (m)	Machinery (ihp)	Speed (kn)	Artillery armament	Torpedo and mine amament	Remarks
					Torpedo boats				
					"251" class				
251	Yarrow Poplar	1880/80	48	29.4x3.8x1.9	500	22.1 (19)	1x37/20²	2 tt 381	
					"254" class				
254	Claparéde Rouen	1883/84	78	37x4.1x2.1	600	17.8 (17.5)	2x37/20²	2 tt 381	
					"255" class				
255	FCM La Seyne	1883/84	75	37.1x3.8x2.1	560	17.5 (18)	2x37/20²	2 tt 381	
					"257" class				
257	Thornycroft Chiswick	1883/83	60	34.4¹x3.8x1.9	700	18 (19.5)	2x37/20²	2 tt 381	
					"258/267" class				
258	Normand La Havre	1883/83	63	38.9¹x3.9x2	575	18.5	2x37/20²	2 tt 381	
267	NAV Nikolaev	1885/86	74	38.9¹x3.7x2.2	550	15.8-17.5			
105	N. Adm. St. Peterburg	1886/87							
106		1887/87							
107		1887/87							
					"101" class				
101	Balt. St. Peterburg	1885/85	67	38x4.4x1.4	500	16.9 (16.5)	2x37/20²	2 tt 381	
					"102" class				
102	Thomson Glasgow	1886/86	125	43.3x5.2x2.4	1300 HP	20.6 (20)	2x47/44	2 tt 381	
					"206" class				
206	Normand. Le Havre	1886/86	96	46.8x3.8x2.6	1010-1020	19.2-19.7 (19)	2x37/20²	2 tt 381	
205		1886/86							
					"108" class				
108	Schichau Elbląg	1886/86	76 t	38.6x4.8x2.1	830-1000	19.6-22 (19)	2x37/20²	2 tt 381	
109		1886/86							
110		1886/86							
261		1886/86							
262		1886/86							
263		1886/86							
264		1886/86							
265		1886/86							
266		1886/86							
201	Nevskiy St. Peterburg	1887/89							+21.08.04. near Vladivostok. grounded
202		1887/89							
					"259" class				
259	Schichau Elbląg	1889/90	135	46.5x5.1x2.1	2300	27.4 (26.5)	2x37/20²	3 tt 381	
					"111" class				
111	Putilov St. Peterburg	1890/91	81	38.4x4.5x2.5	1100	17.2-19 (17)	2x37/20²	2 tt 381	
112		1890/91							
113		1891/91							
114		1891/91							
252	BF Odessa	1891/91							
253		1892/92							

Name	Builder	Year date (launched/ in sernice)	Displacement (t)	Dimensions (m)	Machinery (ihp)	Speed (kn)	Artillery armament	Torpedo and mine amament	Remarks
					"260" class				
260	Schichau Elbląg	1889/90	86	38.6-38.9x4.6-4.9x2-2.1	1000-1300	21	2x37/20²	2 tt 381	
115	Putilov St. Peterburg	1893/93							
116		1893/93							
125	Izhora St. Peterburg	1893/93							
126		1893/93							
121		1894/94	85						
122		1894/94							
131		1895/96	86						
132		1895/96							
268	NAV Nikolaev	1895/95							
					"203" class				
203	Krejton Abö	1889/90	140	46.4x5x2.5	2040	19.6	3x37/20²	3 tt 381	
204		1889/90			2140	20.2			+30.06.04. scuttled near Gensan
					"117" class				
117	Krejton Abö	1890/90	93	41x4.8x2.6	1245	20 (18)	2x37/20²	2 tt 381	
					"118" class				
118	Krejton Abö	1891/92	101	46.8¹x4x2.5	660-1030	16.2-19 (18)	2x37/20²	2 tt 381	
256		1891/92							
123	Izhora St. Peterburg	1891/92		46.5¹x4x2.6					
124		1891/92							
					"103" class				
103	Normand Le Havre	1892/92	117	42x4.4x2.4	1800		2x37/20²	3 tt 381	
119	Krejton Abö	1894/95	120	42x4.5x2.4	2000-2500	22.5-24.5 (21)			
120		1894/95							
127	Izhora Kolpino	1895/98							
133	Nevskiy St. Peterburg	1895/97							
134		1895/97							
270	NAV Nikolaev	1895/97							
271		1895/97							
128	Izhora Kolpino	1895/98							
135	Nevskiy St. Peterburg	1896/97							
136		1896/97							
272	NAV Nikolaev	1896/99							
273		1896/99							
137	Nevskiy St. Peterburg	1897/97							
138		1897/97							
139		1897/97							
140		1897/97							
141		1897/97							
142		1897/97							
129	Izhora Kolpino	1897/99							
130	Izhora St. Peterburg	1897/00							
208	N. Adm. St. Peterburg	1897/99			1460-1500	17.3-18.4 (18.5)			+16.07.04. near Vladivostok. mined
209		1897/99							
210	Izhora St. Peterburg	1898/99							
211		1898/99							

Name	Builder	Year date (launched/ in sernice)	Displacement (t)	Dimensions (m)	Machinery (ihp)	Speed (kn)	Artillery armament	Torpedo and mine amament	Remarks
	"104" class								
104	Normand Le Havre	1893/94	77	35.9x4.2x2.7	1450	24.5 (25)	2x37/20²	3 tt 381	
	"212" class								
212	Krejton Abö	1901/02	186	52.4x5.3x2.4	3500	25-25.6 (24.5)	3x37/20²	3 tt 381	
213		1901/02							
	"214" class								
214	Nevskiy St. Peterburg	1902/03	152	45.1x4.9x2.7	4200 HP	26.1-27 (29)	3x47/44	2 tt 381	
215		1902/03							
216		1902/03							
217		1902/03							
218		1902/03							
219	Krejton Abö	1903/03							
220		1903/03							
221		1902/03							+09.03.04. near Creta. foudered
222		1902/03							
223		1902/03							
	Minelayers								
	"Aleut" class								
Aleut	Nylands Chrliania (Oslo)	1886/86	842	45.7x9.4x3.5	780	11.9 (10)	4x87/24. 4x23²	2 tt 381? 150 mines	
	"Bug/Volga" class								
Bug	Lindholmens Göteborg	1891/92	1382	62.2x10.4x4.4	1930 (1400)	14.2 (13)	6x47/44. 4x37/23²	270-400 mines	+28.11.05. Sevastopol'. scuttled during the bolshevik mutiny
Dunay		1891/92			2080 (1400)	14.7 (13)			
Volga	N. Adm. St. Peterburg	1904/05	1453	64.6x11.9x4.1	1640 HP (1600 HP)	13.8 w (13 w)	4x47/44	230 mines	
	"Amur" class								
Amur	Balt. St. Peterburg	1898/01	2800 (2590)	92.7x14.9x5.2	4890 (4700)	17.9 (18)	5x75/50. 10x47/44	450 mines	+18.12.04. Port Arthur. Jap. land artilley
Yenisiey		1899/01			4960 (4700)	18.1 (18)			+11.02.04. Talien bay. mined
	Submarines								
	"Dzhevecki III" mod. / "Kieta" class								
Keta	Messner St. Peterburg	1881/81 mod.1905	8/?	7.5x1.5x1.5	24	?/?	xxx	2 tl 381	
	"Del'fin" class								
Del'fin	Balt. St. Peterburg	1903/04	113/123	19.6x3.6x2.9	300/120*	9/4.5	xxx	2 tl 381	+29.06.04. Neva. St. Petersburg. explosion; +05.05.05. Vladivostok. eksplosion.
	"Forel'" class								
Forel'	Germania Kiel	1903/04	17/18	12.5x2.1x2.1	60*	4/?	xxx	2 tl 381	
	"Petr Koshka"								
Petr Koshka	Bałt. St. Peterburg	1903/04?	20/?	15.2x1.3x1.3	24*	6.5/3.5	xxx	2 tl ?	Experimental ship
	"Portarturets" class								
Portarturets	Port Arthur	1904/04?	25/?	10x1.9x1.3	?	?/?	xxx	2 tl ?	Experimental ship
	"Chelim" class								
Chelim	Balt. St. Peterburg	1904/05	14/?	8.7x2x?	14*	7/4	xxx	2 tt 381	
	"Kasatka" class								

Name	Builder	Year date (launched/ in sernice)	Displacement (t)	Dimensions (m)	Machinery (ihp)	Speed (kn)	Artillery armament	Torpedo and mine amament	Remarks
Kasatka	Balt. St. Peterburg	1904/05	142/177	33.4x3.5x3.4	400/60-100*	8.5/5.5	xxx	4 tl 381	
Skat		1904/05							
Nalim		1904/05							
Fel'dmarshal Graf Sheremet'ev		1904/05							
Okun'		1904/05							
Makrel'		1904/08							
"Som" class (American "Holland" class)									
Som	Lewis Nixon Elizabethport (USA)	1904/05	105/124	19.8x3.6x2.9	160/60-70*	8.5/6	xxx	1 tt 381/ 457	
Shchuka	Newskij St. Peterburg	1904/05	110/125						
Losos'		1905/06							
Sudak		1905/07							
Beluga		1905/06	105/124						
Peskar'		1905/06							
Sterlyad'		1905/06							
"Osetr" class (eks American "Protektor")									
Osetr	NNS Bridgeport (Conn. USA)	1905/05	136/174	20.6x3.6x3.7	240/100*	8.5/4.5	xxx	3 tt 381	
Kefal'	NNS/Arsenal Libawa	1905/05			260/130*				
Bychok		1905/							
Plotva		1905/							
Paltus		1905/							
Sig		1905/							
Auxiliary cruisers									
Various classes									
Dniepr (ex *Peterburg*)	Hawthorn.Leslie Hebburn-on-Tyne	1893/94	9460	137.8x15.8x7.7	10500	19	7x120/45. 8x47/43. 8x37/23	xxx	
Lena (ex *Chersoń*)	Hawthorn.Leslie Hebburn-on-Tyne	1896/97	10675	138.7x16.5x7.5 m	12500	19.5	6x120/45. 6x75/50	xxx	12.09.04. interned in San Francisco
Angara (ex *Moskva*)	CSE Glasgow	1897/98	12050	143.3x17.7x8.7	15500	20.2	6x120/45. 6x75/50	xxx	Disarmed since March 1904; +30.10.04. Port Arthur. Jap. land artillery
Rion (ex *Smolensk*)	Hawthorn.Leslie Hebburn-on-Tyne	1900/01			16000	20	8x120/45. 8x75/50. 2x37/23	xxx	
Various classes – bought in Germany									
Kuban' (ex *Augusta Victoria*)	Vulcan Szczecin	1889/90	12000	158.8x17.1x8.5	12500	18.5	2x120/45. 4x75/50. 8x57/40	xxx	
Terek (ex *Columbia*)	Laird Birkenhead	1889/90	10000	139.9x17.1x7.6	13500	19		xxx	29.06.06. interned in Batavia
Ural (ex *Maria Theresa*)	Vulcan Szczecin	1890/91	10500	141.1x15.8x8.2	17500	19		xxx	+27.05.05. the battle of Tsushima. Jap. gunfire
Don (ex *Fürst Bismarck*)	Vulcan Szczecin	1890/91	12130	153.1x17.5x6.8	14000	19		xxx	

1) Full lenght

2) Revolver guns

Ships mobilized for Port Arthur's Squadron auxiliary duties;
  Amur (1901) – 2449 BRT
  Beytang (?) - ?
  Bogatyr' (1900) – 321 BRT → auxiliary unit of Inzhinernoe Vedomstvo → auxiliary minelayer
  Bureya (1901) – 919 BRT
  Tsitsikar (1894) – 1028 BRT
  Eduard Bari (1899) – 3496 BRT; + 04.04, sunk as blockship to protect the entrance of Port Arthur
  Evropa (?) - ?; +03.04, Port Arthur, collision
  Girin (1889) – 1639 BRT
  Inkou (1898) – 150 BRT
  Kazan' (1900) – 6076 BRT → hospital ship
  Khabarovsk (?) - ?
  Khaylar (1882) – 5606 BRT; s+ 9.03.04, sunk as blockship to protect the entrance of Port Arthur
  Kharbin (1881) – 3573 BRT; s+ 9.03.04, sunk as blockship to protect the entrance of Port Arthur
  Mongoliya (1901) – 2937 BRT → hospital ship
  Ninguta (1889) – 980 BRT
  Novik (1887) – 328 BRT
  Nonni (1901) – 2422 BRT
  Silach (1890) – 499 BRT
  Shilka (1900) -2422 BRT; s+04.04, sunk as blockship to protect the entrance of Port Arthur
  Zeya (1901) – 919 BRT

Ships mobilized for Vladyvostok's Squadron auxiliary duties;
  Yaakut (1884) – 701 BRT
  Kamchadal (1892) – 467 BRT
  Kolyma (1893) – 2698 BRT
  Mongugay (1892) – 1012 BRT → minelayer (since the autumn 1904)
  Nakhodka (1901) – 115 t
  Nadezhnyy (1897) – 1212 BRT → ice-breakar
  Selenga (1899) – 3517 BRT (ex Ger. *Claudius*)
  Sungari (1903) – 4243 BRT (ex Ger. *Tiberius*)
  Tobol (1899) – 3741 BRT (ex Brit. *Cheltenham*)

Ships mobilized for II and III Pacific Squadron auxiliary duties; (* - units under mercantile banner)
  Anadyr" (1903) – 16220 t
  German Lerche (1902) – 3126 BRT
  *Graf Strogonov** (1903) – 7016 BRT
  Irtysh (1900) – 7507 BRT; +28.05.05, scuttled after the battle of Tsushima
  Yaroslavl' (1893) – 4495 BRT
  *Yupiter** (1900) – 4896 BRT
  Kamchatka (1902) – 7200 t → repair-ship; +27.05.05, the battle of Tsushima, Jap. gunfire
  Kiev (1896) – 5566 BRT
  Kitay (1898) – 4660 BRT
  *Knjaz' Gorchakov** (1901) – 3882 BRT
  *Koreya** (1899) – 6163 BRT
  Kostroma (1888) – 3513 BRT → hospital ship
  *Kuroniya** (1890) – 4572 BRT
  *Kseniya** (1900) – 3773 BRT → repair-ship
  *Livonya** (1902) – 5782 BRT
  *Malaya** (1898) – 4847 BRT
  *Merkuriy** (1900) – 4046 BRT
  Meteor (1901) – 4259 BRT → fresh water tank-ship
  Orel' (1890) – 4528 BRT →hospital ship; seized by Japanese 27.05.05
  *Rus** (1903) – 611 BRT →tug; +27.05.05, battle of Tsushima, collision
  Svir" (1898) – 542 BRT →tug
  *Tambov** (1893) – 4441 BRT
  *Saratov** (1891) – 5308 BRT
  *Vladimir** (1895) – 5621 BRT
  *Voronezh** (1895) – 5616 BRT

Bibliography

Unpublished documents

Public Record Office (PRO), London

Admirality (ADM): t. 116/969, 189/24, 189/25, 231/37, 231/39, 231/41, 231/42, 231/43, 231/44, 231/45

Cabinet Office (CAB): t. 37/78, 37/79, 41/24

Foreign Office (FO): t. 46/643, 46/644, 46/645, 46/646, 46/647, 46/648, 46/649, 46/650, 46/651, 46/652, 46/653, 46/654, 46/655, 46/656, 46/657, 46/658, 46/659, 46/660, 46/661, 46/662, 46/663, 46/664, 46/665, 46/667, 46/668, 233/122, 233/125, 418/42, 418/50, 881/8076X, 881/9498X

Transport Department (MT): t. 9/776, 9/801, 23/221

War Office (WO): t. 33/294, 33/315, 33/337, 33/1518, 33/1519, 33/1520, 33/1521, 33/1522, 33/1523, 33/1524, 33/1525, 33/1526, 33/1527, 106/181, 106/6351, 106/6352, 106/6353, 106/6354, 106/6355, 106/6356

Rossiyskiy gosudarstvennyy arkhiv voenno-morskogo flota (RGAVMF), St. Peterburg

Glavnyy morskoy shtab: Fond 417

Vrmennyy morskoy shtab namestnika na Dal'nem Vostoke: Fond 467

Morskoy pokhodnyy shtab namestnika na Dal'nem Vostoke: Fond 469

Shtab komanduyushchego flotom v Tikhom okeane: Fond 524

Dnevniki, zametki, zapiski... (kollektsiya sobrannaya Ioricheskoy komissiey pri Morskom General'nom Shtabe po opisaniyu deystviy flota v voynu 1904-1905 gg.): Fond 763

Vakhtennye i shkanechnye zhurnaly: Fond 870

Published documents

Admiral Nebogatoff on the Battle of Tsushima., JRUSI vol. XLb (1906)

The Battle of the Sea of Japan., USNIP Nr 3/1905

Khronika voenno-morskikh dejstvij na dalnem vostokie. Part 1-20, MS Nr 3-12/1904, 1-11/1905

Damages to Russian Ships at Port Arthur., USNIP Nr 4/1905

Lebedev A., Russko-yaponskaya voyna 1904-05 g.g., Materialy dla opisaniua dejstviy flota. Khronologicheskiy perechen voennykh deystviy flota w 1904-05 g.g., Vypusk" I, Perechen vojennykh deystviy flota u Port Artura w 1904 godu. Izdanie Komissii dla sostavleniya opisaniya deystviy flota v voynu 1904-5 gg., St. Peterburg 1910

Novikov, Russko-yaponskaya voyna 1904-1905 gg. Maaterialy dlya opisaniya deystviy Khronologicheskiy perechen' voennykh" deystviy flota v" 1904-5 g.g. Vypusk" II. Perechen' sobytiy pokhoda 2-oy eskadry Tikhago Okeana i eya otryadov" na Dalniy Vostok" i boy v" Tsusimskom" prolive., St. Peterburg 1912

Official History of the Russo-Japanese War. Prepared by the HIorical Section of the Committee of Imperial Defence. vol. I-V, London 1909-1910

Oficjalnyy otdel., MS Nr 1-12/1904, 1-12/1905

Opisanie voennykh deystviy na more v 37 i 38 gg. Meydzi (v 1904-1905 gg.). Sostavleno morskim general'nym shtabom v Tokio, tt. I - IV, St. Peterburg 1909-1910

Russko-yaponskaya voyna 1904-1905 gg. Deystviya flota. Dokumenty. (Otdel' III-IV). Izdannye Ioricheskoy komissiey po opisaniyu deystviy flota v voynu 1904-1905 gg. pri Morskom General'nom Shtabe, St. Peterburg 1907-1914

Books & Articles

Afonin N.N., Balakin S.A., "Vnimatel'nyy" i drugie (port-arturskie minonostsy zarubezhnoy postroyki)., Moskva 2000

Afonin N.N., Na puti k Tsusime (Minonostsy Nevskogo zavoda tipa "Buynyy" v Russko-yaponskoy voyne)., "Morskoy Ioricheskiy Sbornik" Nr 1/1990

Afonin N.N., "Retvizan"., "Gangut" Nr 1

Afonin N.N., "Steregushchiy"., "Gangut" Nr 4

Alliluev A.A., Kreyser "Novik". cz. 1-2, "Gangut" Nr 2-3

Alliluev A.A., Kreysery "Zhemchug" i "Izumrud". Part 1-2, "Gangut" Nr 5-6

Beglyy, A.N., Ocherk" morskikh operatsiy russko-yaponskoy voyny. Part 1-6, MS Nr 4, 6-7, 9/1912, 2-3/1913

Anderson R. M., Sea battles. A reference guide., Newton Abbot 1975

Anderson R. M., Flatirons, the Rendel gunboats., WI Nr 1/1976

Apushkin V.A., Russko-yaponskaya voyna 1904-1905., St. Peterburg 1911

Arbuzow V.V., "Borodino" class armored ships., St.Peterburg 1993

Arbuzov V.V., The Battleship "Dvenadtsat' Apostolov"., WI Nr 4/1992

Arbuzov V.V., Bronenostsy tipa "Yekatyerina II"., St. Peterburg 1994

Ballard G.A., The Influence of the Sea on the Political History of Japan., London 1921

Balakin S., Byvshie russkie korabli v yaponskom flote (Trofei voyny 1904-1905 g.g.), "Naval" Nr 1 (1991)

Balakin S., Port-arturski kwartet (rosyjskie niszczyciele typu "Kasatka")., OW nr 4-6/1992

Bartlewicz J., Broń podwodna., Warszawa1934

Beskrovnyy L.G., Armiya i flot Rossii v nachale XX v., Moskva 1986

Beskrovnyy L.G., Russkaya armiya i flot v XIX veke., Moskva 1973

Bestuzhev N.A., Opyt' Iorii rossiyskogo flota., Leningrad 1961

Bogart C.H., "Fuso"., WI, Nr 3/1972

Bogdanov M.A., "Navarin"., "Gangut" Nr 4

Bogdanov M.A., "Sisoy Velikiy"., "Gangut" Nr 3

Bozhenko P., Podvodnye minonostsy: Russkie podvodnye lodki v voyne 1904-1905 g.g. Boevoy debyut., "Naval" Nr 1 (1991)

Brassey's Naval Annual 1886, 1894 - 1905

Bridge C.A.G., The Russo-Japanese War, 1904., BNA 1905

Brook P., Armstrong Battleships built for Japan., WI Nr 3/1985

Brook P., The Armstrong Torpedo Gunboats., WI Nr 2/1978

Brook P., The Elswick Cruisiers. Part 1-4, WI Nr 2/1970, 3/1971, 3/1972, 3/1973

Bubnov M., Port Artur. Part 1-16, MS Nr 4-12/1906, 1-7/1907

Burt R.A., British Battleships 1889-1904., London 1988

Bykov P.D., Russko-yaponskaya voyna 1904-1905., Moskva 1942

Campbell J.P., The Nort Sea Incident of 1904., USNIP Nr 3/1974

Campbell N.J.M., The battle of Tsu-Shima. cz. 1-4, "Warship" 1978 (Nr 5-8)

Cieślak M., Rosyjski pancernik "Cesariewicz". Cz. 1-2, MSiO Nr 4-5/2003, 6/2003

Colomb P.H., Morskaya voyna., Moskva 1940

Comparative losses in the Russo-Japanese War., USNIP Nr 3/1905

Conway's All the World's Fighting Ships 1860-1905., London 1979

Conway's All the World's Fighting Ships 1906-1921., London 1985

Corbett J.S., Maritime Operations in the Russo-Japanese War 1904-1905. vol. I-II, Annapolis 1994

Custance R., The Ship of the Line in Battle., London/Edinburgh 1912

Curtis A., The Sige of Port Arthur from a Naval Aspect., JRUSI vol. XLa (1906)

Chagin, Ocherk razvitiya yaponskogo flota., MS Nr 7/1898

Chestyakov V., Do pervogo zalpa., "Naval" Nr 1 (1991)

Davelyui P., Uroki russko-yaponskoy voyny. Bor'ba za ovladenie morem., St. Peterburg 1908

Denisov B., Minnaya voyna u Port-Artura v 1904 g., MS Nr 6/1935

Denisov B., Minnaya voyna u Vladivostoka v 1904-1905 gg., MS Nr 10/1935

Denisov B.,Ispol'zovanie torpednogo oruzhiya v russko-yapon-suyu voynu., MS Nr 11/1935

Drashpil B.V., Tamura T., Wright C.C., The Fate of the Four Chinese Torpedo Boat Destroyers., WI Nr 2/1987

Drashpil B.V., The Russian Rendels., WI Nr 2/1980

Drashpil B.V., Surface Torpedo Craft of the Imperial russian Navy. cz. 1, WI Nr 3/1982

Dyskant J.W., Cuszima 1905., Warszawa 1979

Dyskant J.W., Port Artur 1904., Warszawa 1996

Dzienisiewicz S., Rozwój idei użycia torpedy., PM Nr 1/1934

Evans D.C., Peattie M.R., Kaigun. Strategy, Tactics, and Technology in the Imperial Japanese Navy, 1887-1941., Annapolis, Maryland 1997

Egor'ev V.E., Operatsii vladivostokskikh kreyserov v russko-yaponskuyu voynu 1904-1905 gg., Moskva 1939

Egor'ev V.E., Operatsiya vladivostokskogo otryada kreyserov v iyule 1904 g., MS Nr 4/1937

Egor'ev V.E., Pervyy pokhod vladivostokskikh kreyserov v korey-skiy proliv i russkikh minonostsev k o-vu Khokkaydo v iyune 1904 g., MS Nr 7/1937

Egor'ev V.E., Vladivostokskiy otryada kreyserov v russko-yapon-skuyu voynu., MS Nr 3/1937

Falk E.A., Togo and Rise of Japanese Sea Power., New York 1936

The First Year of the War. A Russian Critique of the Present Situation by Sea., JRUSI vol. XLXIXa (1905)

Fisher E.C., Battleships of the Imperial Russian Navy. cz.1-4, WI Nr 3-4/1968, 1-2/1969

Fitzgerald C.C.P., The Imperial Japanese Navy., USNIP Nr 2/1900

Fokeev K.F., Voenno-morskoe isskustvo parovogo flota vo wtoroy polovine XIX w.. Petrodvorec 1962

Frankowski S., Mina zagrodowa w wojnie na morzu., PM Nr 4/1929

Glock M., Japoński pancernik "Mikasa"., OW Nr 3/2005

Glock M., Rosyjskie pancerniki typu "Połtawa". Cz. 1-2, OW Nr 3-4/2007

Gomm B., Die russischen Kriegsschiffe 1856-1917. Band I-IX, Wiesbaden 1989-1999

Goncharov L., Nekotorye takticheske uroki Tsusimy., MS Nr 6/1935

Gozdawa-Gołębiowski J., Od wojny krymskiej do bałkańskiej., Gdańsk 1985

Gribovskiy V.Yu., "Tsesarevich" v boyu 28 ijulja 1904 goda., "Gangut" Nr 19

Gribovskiy V.Yu., Bronenosec beregovoy oborony "General-admiral Apraksin"., "Gangut" Nr 18

Gribovskiy V.Yu., Eskadrennye bronenostsy tipa "Borodino" v Tsusimskom srazhenii., "Gangut" Nr 2

Gribovskiy V.Yu., Eskadrennyy bronenosec "Borodino"., St. Peterburg 1995 (bibl. "Gangut")

Gribovskiy V.Yu., K Iorii sozdanija bronenoscev rossiyskogo i yaponskogo flotov nakanune voyny 1904-1905 gg., "Gangut" Nr 1

Gribovskiy V.Yu., Katastrofa 31 marta 1904 goda (gibel bronieno-sca "Petropavlovsk")., "Gangut" Nr 4

Gribovskiy V.Yu., Krestnyy put' otryada Nebogatova., "Gangut" Nr 3

Hart S., The Russo-Japanese War, 1904-05., London 1958

Holman H.W.L, The Russian Navy., JRUSI vol. XXXIV (1892)

Hough R., The great admirals., London 1977

Hubert W., HIoria wojen morskich., Warszawa 1935

Hubert W., Zwycięstwa Japończyków pod Yalu i Cuszimą., "Bellona" Nr 4/1936

Ignatev E.P., Vzryvy v bukhte Zolotoy Rog., "Gangut" Nr 1

Ignatev E.P., K zyuydu ot ostrova Russkiy., "Gangut" Nr 2

Istoriya russko-yaponskoy voyny 1904-1905 (edited by. I.I. Rostunov)., Moskva 1977

Istoriya russkoy armii i flota. vol.XII Moskva 1913

Istoriya voenno-morskogo isskustva. vol. I-III, Moskva 1954

Istoriya voenno-morskogo isskustva. Uchebnik., Moskva 1969

Itani J., Lengerer H., Rehm-Takahara T., Sankeikan: Japan's coast defence ships of the "Matsushima" class., "Warship" Nr 49 (1990)

Jane F.T., The Imperial Japanese Navy., London 1904 (rep. 1984)

Jane's All the World's Fighting Ships 1898

The Japanishe torpedo boats in the battle of Tsushima., WI No 2/1972

Yarovoy V.V., Kratkiy ocherk Iorii Dobrovolnogo flota., "Gangut" Nr 3

Jentschura H., Yung D., Mickel P., Warships of the Imperial Japanese Navy 1869-1945., London 1977

Klado N.L., The Battle of the Sea of Japan., London 1906

Klado N.L., The Russian navy in the Russo-Japanese War., London 1905

Klimczyk T., Juene Ecole admirała Aube., MSiO Nr 6/2003

Klimczyk T., Hloria pancernika., Warszawa 1994

Klimczyk T., Zanim wymyślono krążowniki liniowe., MSiO Nr 3/2006

Klimovskij S.D., Port Artur., "Gangut" Nr 2

Kodrębski W., Eksplozje amunicji na okrętach wojennych., PM Nr 11-12/1930

Kofman V., Tsusima: analiza protiv mitov., "Naval" Nr 1 (1991)

Kolpakov A.M., Krestyaninov V.Ya., Shubochkin E.F., Opyt boevogo primenenya buksiruemykh kotaktnykh tralov v Port-Arture., "Gangut" Nr 7

Korotkin J.M., Boyevoye povrezhdeniya navodnych korabley., Leningrad 1960

Korshunov J.L., Djakonov J.P., Miny rossiyskogo flota, St. Peterburg 1995 (bibl. "Gangut")

Korshunov Yu.L., Uspenskiy G.V., Torpedy rossiyskogo flota.

Kosiarz E., Bitwy morskie., Gdańsk 1970

Kosiarz E., Wojny na Bałtyku X-XIX w., Gdańsk 1978

Kostenko V.P., Na "Orle" v Tsusime., Leningrad 1968

Kotten A., Morskaya strategiya v russko-yaponskuyu voynu., MS Nr 6/1910

Kowner R., Hlorical Dictionary of the Russo-Japanese War., Lanham, Maryland-Toronto-Oxford 2006

Krestjaninov V.J., Molodcov S.V., Kreyser "Askol'd"., St. Peterburg 1994

Lacroix E., The Development of the Imperial Japanese Navy. Part.1-19, TBS Nr 3/1962, 6/1963, 1-6/1968, 1-6/1969, 1-6/1970

Laskowski H., Artyleria morska., Warszawa 1934

Leather J., World warships in review 1860-1906., London 1976

Lloyd A., Admiral Togo., Tokyo 1905

Mahan A.T., Mahan on Naval Warfare. Selections from writings of rear admiral Alfred T. Mahan., Boston 1941

Mahan A.T., Naval Strategy., London 1911

Marder A.J., The Anatomy of British Sea Power 1880-1905., New York 1940

Matthei D., Russische Seemachtbestrebungen in der Epoche des Navalismus., MR Nr 1/1978

McLaughlin S., From "Riurik" to "Riurik": Russia's Armoured Cruisiers., "Warship" 1999-2000

Melnikov R.M., Bronenosec "Potemkin"., Leningrad 1981

Melnikov R.M., Eskadrennye bronenoscy tipa "Peresvet"., cz. I-III, "Gangut" Nr 11-13

Melnikov R.M., Kreyser "Bogatyr'"., St. Peterburg 1995 (bibl. "Gangut")

Melnikov R.M., Kreyser "Ochakov"., Leningrad 1986

Melnikov R.M., Kreyser I ranga "Dmitriy Donskoy"., St. Peterburg 1995 (bibl. "Gangut")

Melnikov R.M., "Rostislav"., "Gangut" Nr 7

Moiseev S.P., Spisok korabley russkogo parovogo i bronenosnogo flota (s 1861 po 1917 g.)., Moskva 1948

Morskie srazheniya russkogo flota., Moskva 1994

Nakamura K., Admiral Togo. A Memoir., Tokyo 1937

Nikitin D.V., Boy 1 avgusta 1904 g., "Chasavoj" Nr 23/1930

Nikitin D.V., Zaniyate nami Port Artura., "Chasavoy" Nr 37/1930

Novikov N.V., Gulskiy incident i carskaya okhranka., MS Nr 6/1935

Novikov-Priboj A.S., Tsuszima. vol. I-II, Warszawa 1979

Notes on the Battle of Sea of Japan., JRUSI vol. XLa (1906)

Olender P., Artyleria w wojnie rosyjsko-japońskiej 1904-1905. Bitwa pod Cuszimą., MSiO Nr 2/1996

Olender P., Artyleria w wojnie rosyjsko-japońskiej 1904-1905. Działania pod Port-Arturem i Władywostokiem., MSiO Nr 1/1996

Olender P., Bitwa pod Cuszimą – mity i rzeczywłość., "Przegląd historyczno-Wojskowy" Nr 1/2008

Olender P., Miny w wojnie rosyjsko-japońskiej, 1904-1905., MSiO Nr 5/1998

Olender P., Wojny morskie 1883-1914., Warszawa 2005

Ono G., War and Armament Expenditures of Japan., New York 1922.

Otryad vladivostokskikh kreyserov v boyu 1 avgusta 1904 goda., "Gangut" No. 55 (2009)

Parkes O., British Battleships 1860-1950., London 1957

Partala M. A., "Oslyabya": sudba ekipazha., "Gangut" Nr 18

Petrov M.A., Obzor glavnieyshikh kampanyi i srazhienyi parovogo flota v svyazi s evolucey voenno-morskogo iskusstva., Leningrad 1927

Polenov L.L., Kreyser "Avrora" v Velikom srezhenii Yaponskogo morya., "Gangut" Nr 2

Polnaja illustrirovannaya Istoriya russko-yaponskoy voyny., vol I-VII., St. Peterburg

Potemkin W., Gibel "Gromkogo"., "Chasavoj" Nr 32/1930

Potter E.B., Nimitz Ch.W., Sea Power. A Naval History., Engliwood Clifs 1950

Rauch G. von, Cruisiers for Argentina., WI Nr 4/1978

Rjagin S.K., Morskie pogranichniki Rossii., "Gangut" Nr 4

Robinson S., History of Naval Tactics., Annapolis 1942.

Rodgers W.L., A Study of Attacks upon Fortified Harbours., USNIP Nr 4/1904, 1/1905

Rossiyskiy gosudarstvennyy arkhiv voenno-morskogo flota (RGAVMF) – dokumenty.

Russian Auxilary Cruisiers in the Red Sea during 1904., WI Nr 2/1972

Sanderson M., Sea battles. A reference guide., Newton Abbot 1975

Santi-Mazzini G., La Tecnologia Militare Marittima, 1776-1916. vol. I-II, Sanremo 1994

Schencking J.Ch., Making Waves. Politics, Propaganda, and the Emergence of the Imperial Japanese Navy, 1868-1922., Stanford, California 2005

Smirnov M., Srazhenie v Koreyskom prolive 14-go i 15-go maya 1905 g., MS Nr 4/1913

Solski E., Sprzęt a wola zwycięstwa., PM Nr 6/1934

Sorokin A.I., Oborona Port-Artura. Russko-yaponskaya voyna 1904-1905., Moskva 1952

Sorokin A.I., Russko-yaponskaya voyna, 1904-1905 godov. Moskva 1956

Staniul Z., Druga eskadra Oceanu Spokojnego. cz.1-3, PM Nr 4-6/1929

Staniul Z., Rozwój taktyki torpedowej w świetle retrospektywy hIorycznej., PM Nr 31-32 (1931)

Stankiewicz J., Zagadnienia marynarki wojennej w Rosji Carskiej na tle stosunków międzynaro- dowych w końcu XIX i na początku XX w. cz.1-2, PM Nr 11-12/1931, 1-2/1932

Steam, Steel and Shellfire. The Steam Warship 1815-1905., London 1992

Stecki T., Z dziennika marynarza - wspomnienia z wojny rosyjsko-japońskiej. cz.1-4, "Morze" Nr 6-9/1927

Stenzel A., Seekriegsgeschichte in ihren wichtigsten Abschnitten., vol. V, Hanover 1911

Stevens W.O., Westcott A., A History of Sea Power., New York 1944

Sueter M.F., The Evolution of the Submarine Boat, Mine and Torpedo., Portsmouth 1907

Suliga S., Bronenosnyy kreyser "Admiral Nakhimov"., Moskva 1995

Suliga S., Korabli russko-yaponskoy voyny. Japonskij flot., Moskva 1995

Suliga S., Korabli russko-japonskoy voyny. Rossiyskiy flot., Moskva 1993

Supiński W., 100 lat okrętów wojennych., Warszawa 1965.

Supiński W., Błaszczyk K., Okręty wojenne 1900-1966., Warszawa 1967.

Supiński W., Lechowski M., Torpedowce i niszczyciele., Gdańsk 1971.

Supłat M., Rosyjskie stawiacze min 1854-1917., cz. 1-2, OW nr 6/1999 i 2/2000

Shirokorad A.B., Russko-yaponskie voyny 1904-1945 gg., Minsk 2003

Shhesnovich E.N., Plavane eskadrennogo bronenosca "Retvizan" 1902-1904., St. Peterburg 1999

Titushkin S.I., Korabel'naya artilleriya v russko-yaponskoy voyne., "Gangut" Nr 7

Tomblin B.B., High Noon at Chemulpo., USNIP Nr 8/1969

Tomitch V.M., Warships of the Imperial Russian Navy. Battleships., 1968

Towle P., Battleship Sales During the Russo-Japanese War., WI Nr 4/1986

Tyrtov D., Bronenosec beregovoy oborony "Admiral Ushakov"., "Chasavoy" nr 32/1930

Ugryumov A.I., Zheleznyy admiral., "Gangut" Nr 6

Urbański P., Dwa wieki napędu mechanicznego statków., Gdańsk 1997

Usov V.J., Port-arturskie "sokoly"., "Gangut" Nr 2

Usov V.J., "Tri Svyatitelya"., "Gangut" Nr 6

Wainwright R., The Battle of the Sea of Japan., USNIP Nr 4/1905

Walczyk T., Pancerniki typu "Ting Yuan"., OW 1999 (numer specjalny)

Warner D. and P., The tide at sunrise. A history of the russo-japanese war 1904-1905., Norwich 1975

Watts A.J., The Imperial Russian Navy., London 1990

Welch P.P., Tsushima and Jutland., USNIP Nr 7/1930

Weyer's Taschenbuch der Kriegsflotten 1901, 1905, 1906, 1907

Wieczorkiewicz P.P., HIoria wojen morskich. Wiek pary (vol. II)., Londyn 1995

Wilson H.W., Battleships in Action. vol. I, London 1926

Wilson H.W., Ironclads in Action. vol. I-II, London 1896

Wright C.C., Cruisers of the Imperial russian Navy. cz.1, 3-4, WI Nr 1/1972, 2/1976, 1/1977

Wright C.C., A Photographic Memoir of the Imperial Russion Navy., WI Nr 4/1987

Zolotarev V.A., Kozlov I.A., Tri stoletya rossiyskogo flota, XIX-nachalo XX veka. Moskva-St. Petersburg 2004

Zuev G.I., Kreyser "Almaz"., "Gangut" Nr 7

Zuev G.I., Okhranu puti sledovaniya 2-y Tikhookeanskoy eskadry vozlozhit' na kollezhskogo sovetnika Gartinga

Magazines

BNA - Brassey's Naval Annual

JRUSI - Journal of the Royal United Service Institution

MR - Marine Rundschau

MS - Morskoj Sbornik

MSiO - Morza, Statki i Okręty

OW - Okręty Wojenne

PM - Przegląd Morski

TBS - The Belgian Shiplover

USNIP - United States Naval Institute Proceedings

WI - Warship International

RUSSIAN NAVY SCALE DRAWINGS

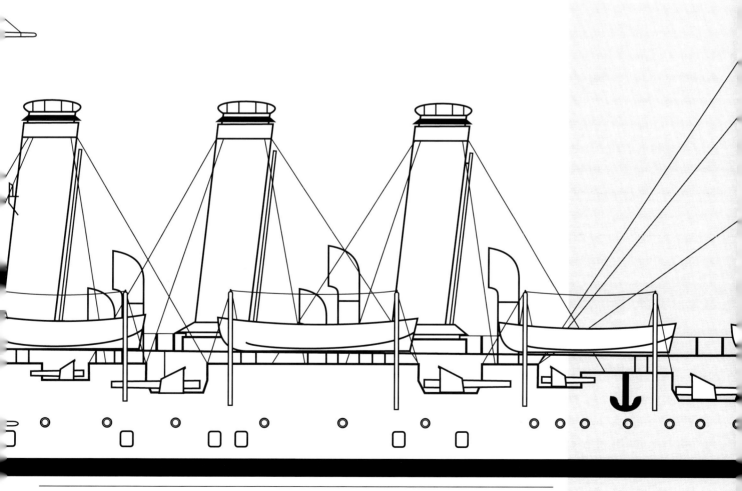

BATTLESHIPS

ЕКАТЕРИНА II

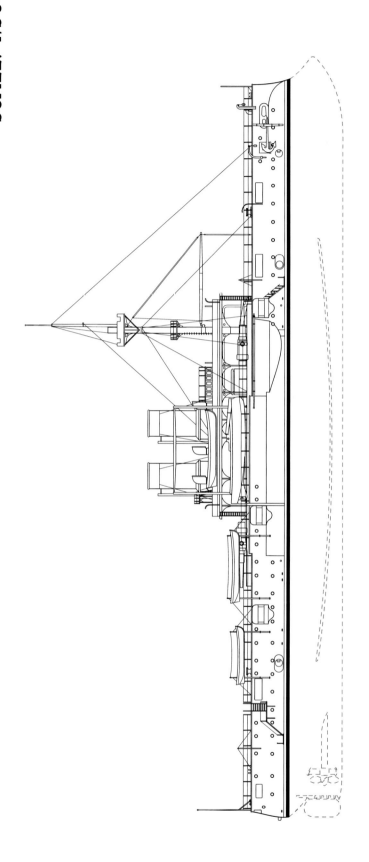

<u>YEKATYERINA II</u>
SCALE: 1/500

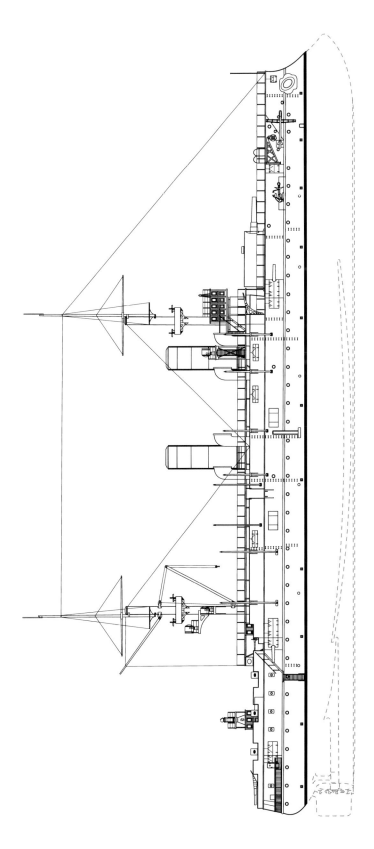

IMPERATOR NIKOLAY I
SCALE: 1/500

ИМПЕРАТОР НИКЛАЙ I

ДВЕНАДЦАТЬ АПОСТОЛОВ

DVENADCAT' APOSTOLOV

SCALE: 1/500

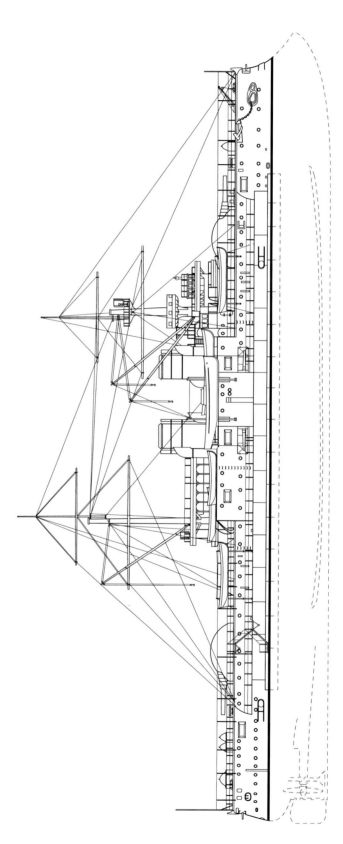

НАВАРИН

NAVARIN
SCALE: 1/500

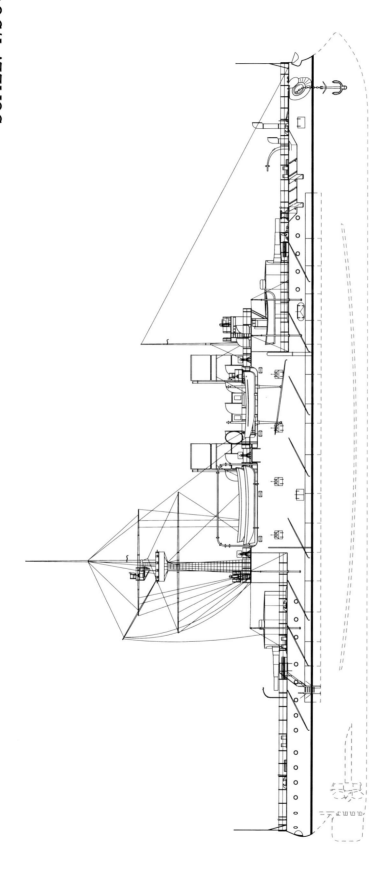

BATTLESHIPS

ТРИ СВЯТИТЕЛЯ

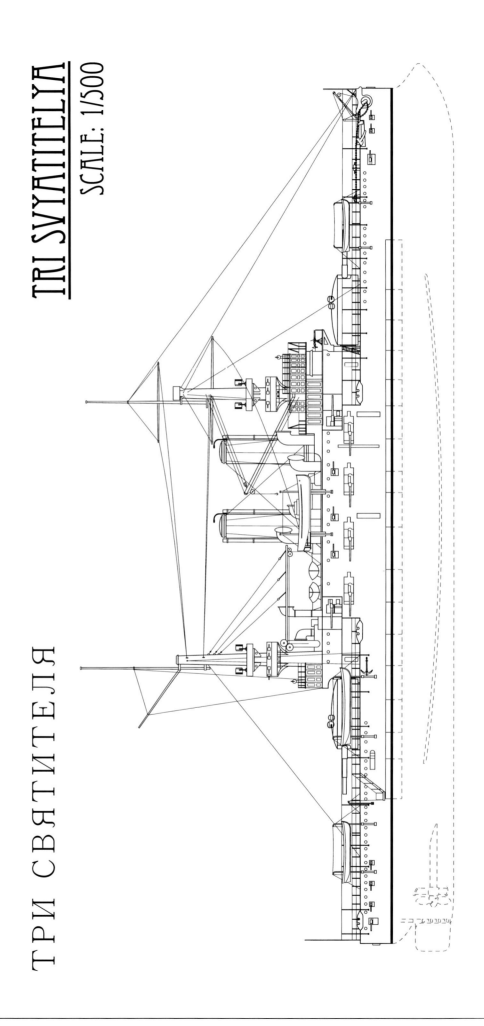

TRI SVYATITELЯ

SCALE: 1/500

СИСОЙ ВЕЛИКИЙ

SISOY VELIKIY
SCALE: 1/500

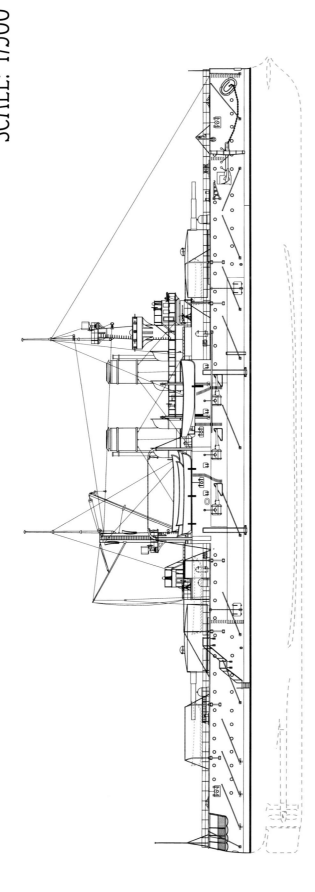

POLTAVA

SCALE: 1/500

ПОЛТАВА

РОСТИСЛАВ

ROSTISLAV
SCALE: 1/500

ПЕРЕСВЕТ

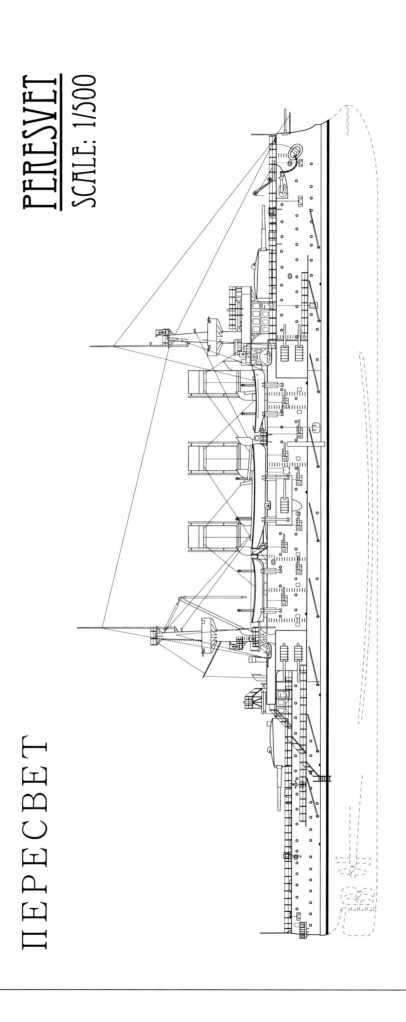

PERESVET
SCALE: 1/500

ПОБЕДА

POBEDA
SCALE: 1/500

РЕТВИЗАН

RETVIZAN
SCALE: 1/500

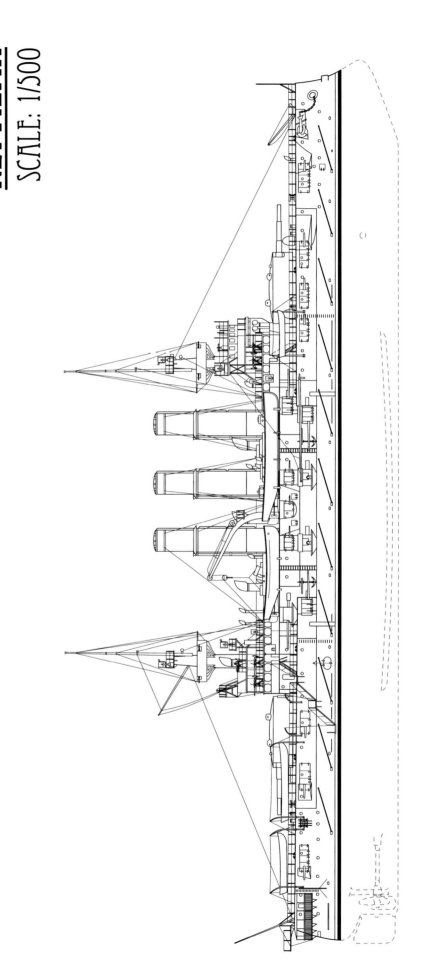

KNYAZ' POTEMKIN-TAVRICHESKIY
SCALE: 1/500

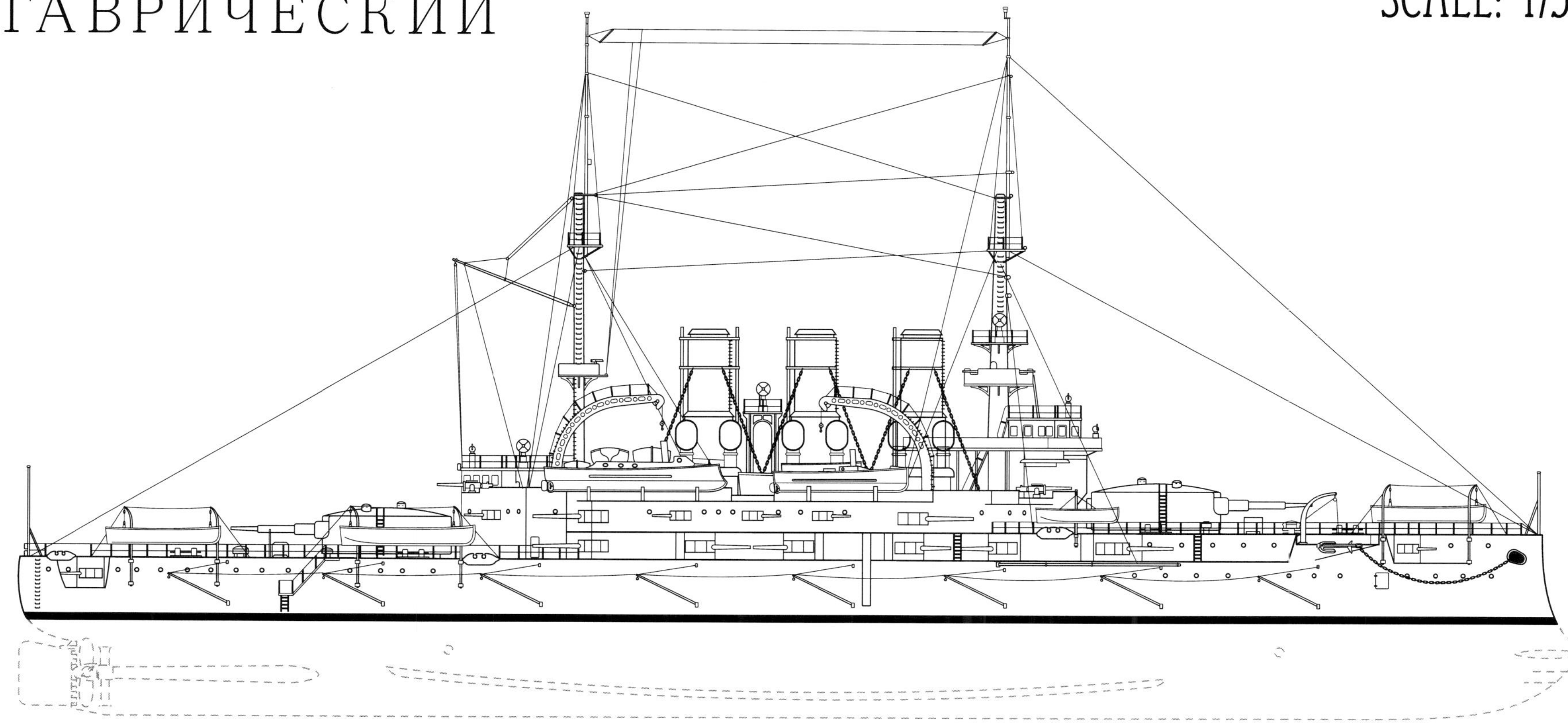

КНЯЗЬ ПОТЕМКИН-
ТАВРИЧЕСКИЙ

BATTLESHIPS

БОРОДИНО

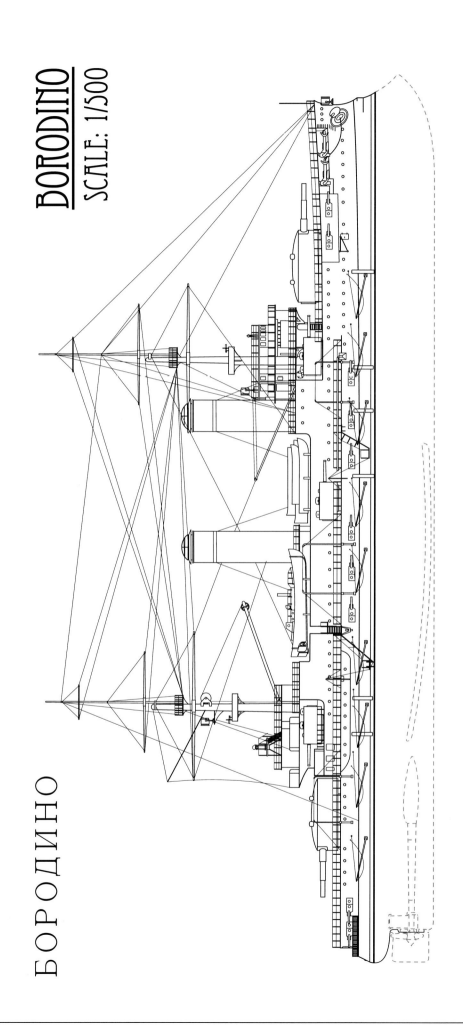

BORODINO
SCALE: 1/500

ADMIRAL USHAKOV
SCALE: 1/500

АДМИРАЛ УШАКОВ

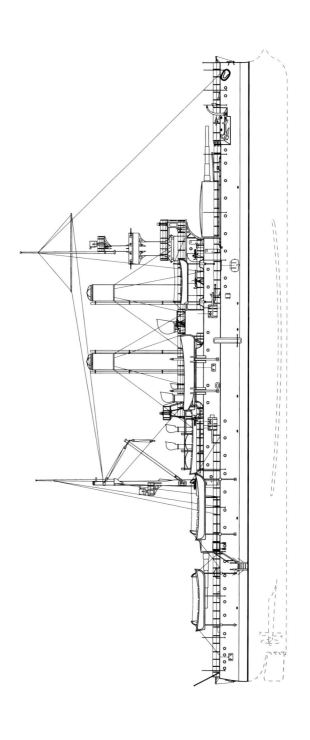

VLADIMIR MONOMAKH

SCALE: 1/500

ВЛАДИМИР МОНОМАХ

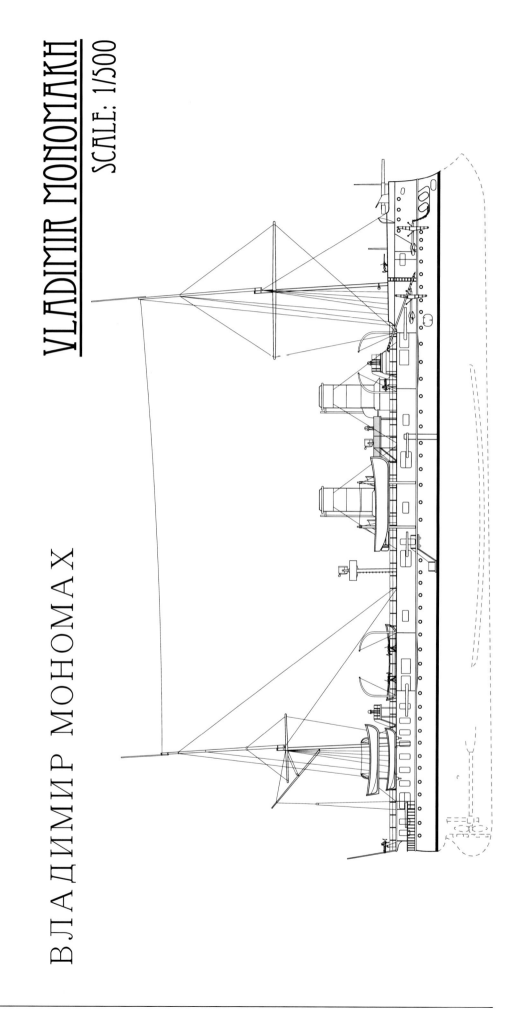

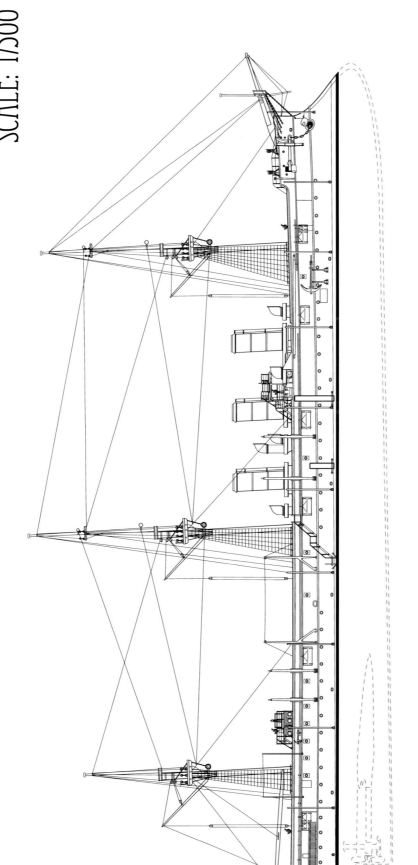

ПАМЯТЬ АЗОВА

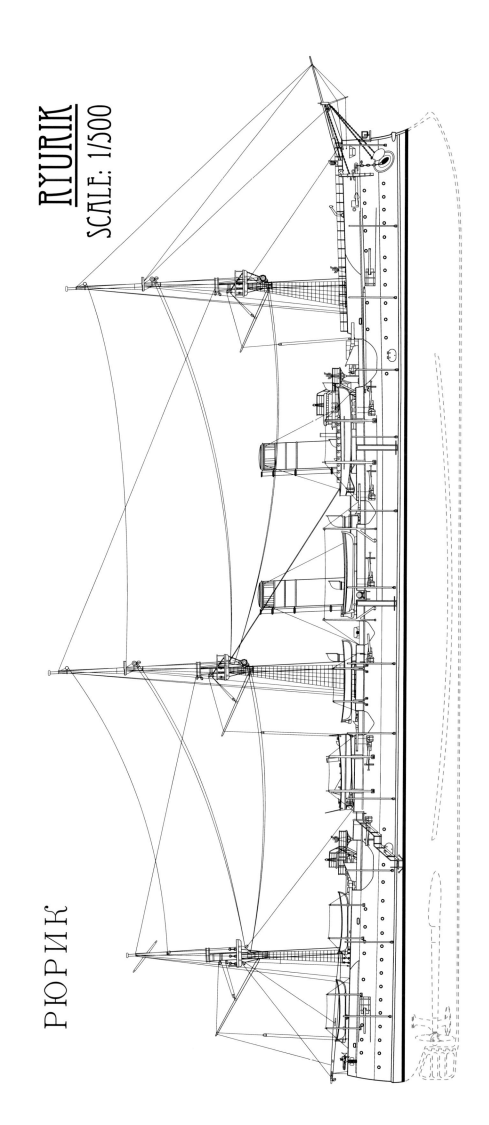

РЮРИК

RYURIK
SCALE: 1/500

ADMIRAL KORNILOV

SCALE: 1/500

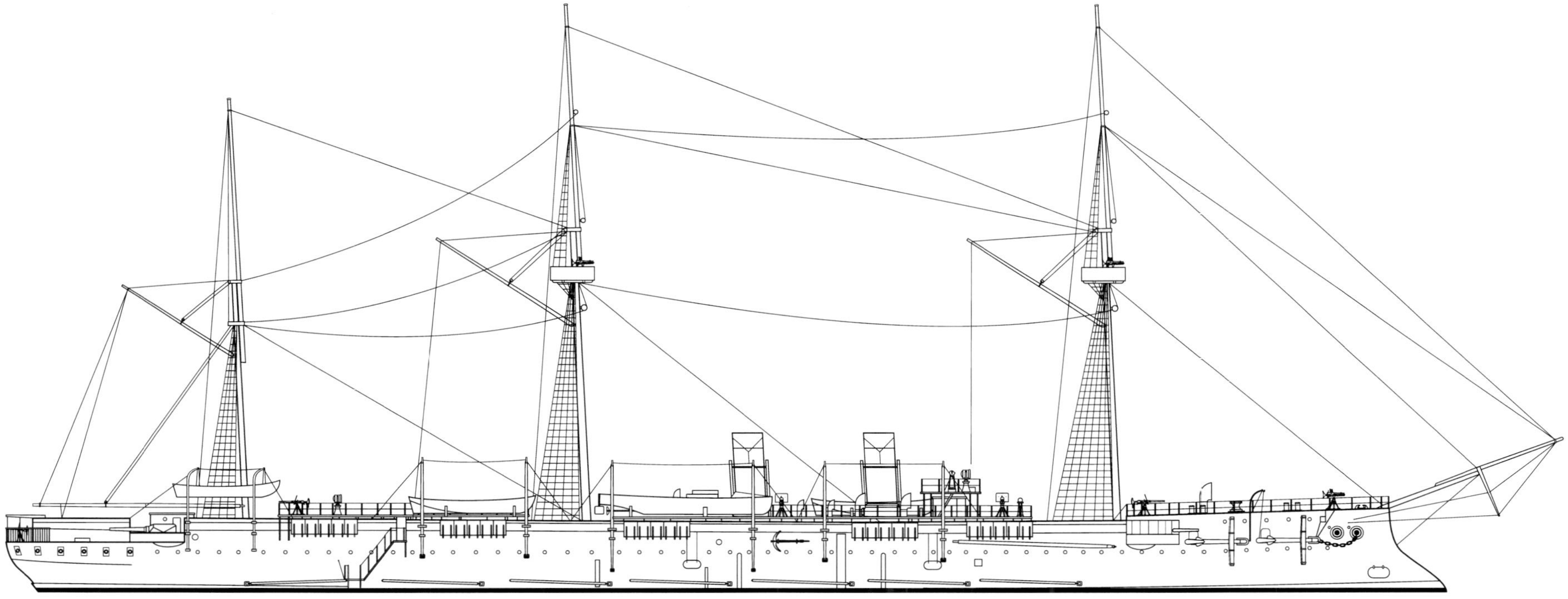

АДМИРАЛ КОРНИЛОВ

CRUISERS

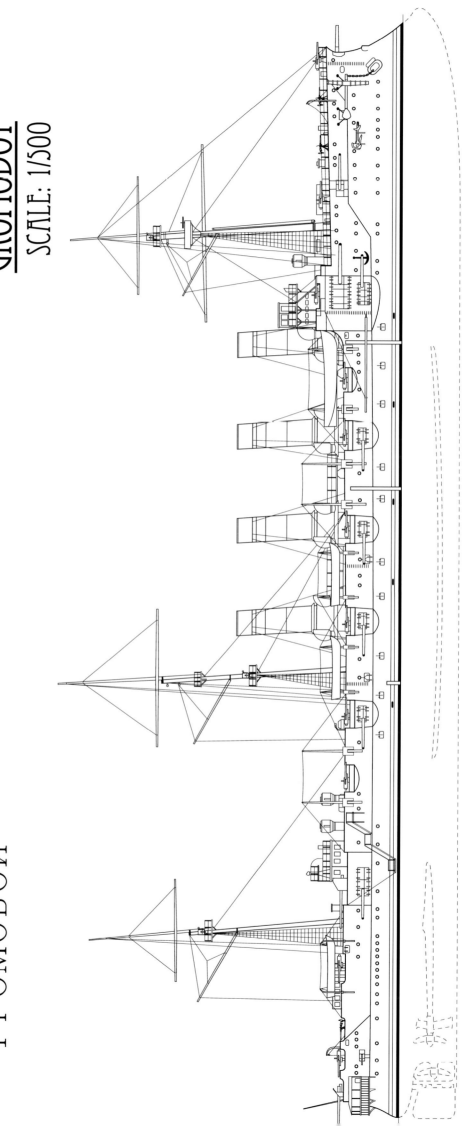

ГРОМОБОЙ

GROMOBOY
SCALE: 1/500

РОССИЯ

ROSSIYA

SCALE: 1/500

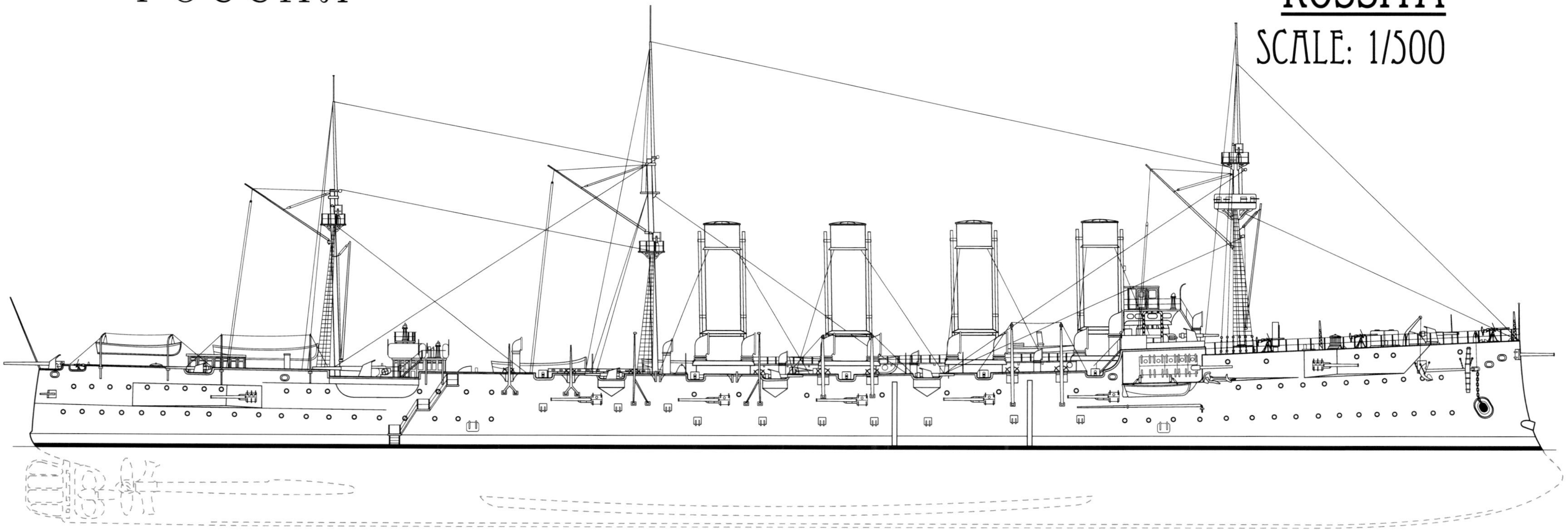

ARMOURED CRUISER

БАЯН

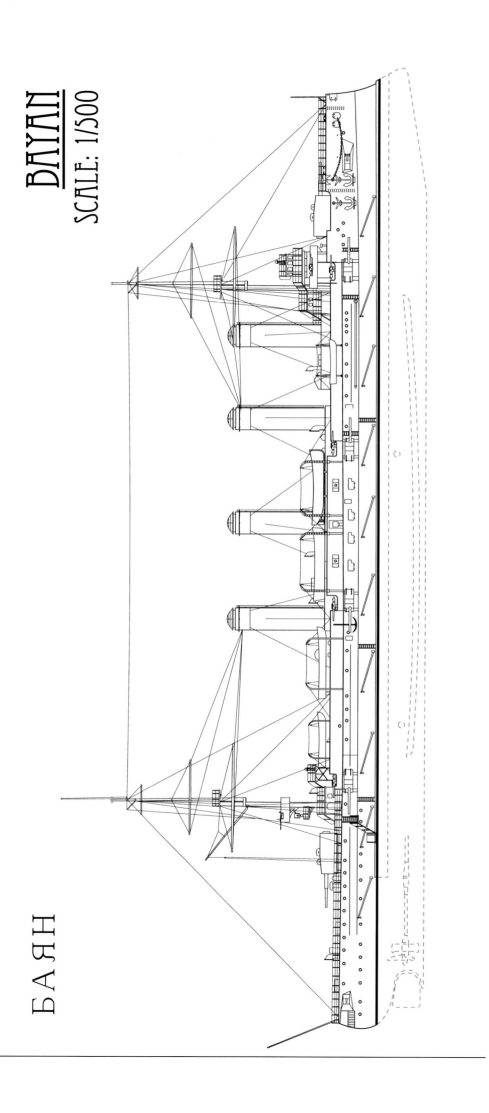

БАЯН
SCALE: 1/500

ВАРЯГ

VARYAG
SCALE: 1/500

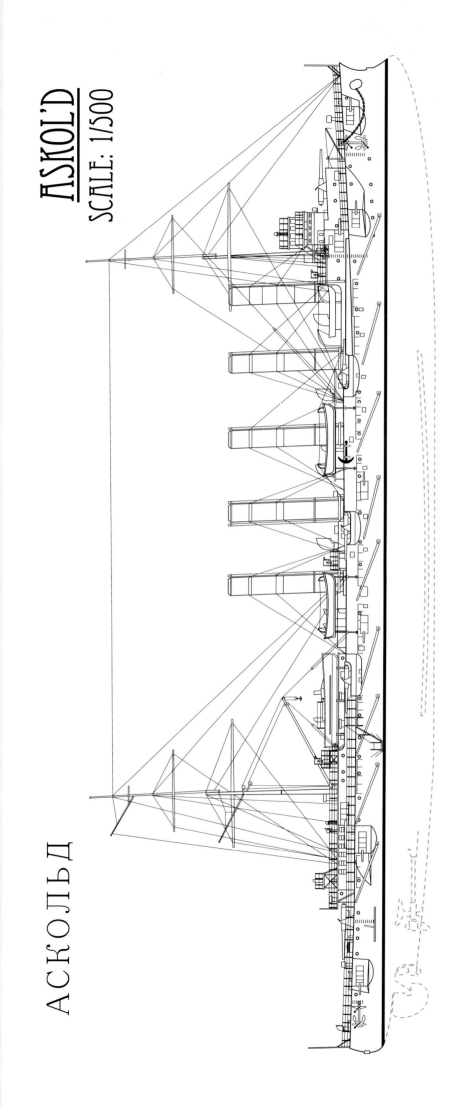

ASKOL'D

SCALE: 1/500

АСКОЛЬД

БОГАТЫРЬ

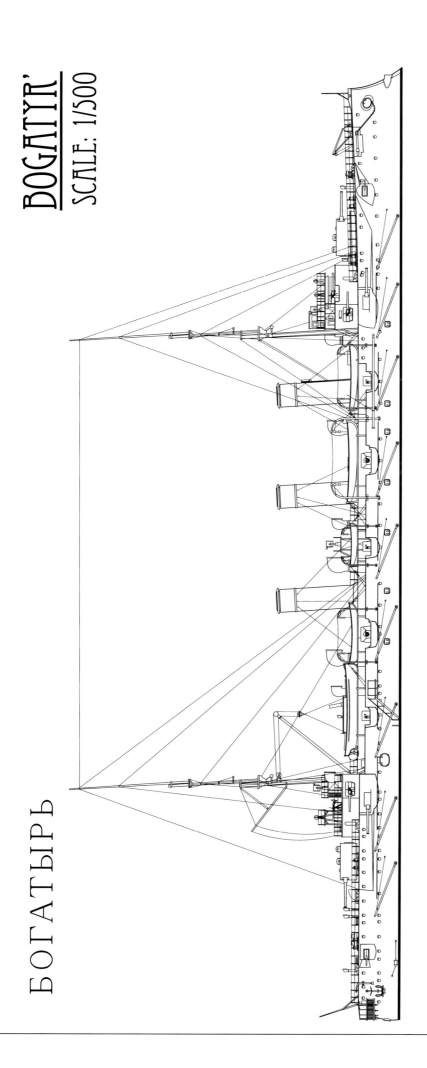

BOGATYR'
SCALE: 1/500

НОВИК

NOVIK
SCALE: 1/500

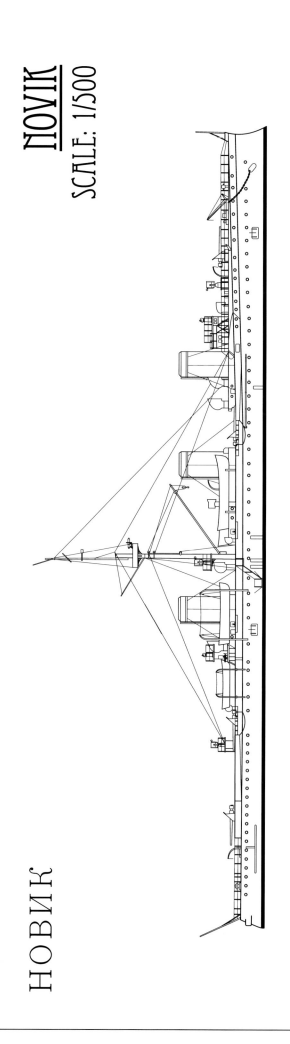

ЖЕМЧУГ

ZHEMCHUG
SCALE: 1/500

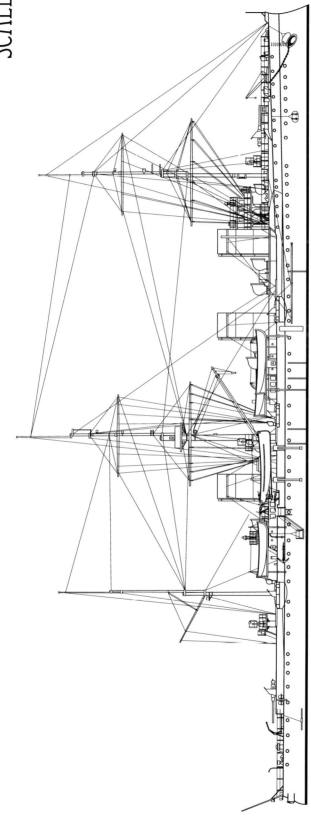

GUNBOATS

ALMAZ

SCALE: 1/350

AJIMA 3

286

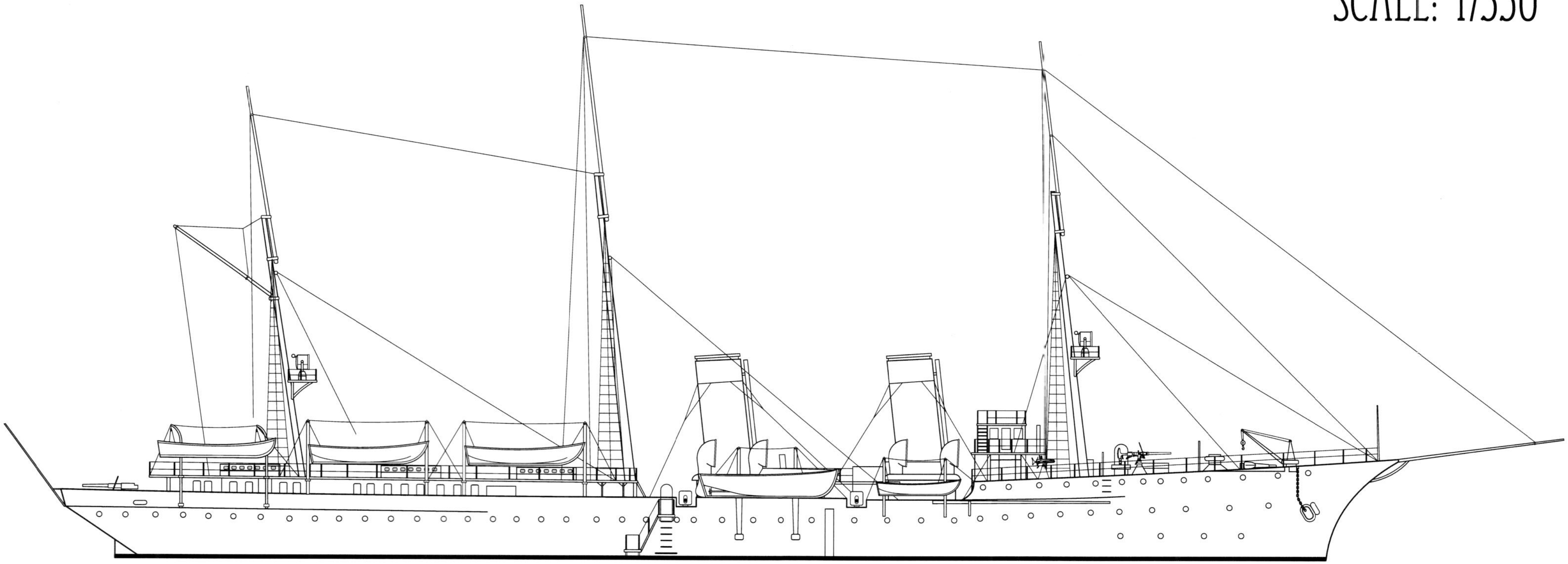

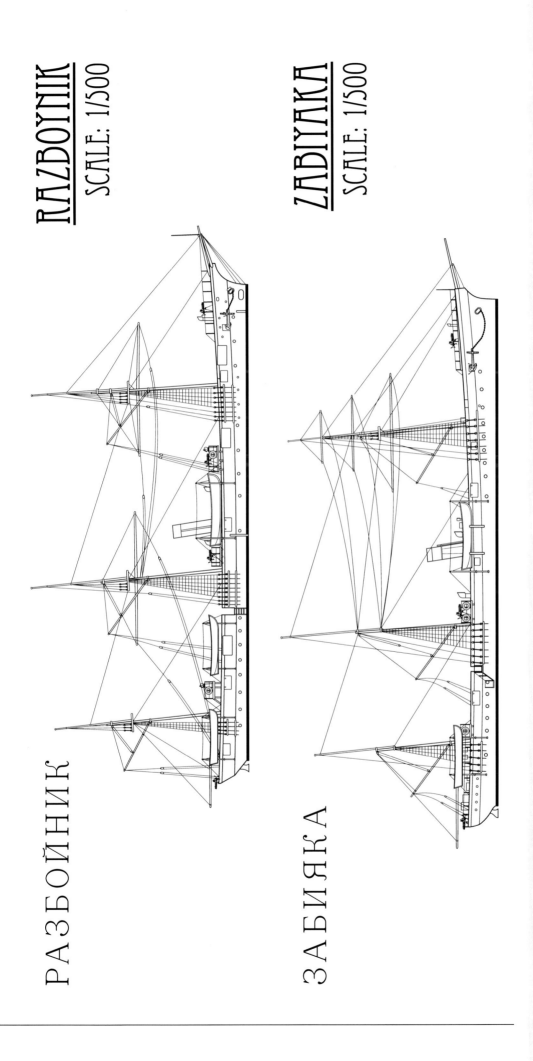

RAZBOYNIK
SCALE: 1/500

РАЗБОЙНИК

ZABIYAKA
SCALE: 1/500

ЗАБИЯКА

SMALL CRUISERS

SIVUCH

SCALE: 1/350

СИВУЧ

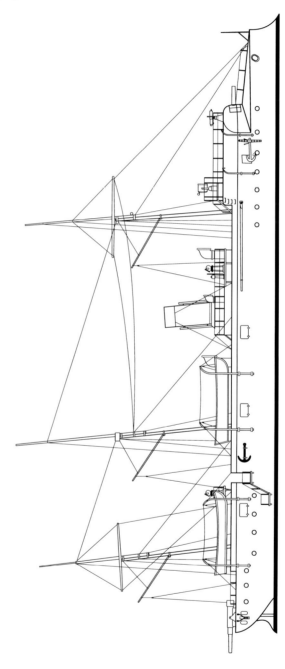

KORYETS
SCALE: 1/350

КОРЕЕЦ

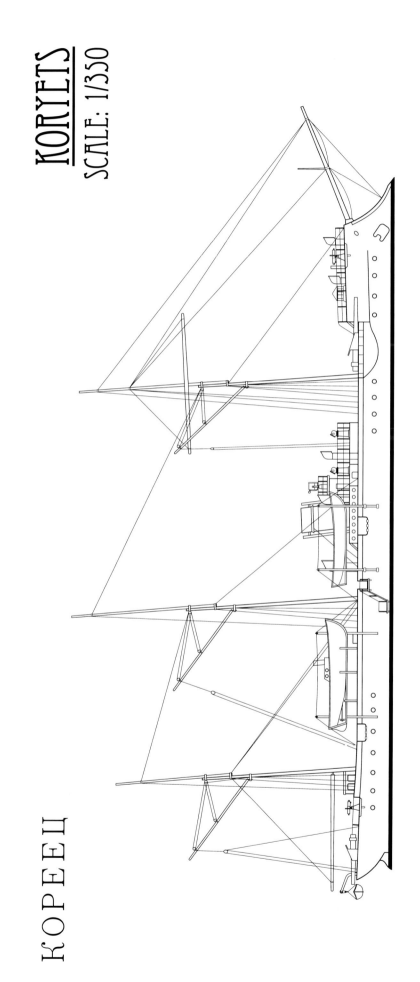

GUNBOATS

MANDZHUR
SCALE: 1/350

МАНДЖУР

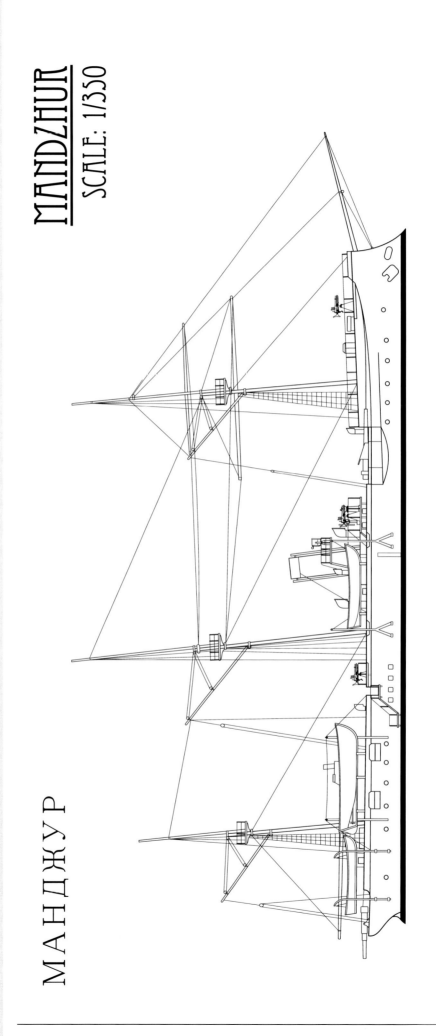

GREMYASHCHIY
SCALE: 1/350

ГРЕМЯЩИЙ

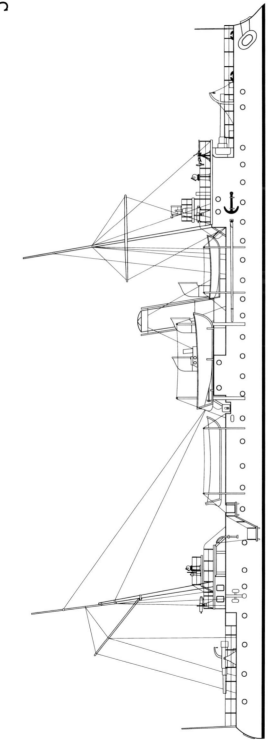

GUNBOATS

TORPEDO BOATS

GILYAK
SCALE: 1/350

ГИЛЯК

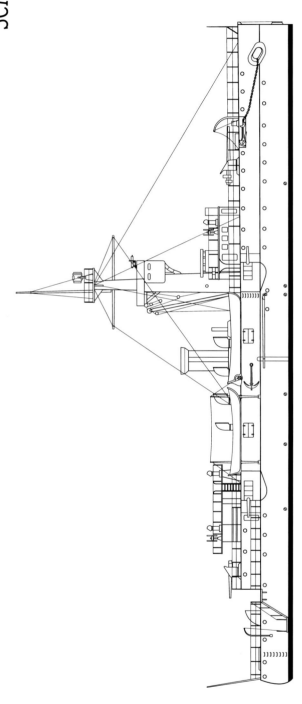

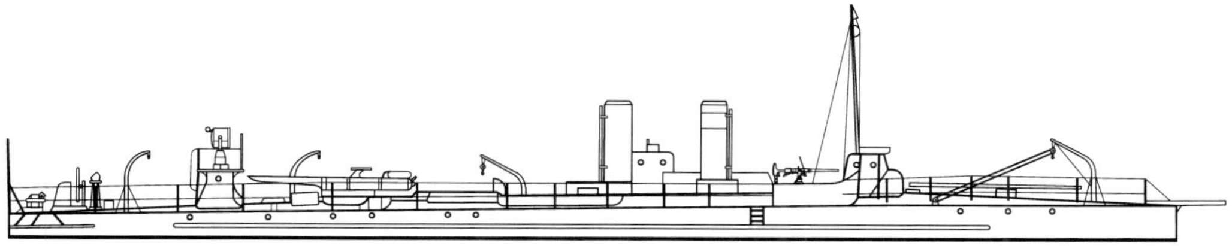

214
SCALE: 1/350

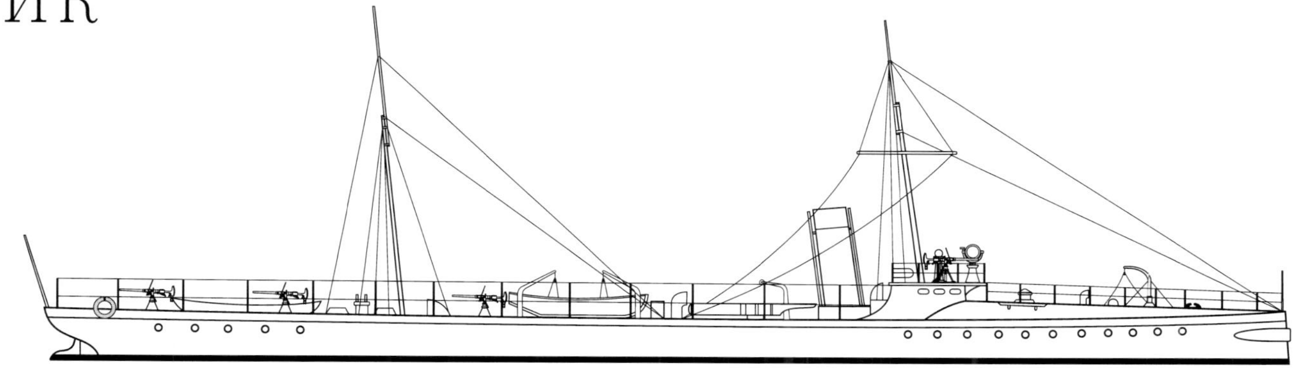

VSADNIK
SCALE: 1/350

ВСАДНИК

LEYTENANT IL'IN
SCALE: 1/500

ЛЕЙТЕНАНТ ИЛЬИН

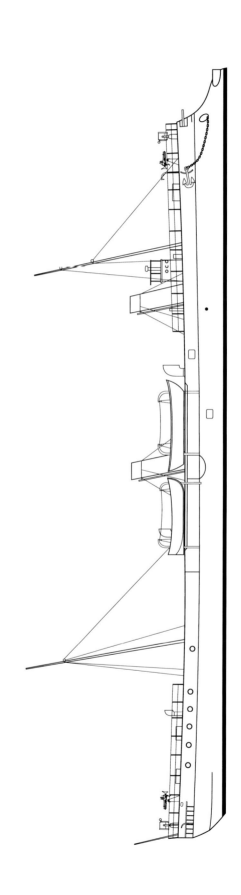

STEREGUSHCHIY
SCALE: 1/350

СТЕРЕГУЩИЙ

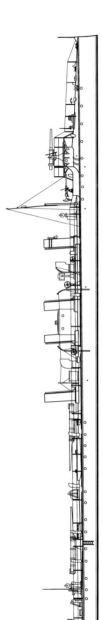

BOYEVOY
SCALE: 1/350

БОЕВОЙ

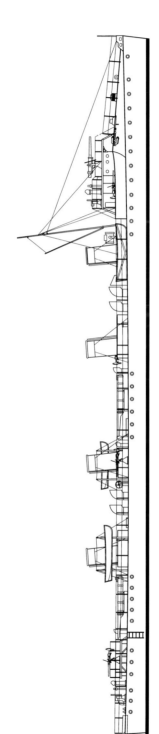

DESTROYERS

DESTROYERS

LEYTENANT BURAKOV
SCALE: 1/350

VNIMATEL'NYY
SCALE: 1/350

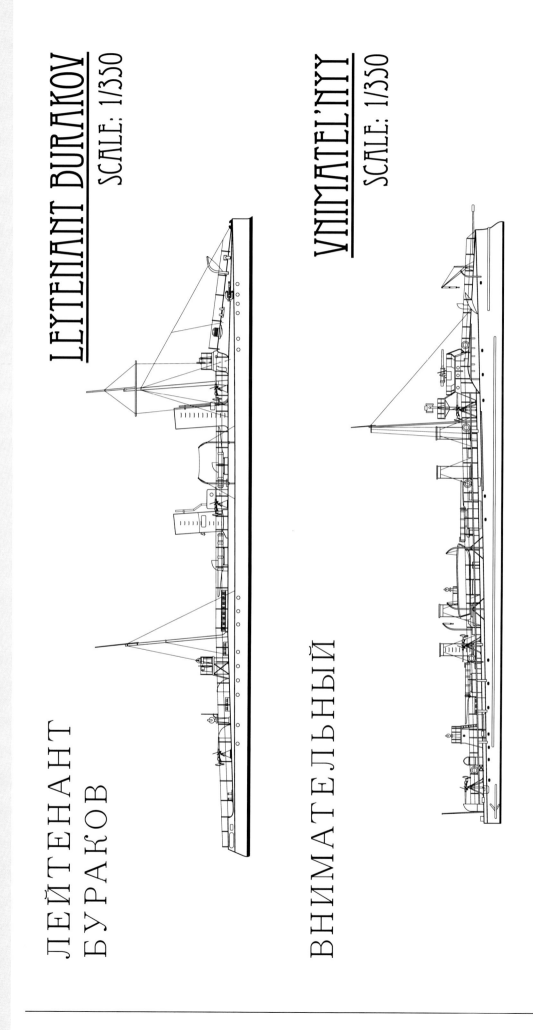

ЛЕЙТЕНАНТ
БУРАКОВ

ВНИМАТЕЛЬНЫЙ

BDITELNY
SCALE: 1/350

БДИТЕЛНЫЙ

BUYNY
SCALE: 1/350

БУЙНЫЙ

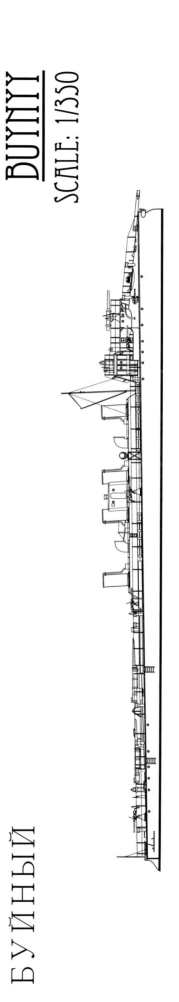

DESTROYERS

103
SCALE: 1/350

108
SCALE: 1/350

111
SCALE: 1/350

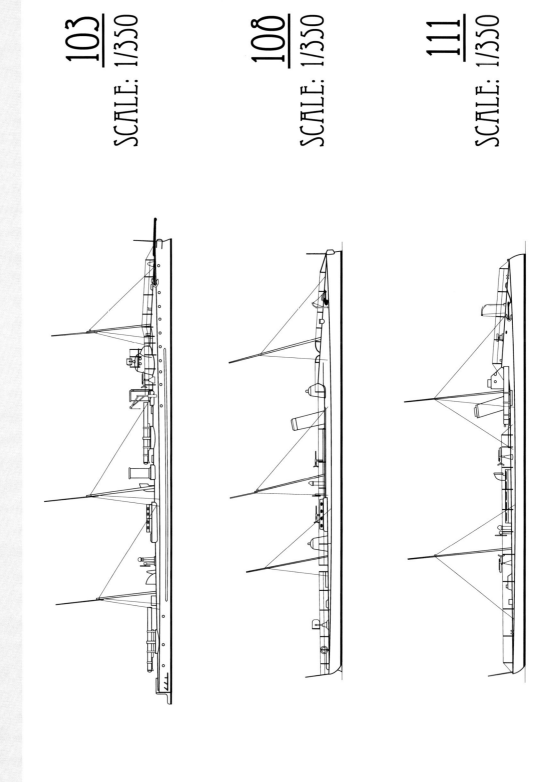

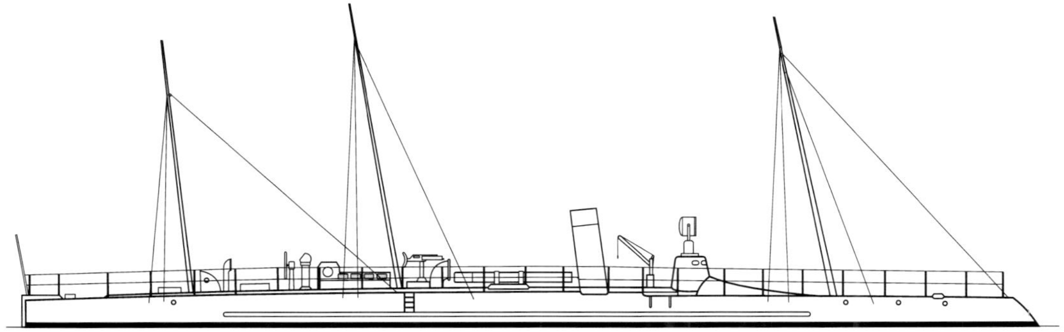

110

SCALE: 1/350

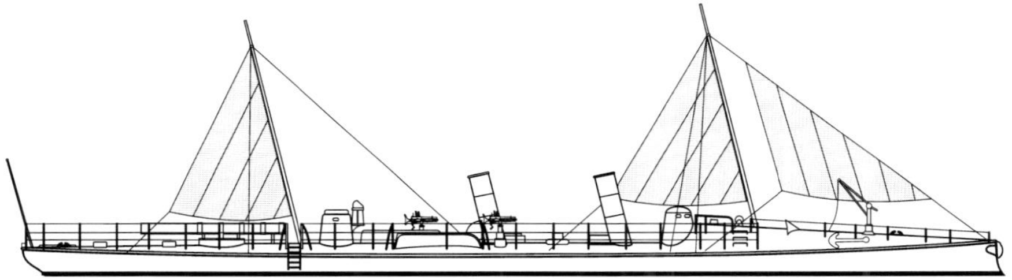

131

SCALE: 1/350

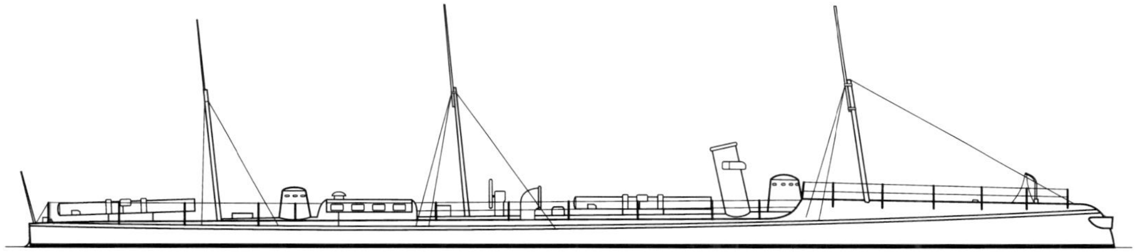

203

SCALE: 1/350

TORPEDO BOATS

206
SCALE: 1/350

212
SCALE: 1/350

267
SCALE: 1/350

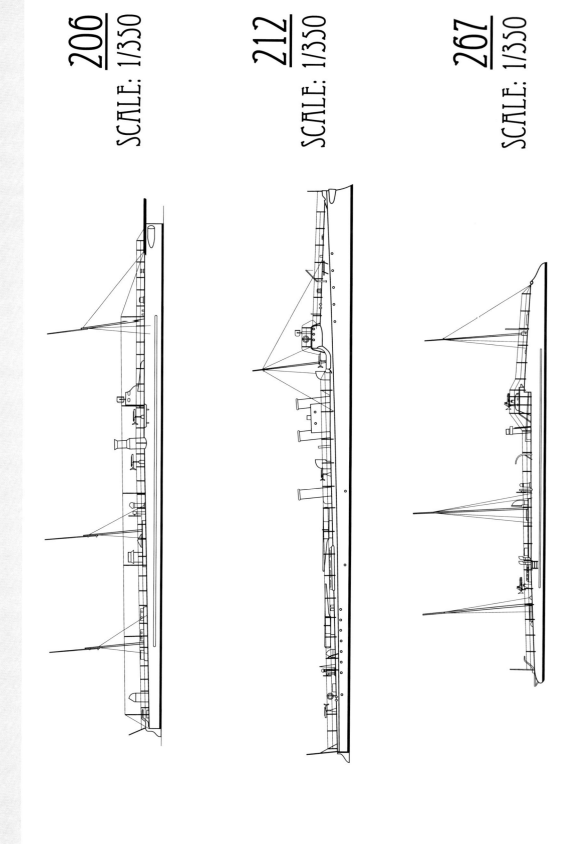

AMUR

АМУР

AMUR
SCALE: 1/350

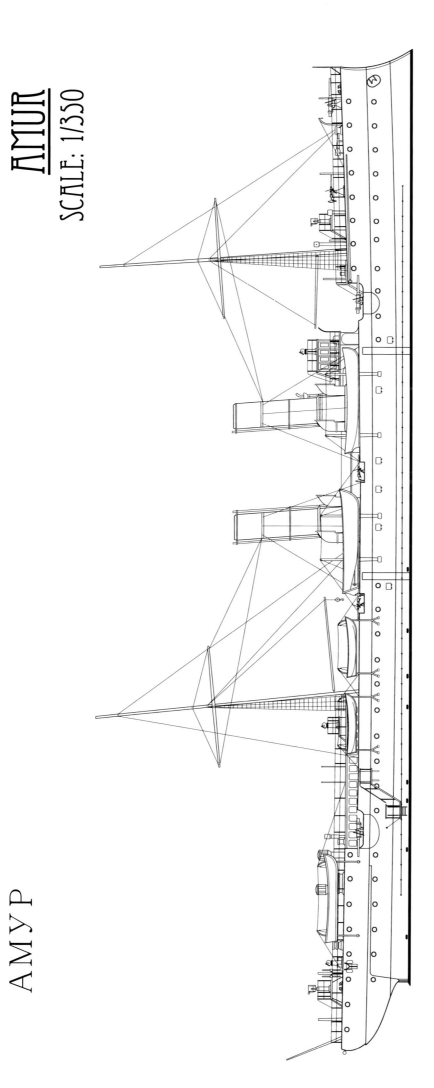

SUBMARINES

DEL'FIN
SCALE: 1/150

ДЕЛЬФИН

FOREL'
SCALE: 1/150

ФОРЕЛЬ

KETA
SCALE: 1/150

КЕТА

KASATKA

SCALE: 1/150

КАСАТКА

OSETR

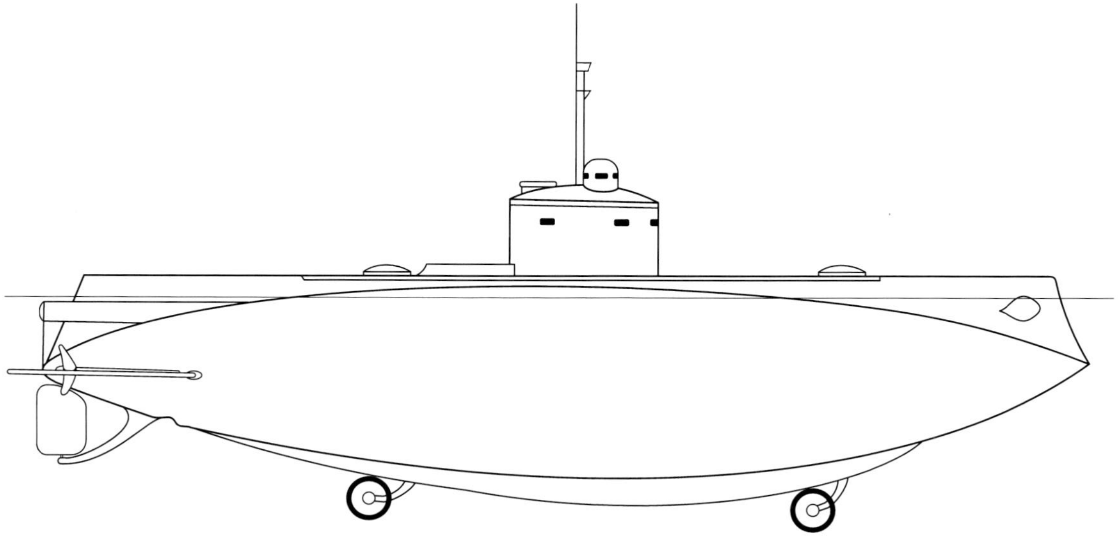

SCALE: 1/150

OCETP

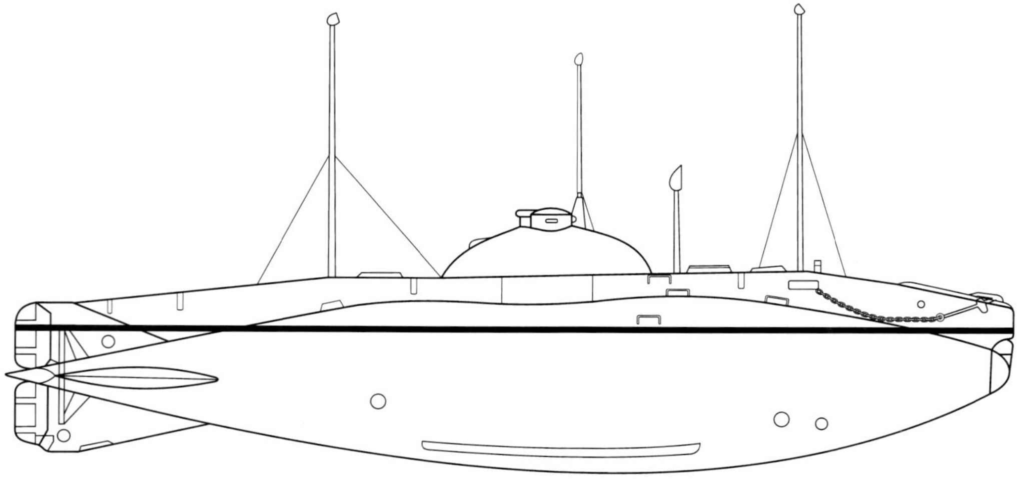

SOM

SCALE: 1/150

COM

INDEX

Warships

114 (Russ. Torpedo boat) 249

115 (Russ. Torpedo boat) 250

116 (Russ. Torpedo boat) 250

117 (Russ. Torpedo boat) 250

118 (Russ. Torpedo boat) 250, 299

119 (Russ. Torpedo boat) 250

120 (Russ. Torpedo boat) 250

121 (Russ. Torpedo boat) 250

122 (Russ. Torpedo boat) 250

123 (Russ. Torpedo boat) 250

124 (Russ. Torpedo boat) 250

125 (Russ. Torpedo boat) 250

126 (Russ. Torpedo boat) 250

127 (Russ. Torpedo boat) 250

128 (Russ. Torpedo boat) 250

129 (Russ. Torpedo boat) 250

130 (Russ. Torpedo boat) 250

131 (Russ. Torpedo boat) 250, 299

132 (Russ. Torpedo boat) 250

133 (Russ. Torpedo boat) 250

134 (Russ. Torpedo boat) 250

135 (Russ. Torpedo boat) 250

136 (Russ. Torpedo boat) 250

137 (Russ. Torpedo boat) 250

138 (Russ. Torpedo boat) 250

139 (Russ. Torpedo boat) 250

140 (Russ. Torpedo boat) 250

141 (Russ. Torpedo boat) 250

142 (Russ. Torpedo boat) 250

201 (Russ. Torpedo boat) 249, 174

202 (Russ. Torpedo boat) 15, 249

203 (Russ. Torpedo boat) 15, 166, 174, 250, 299

204 (Russ. Torpedo boat) 15, 250

205 (Russ. Torpedo boat) 15, 163, 166, 174, 236, 249

206 (Russ. Torpedo boat) 15, 163, 166, 174, 249, 300

208 (Russ. Torpedo boat) 15, 163, 177, 250

209 (Russ. Torpedo boat) 15, 250

210 (Russ. Torpedo boat) 15, 250

211 (Russ. Torpedo boat) 15, 250

212 (Russ. Torpedo boat) 182, 251, 300

213 (Russ. Torpedo boat) 181, 182, 251

214 (Russ. Torpedo boat) 251, 293

215 (Russ. Torpedo boat) 251

216 (Russ. Torpedo boat) 251

217 (Russ. Torpedo boat) 251

218 (Russ. Torpedo boat) 251

219 (Russ. Torpedo boat) 251

220 (Russ. Torpedo boat) 251

221 (Russ. Torpedo boat) 251, 182

222 (Russ. Torpedo boat) 251, 182

223 (Russ. Torpedo boat) 251

251 (Russ. Torpedo boat) 249

252 (Russ. Torpedo boat) 249

253 (Russ. Torpedo boat) 249

254 (Russ. Torpedo boat) 249

255 (Russ. Torpedo boat) 249

256 (Russ. Torpedo boat) 250

257 (Russ. Torpedo boat) 249

258 (Russ. Torpedo boat) 249

259 (Russ. Torpedo boat) 249

260 (Russ. Torpedo boat) 250

261 (Russ. Torpedo boat) 249

262 (Russ. Torpedo boat) 249

263 (Russ. Torpedo boat) 249

264 (Russ. Torpedo boat) 249

265 (Russ. Torpedo boat) 249

266 (Russ. Torpedo boat) 249

267 (Russ. Torpedo boat) 249, 300

268 (Russ. Torpedo boat) 249

270 (Russ. Torpedo boat) 250

271 (Russ. Torpedo boat) 250

272 (Russ. Torpedo boat) 250

273 (Russ. Torpedo boat) 250

A

Abrek [Абрек] 246

Admiral Kornilov [Адмирал Корнилов] 244, 277

Admiral Nakhimov [Адмирал Нахимов] 186, 189, 201, 207, 210, 211, 218, 219, 220, 221, 244, 257

Admiral Senyavin [Адмирал Сенявин] 195, 196, 201, 207, 211, 212, 215, 218, 219, 223, 225, 230, 243

Admiral Ushakov [Адмирал Ушаков] 195, 201, 206, 207, 211, 212, 215, 219, 220, 222, 223, 225, 243, 257, 273

Adzuma [吾妻] 29, 31, 110, 129, 161, 162, 167, 172, 175, 199, 207, 208, 225, 228, 235, 237

Akagi [赤城] 37, 46, 48, 51, 53, 55, 63, 84, 85, 112, 199, 228

Akashi [明石] 9, 62, 68, 70, 74, 95, 111, 137, 199, 215, 226, 228, 238

Akatsuki [暁] 9, 40, 51, 87, 102, 106, 112, 113

Akebono [曙] 9, 38, 39, 104, 112, 145, 199, 221, 228, 235, 236

Akitsushima [秋津洲] 9, 55, 62, 68, 70, 74, 111, 136, 179, 199, 202, 226, 228, 238

Aleut [Алеут] 15, 176, 251

Almaz [Алмаз] 182, 186, 189, 201, 216, 221, 225, 257, 297

Amur [Амур] 6, 15, 32, 51, 52, 54, 89, 90, 94, 95, 97, 98, 174, 175, 237, 251, 253, 301

Angara ex Moskva [Ангара ex Москва] 15, 27, 237, 252

Aotaka [蒼鷹] 9, 42, 104, 105, 114, 199, 228, 235

Arare [霰] 113, 199, 228, 235

Ariake [有明] 113, 117, 199, 219, 228, 235

Asagiri [朝霧] 9, 102, 103, 104, 113, 199, 221, 228, 235, 236

Names